The Rise of Modern Japan

The Rise of Modern Japan

W. G. BEASLEY

Emeritus Professor of the History of the Far East,
University of London

Third edition

PHŒNIX

A PHOENIX PAPERBACK

First published in Great Britain in 1990
by Weidenfeld & Nicolson

Reprinted in 1993
Second edition 1995
Third edition 2000

This paperback edition published in 2001
by Phoenix,
an imprint of Orion Books Ltd,
Orion House, 5 Upper St Martin's Lane,
London WC2H 9EA

A CIP catalogue record for this book
is available from the British Library.

ISBN 0 75381 123 5

Printed and bound in Great Britain by
The Guernsey Press Co. Ltd, Guernsey, C.I.

CONTENTS

ACKNOWLEDGEMENTS

Since this book incorporates work which I have carried out over a span of forty years, I shall not attempt to list all those who at one time or another have given me help and advice about various parts of its subject-matter. However, there are some debts which I do wish particularly to acknowledge. Among the many Japanese scholars to whom my thanks are due, pride of place must undoubtedly be accorded to the late Professor Iwao Seiichi of Tokyo University, who introduced me to that university's Historiographical Institute in 1950, and remained a valued friend and adviser until his death. Three other historians of Tokyo University have also made a continuing contribution to my studies: Professor Numata Jiro, who taught me to read Tokugawa documents; Professor Oka Yoshitake, through whom many doors were opened to me; and Professor Hayashi Shigeru, a most knowledgeable guide to modern bibliography. Outside Japan, my colleagues at the School of Oriental and African Studies in London, in addition to making useful suggestions about my research on a number of occasions, provided a congenial intellectual environment in which to pursue it. To them all I express my thanks. So I do above all to my wife, who has not only given me much practical help over the years, but has also opened an alternative route to the understanding of Japan through her friends and interests there, which have often been different from my own.

W. G. Beasley

London
May 1989

PREFACE

In 1987, when I started to prepare a thorough revision of *The Modern History of Japan*, first published in 1963, it was clear that much had to be changed. Not only was there a need to introduce more material on the period since 1945, preferably abbreviating some of the nineteenth-century sections to make room for it, but also account had to be taken of the fact that scholarly writing over the previous twenty years had brought new perceptions of the subject. For example, it was necessary to pay more attention to economic growth, in view of the importance which the 'economic miracle' has played in recent Japanese history; there is now a range of writing about Japanese social and cultural responses to the West, adding greatly to our knowledge of the processes of modernization; and much research has been published about the conflicts and decisions which led to the Pacific War.

The present volume is the result of trying to incorporate the substance of this into a volume no longer than the old one, while retaining as many as possible of the general characteristics of the earlier version. The bibliography is less complete, because there are many more works it would now be possible to cite. There is an additional appendix, listing Japanese Prime Ministers since 1885, partly to make good the loss of some political narrative from the main part of the text. There is a different concluding date: early 1989, when the death of Emperor Hirohito brought the Showa era to an end. And there is a new title. The changes in specific subject-matter, and in the allocation of space to the various topics, are so considerable that to have used the same title might have been misleading.

W.G.B.

PREFACE TO THE SECOND EDITION

A new chapter, Chapter 17, carries the narrative down to the end of 1994, but no revisions have been made to earlier chapters. Some additions have been made to the index and the list of prime ministers. Since the new material derives almost entirely from articles in contemporary newspapers and magazines, no attempt has been made to revise the bibliography.

W.G.B.

London
January 1995

PREFACE TO THE THIRD EDITION

I have confined my changes to extending Chapter 17 to cover the years 1994–1999, and updating the list of Japanese prime ministers on page 296.

W.G.B.

London
January 2000

CHINESE AND JAPANESE WORDS AND NAMES

Chinese and Japanese personal names are given in the order which is traditional in those two countries, that is, family name, followed by given name (e.g. Mao Tse-tung, Iwakura Tomomi, where Mao and Iwakura are family names).

Chinese words and names are romanized according to the Wade–Giles system, which is more often to be found in books relevant to Japanese history. Alternatives in the Pinyin system, now becoming standard for references to contemporary China, are given in the index.

Japanese words and names are romanized according to the modified Hepburn system, save that macrons, indicating long vowel sounds, are omitted from names of persons, places and institutions (e.g. Tojo, instead of Tōjō; Choshu, instead of Chōshū; Dajokan, instead of Dajōkan), as well as from some familiar terms like Shinto (properly Shintō). Macrons are given in all such cases in the index.

1

THE TOKUGAWA LEGACY

It is now generally recognized that Japan has been much the most successful of the countries outside Europe and North America in achieving modernization. Much of this book will be concerned with how that came about. One context in which such a discussion has to be put is that of the relationship between tradition and modernity. Like other peoples, the Japanese have faced problems in adjusting their values and their social institutions to the industrial age; but for them the experience has been exceptionally disturbing, because the discontinuities have been cultural as well as social. What they left behind was both traditional and Asian. What they moved towards was both modern and Western. The transformation therefore required them, not merely to abandon past modes of thought and ways of doing things, but also to sacrifice a part of their cultural identity. It posed the question, can one be simultaneously 'modern' and Japanese?

That is one reason why an account of Japan in the past hundred years or so should start with some assessment of Japan as it was before modernity began. It is necessary to identify points of departure. One needs to do so, moreover, because they have had an influence on the processes of change itself. A ruling class which, in the third quarter of the nineteenth century, incorporated several hundred thousand samurai families could not be expected to develop social and political structures identical with those of contemporary Britain or France or Germany, still less those of the United States. An economy which leapt in little more than a generation from late feudal to early industrial forms of organization was hardly likely to behave in strict accordance with Western economic doctrine. A religious and philosophical tradition based on Shinto, Buddhism and the Confucian ethic was bound to react to the challenge from scientific thought and nationalism in ways which differed from that of Christianity. In other words, there is an element of Japaneseness, as well as of universality, in what has happened in modern Japan.

Inevitably the interpretation of it has provoked controversy. All the same, there is a wide measure of agreement about where one should begin, which is with Japan under Tokugawa rule (1600–1868). This was the formative age for institutions which contributed to both social stability and oppression in later years. It gave rise to an embryo capitalism, which was the prerequisite for Western-style industrial growth. It shaped in a definitive form the national traditions of culture and ideas, on which subsequent generations were to depend, or from which they were to detach themselves. Moreover, the overthrow of the Tokugawa, and the events surrounding it, comprise by common consent the first phase in the transition from pre-modern to modern in Japanese history. Tokugawa society and the manner of its end will therefore form the subject of the first three chapters of this book.

POLITICAL SOCIETY

Britain's first diplomatic representative in Japan, Rutherford Alcock, writing in 1863 after spending three years in the country, described Japanese government in terms of Europe's middle ages. Feudalism, he said, 'after time and out of place', was to be found in Japan 'with sufficient identity and analogy in all its leading features to make the coincidence striking'.[1] Scholars would still accept the statement as valid in some degree. In 1850 members of Japan's ruling class, the lords and their samurai, remained bound to each other by ties of vassalage and for the most part exacted from the peasantry a portion of the crop as feudal dues. On the other hand, it would now more often be argued that in other respects Japan was ceasing to be feudal, having developed in ways for which medieval Europe offers no close parallel. Central authority was stronger than in England or France before 1450. The lords' domains were in size and organization more like princedoms than fiefs. Most samurai did not themselves hold land in return for service, or live in villages as lords of a manor. Indeed, the exercise of power, both nationally and locally, was substantially bureaucratic.

The system derived from a period of civil wars in the fifteenth and sixteenth centuries, when men of military ability and administrative skill had carved out for themselves large territories, and secured formal recognition of their authority within them. The last and greatest of these men was Ieyasu, founder of the Tokugawa house. In 1600 he won national hegemony by a victory over the lords of west Japan. In 1603 he took the office of Shogun, nominally the emperor's military deputy, but for some centuries held by *de facto* rulers of Japan (from whom Ieyasu claimed descent). It gave him an overlordship which extended to all men and all places, even to the Imperial Court itself. In Kyoto, the emperor's capital, the Shogun was represented by a governor, chosen from among his own relatives or vassals. Court nobles appointed to act in his interests had to swear a special oath of allegiance to him. Senior officials at the Court, though their titles recalled the days when emperors had ruled as well as reigned, were left to perform duties which were no more than ceremonial, bearing hardly at all on government; and for recompense they depended on the Shogun's favour, which was not generous. Even those whose rank was the highest in the land enjoyed an income, measured in rice, smaller than that of many of the Shogun's own household officers. Moreover, their life was regulated in its every detail – dress, marriages, codes of behaviour, even literary pursuits and pastimes – by laws which the Shogun issued. The emperor himself was a Tokugawa pensioner, virtually a prisoner in his palace.

In sharp contrast were the men in the Shogun's capital of Edo (later to be Tokyo). These were the real rulers of Japan. Most powerful among them, the Shogun held as feudal lord lands whose estimated yield was some 15 per cent of that of Japan at large. His samurai, excluding those who were vassals-in-chief, held 10 per cent more. The running of these vast estates involved thousands of officials, great and small, whose labours brought together the revenues from which were paid the Shogun's household expenses, salaries, stipends for those officers who had no land, and occasional grants in aid to the loyal but impoverished. From the same source came the funds for governing Japan, in so far as these were not provided by feudal lords from their own resources.

In theory the office of Shogun was both hereditary and autocratic, but after 1650 the Tokugawa line rarely produced a man capable of absolute rule. For the most part, decisions were taken by those who held posts in his central administration, which was known as the Bakufu. At the head of it were the councillors (*Rōjū*), usually four or five in number, who were responsible for general policy and for supervision of the country's other lords. All were Tokugawa henchmen, ranking as vassals-in-chief. Below them came men of lesser standing, also vassals of the Shogun, who administered (in descending order of rank) shrines and temples, finance, the two capitals, Edo and Kyoto, other important urban centres, like Osaka and Nagasaki, and the Tokugawa estates.

Throughout the country feudal lords (*daimyō*) were classified in terms of their relationship to the Tokugawa. Those of Tokugawa blood (most bore the older family name of Matsudaira) were excluded from office as a rule, but exercised a good deal of influence by virtue of their wealth and birth. Below them were the *fudai*, numbering nearly 150 by the end of the period. These were Tokugawa vassals of long standing, from whose ranks were filled the Bakufu's main offices. The rest of the *daimyō* were the hundred or so *tozama*, or 'outside' lords, who were independent, save for the powers the Shogun had over them by virtue of the emperor's commission, and excluded from central government posts.

All *daimyō* were in some degree free from Edo's interference. Within the boundaries of his domain – an area which might contain anything from a dozen or so villages up to a complete province, sometimes more – the lord was absolute master. His administration was usually patterned on that of the Tokugawa, senior councillors being chosen from collateral branches of his own house or from a few families of leading retainers, while other posts were filled by samurai of middle or lower rank, who served as bureaucrats in the castle town or as intendants governing rural districts. In none of their duties were they directly accountable to the Shogun or his representatives. Nor did the domain owe taxes to the Bakufu. On the other hand, the lord as a person had no such freedom: the Shogun had the right to transfer him from one fief to another, to reduce the size of his holding, or even to confiscate it altogether, if he gave cause. Once in a generation or so his house was likely to be called upon to carry out expensive public works, like flood control, road-building, or repairs to one of the Shogun's castles. Its marriage alliances were subject to Bakufu approval. So were its defences. Most important of all, each lord was required to spend half his time – six months or twelve months at a stretch – in Edo, leaving members of his family there as hostages when he returned to his province. This system of 'alternate attendance' (*sankin-kōtai*) was fundamental to the maintenance of political authority. Its cost was a regular burden on a lord's finances.

In the last resort it was the distribution of land which enabled the Tokugawa to enforce these rules, for land was the basis of the feudal army. It was measured, not by area, but by estimated yield, stated in *koku* of rice (1 *koku* equals about 5 bushels); and contemporary writers assumed a rough equivalence between land assessment in *koku* and numbers in the population, so that a domain of 100,000 *koku* would be expected to have about 100,000 inhabitants. The first three Tokugawa rulers had carried out a major redistribution of fiefs, by which they and their adherents acquired, not only the lion's share of the whole, but also a dominant position in strategic areas. In addition to the 25 per cent of the national total of land which belonged to the Shogun and his direct retainers, Tokugawa branch families had another 10 per cent and Tokugawa vassals-in-chief, the *fudai*, twice as much again. Most of these estates were concentrated in the central region of Japan, constituting a 'central fortress' which gave the Bakufu control of the area round Edo and Kyoto, plus the routes connecting them. The *tozama* lords were left with about 40 per cent of the country's territory, mostly in the south and west or in the north-east, the most powerful of them, the so-called 'province-holders', being subject to the watchful attentions of a *fudai* established on their borders.

Because domains played a major part in the political turbulence with which the early chapters of this book will be concerned, it may be useful to identify a few of them. Only one *fudai* had a holding over 200,000 *koku*. This was Ii of Hikone, whose lands straddled the eastern approaches to Kyoto. Of the Tokugawa branch houses, Mito was about the same size as Hikone, while Wakayama (Kii) and Nagoya (Owari) each exceeded half a million *koku*. Kanazawa (Kaga) on the Japan Sea coast was the largest of the *tozama*, rated at just over a million. Kagoshima (Satsuma) came next at nearly 800,000; and there were fourteen more at 200,000 and over, of which Saga (Hizen) in northern Kyushu, Yamaguchi (Choshu) on the straits between Kyushu and Honshu, and Kochi (Tosa) in southern Shikoku were to be particularly important in the nineteenth century.

Within the towns and villages which made up these territories, pride of place went always to the samurai. Originally he had often been a farmer-warrior, tilling the soil in times of peace and following his lord into battle in times of war; but with the increasing scale and complexity of warfare in the fifteenth and sixteenth centuries, fighting became something for specialists, so that the functions of the samurai and the farmer became distinct. In the end – the change was made formal in 1588 – the farmer was forbidden to carry arms, the samurai was incorporated into something very like a garrison, living in a strongly-defended castle from which the surrounding countryside was governed. It was in this way that the typical domain of the Tokugawa period took shape. It was large and usually compact. Within its frontiers the lord brooked no challenge to his authority over men and land, whether from the once-powerful shrines and temples, or from his own followers. Only a few of the latter were allowed to retain fiefs of their own and these were subject to a system of control which was a replica in miniature of that which Edo imposed on *daimyō*. Most samurai lost their land entirely. In return they received stipends from the domain treasury, payable in rice, or in some instances in cash.

The transformation of the samurai was carried a stage further by the Tokugawa success in restoring and then maintaining law and order after centuries of civil war. He was no longer so much needed as a soldier. On the other hand, the nature of the new domain made him all the more important as a civil official. In every castle-town there was a multitude of posts to be filled, their duties ranging from the making of policy to the administration of a rural district, from supervision of finance and archives to service as attendants and messengers. All were filled by samurai, in most cases samurai of a specified rank. The insistence on status qualifications for appointment made the system stiff and cumbersome, but it enabled many thousands of men – there were 400,000 samurai families – to enter the modern age with a knowledge of office routine and some experience in dealing with regulations. This made them suitable recruits to a modern bureaucracy. As we shall see later in this chapter, they had also developed an ideology appropriate to such functions.

This is not to say that Japan had an effective governmental service before the Tokugawa fell. Many samurai had nothing to do but garrison duties. Most were underemployed: it was a common complaint among reformers that there were more jobs than work. For a majority, indeed, appointment was principally a means of supplementing inadequate hereditary stipends. It normally carried modest allowances, but salary, in the form of a temporary addition to stipend, was paid only to those few whose promotion carried them above the level of posts identified with their rank. Thus a significant rise in income had to depend on achieving higher status, something which might come through marriage or adoption, or through favouritism, but not often through merit.

The relationship between samurai and the rest of the population was also very much a matter of status. The classic description of Tokugawa society is one of fixed stratification: a descending hierarchy of samurai, farmer, artisan, and merchant, each segment subdivided and the differences between them rigidly maintained. In reality this is misleading. Overwhelmingly the most important distinction was that between samurai and the rest.

The key to the relationship was that samurai lived in towns, from which they governed villages. In some areas, it is true, there were 'rural samurai' (*gōshi*), who had been allowed to retain their original lands and live in the countryside; but in order to do so they had sacrificed most of the privileges of samurai rank, including that of holding office, so they were not in any sense the equivalent of European lords of the manor. Nor were they part of the regular village community, which consisted ideally – from the lord's viewpoint – of peasant farmers, bound to the soil, each cultivating a plot large enough to support his family and paying any surplus of his crop as feudal dues. It was a system of equality in misery. The local representative of authority was the village headman, always a farmer, usually one of more substance than the rest. It was his duty to apportion individual shares of taxation, which the domain imposed on the community as a whole. He was answerable to his lord for the village's good order; settled civil disputes between its inhabitants; arranged details of irrigation use; organized festivals. Samurai from the domain's administrative centre, holding office as steward or local magistrate, came only to deal with crises (natural disasters and human disturbances), or when the crop was to be assessed for tax. They were outsiders, held much in awe.

One consequence of this was that samurai, though they governed, were not involved in the day-to-day management of agriculture, a fact that was to prove crucial to their economic standing. Their position in the towns was, on the face of it, much stronger. With few exceptions, Tokugawa towns were castle-towns, the result of detaching samurai from the land and assembling them round the *daimyō*'s stronghold in the sixteenth and seventeenth centuries. The merchants and artisans who gathered to serve them there, providing goods for their use and financial expertise for their tax-collecting, had much less chance of escaping supervision than the farmers had. They lived in the shadow of the castle, occupying districts separate from those of the samurai, each with its headman, who was responsible to castle officials; and even though they protected themselves as best they could against oppression and bad debts by forming guilds, which paid modest fees in return for market rights and monopolies, they were never able to escape from the authority of the samurai, beside whom they lived. Against that, propinquity gave the town dwellers some leverage to use against their masters. As contemporary conservatives were quick to point out, samurai, because they lived in towns, were open to corruption by urban extravagance. As a result, long before the nineteenth century, feudal debt had become a feature of Japan's political economy.

THE ECONOMY

There are two ways of looking at the significance of the Tokugawa economy for later history. One can describe it as a cause of the Bakufu's collapse, focusing one's attention on such things as shifts in the regional and social distribution of wealth, the failure of government, both nationally and locally, to come to terms with economic change, and the proliferation of economic discontents. Or one can treat it as a phase in the development of Japanese capitalism, to which the fate of the Tokugawa is almost irrelevant: a matter of economic motivation, skills, and institutions. Both approaches are separately subjects of controversy. So is the allocation of priority between them.

The seventeenth century was a period of rapid economic growth. Feudal officials did not often collect the kind of information needed by modern statisticians, but the outlines of what occurred are clear enough from such evidence as we have. There was a rapid rise in population and in land under cultivation, once stability had been restored after the long years of civil war; this was accompanied by an increase in agricultural production, which stimulated domestic commerce; and commerce meant more and larger towns. Most of these, as we have said, were castle-towns, each bound to its local hinterland by the needs of tax-collecting and food supply. They were all linked to Edo by the rules of 'alternate attendance'. The requirement that each lord and members of his family, accompanied by substantial numbers of servants and retainers, must live in the Shogun's capital half the year made necessary not only a regular transfer of resources from the domain, but also facilities for the movement of goods and people. Osaka became the centre for the commercial and financial aspects of the system, Edo a huge consumer market, housing at any one time a large proportion of the ruling class. There were several corollaries: a high degree of functional differentiation among the merchants of Edo and Osaka; the development of roads and shipping routes to link the two cities with each other and with the rest of the country; and the creation of a national market in some commodities.

The character of agriculture was much influenced by these changes. In parts of Japan villages began to move away from subsistence farming in favour of production for the market. Some cash crops became regional specialities: silk in the mountains to the north of the road between Edo and Nagoya; cotton to the west of Nagoya as far as the Osaka region; sugar round Kagoshima and in the islands to the south. Farmers turned to more efficient methods of production, involving greater use of farm animals and fertilizer. And once started, the process of development continued – at varying pace – for the rest of the Tokugawa period. By the nineteenth century, Thomas Smith concludes, farmers, except those in backward areas, 'typically grew what soil, climate, and price favored, regardless of what they themselves happened to need'.[2]

One cannot estimate the country's production accurately, of course, though on Malthusian principles population is an indicator of sorts: it grew from about 18 million in 1600 to something like 30 million by 1850. So is urbanization. Rozman estimates that at the beginning of the period some 7 per cent of Japanese lived in towns. By the end of it this had risen to nearer 16 per cent, the densest concentration being in the plains round Edo and Osaka. Edo itself had a population of a million persons (half a million being samurai) in the early eighteenth century; Kyoto had 400,000; Osaka, which was almost wholly a commercial city, had 300,000.

It is clear from these very broad-brush statements that well before there was any stimulus from Western capitalism Japan had reached a stage of development from which modern economic growth was within its reach. The national economy had a high degree of integration. In the more advanced regions villagers were already making use of cash for purchases, rather than subsisting on what they grew and made themselves. Some of them were becoming landlords and entrepreneurs, marketing crops and fertilizer, manufacturing saké or textiles. In the towns there were merchants capable of handling large wholesale deals, organizing regular shipping routes, raising loans and transferring credits of significant size.

There are some points on which it is impossible to be so definite, though their importance warrants speculation. One is the relationship between urban and rural growth. After about 1720 the overall increase in population was slow. There was some expansion in regions which scholars now classify as 'intermediate' – mostly in south and west Japan – but this was balanced by static or even declining figures for urban areas at the centre. Thomas Smith has put forward an explanation of this in terms of the transfer of manufacturing activities from towns, where they were more closely under the scrutiny of tax officials and the monopoly powers of guilds, to the nearby countryside, where they had greater freedom and could benefit from the use of part-time rural labour. Since this labour came in the form of farm by-employment, taking up the slack not required for agriculture at certain seasons of the year, there was no need for an expanding population in order that levels of production might be maintained, or even enlarged. As a result, one assumes, there would have been an increase in rural incomes and spending power. Hanley and Yamamura cite evidence that in some areas production outpaced population growth, which implies an average improvement in standards of living and personal wealth (though there remains a problem about its distribution).

These arguments are relevant to an understanding of how Japan was able to industrialize after 1870. They do, however, rest on uncertain statistical foundations, as inevitably they must when much of the material is scattered and anecdotal. Nor should one overlook the factors which still held back any move towards industrial capitalism: the narrowness of Japan's domestic market, fragmented by feudal separatism; limitations on the movement of labour, arising from the determination of the lords to keep men on the land; the backwardness of manufacturing technology, which had not yet advanced beyond the use of water for power; and the close ties between merchant capital, monopoly guilds, and political authority in the towns. All these things had to be modified or ended before the economy reached a point of take-off.

About the short-term consequences of Tokugawa economic change there is less uncertainty. The most conspicuous was its effect on government finance. Both Bakufu and domains raised much the greatest part of their revenues in rice. Leaving aside the stipends they paid to samurai, their expenditures were largely in the money economy of the towns, where prices not only drifted steadily upward over the years, but also fluctuated widely at quite short intervals. Matching expenditure to revenue in these circumstances was beyond the capacity of most feudal officials, who turned to merchants for advice and to borrowing as a means of making good the occasional deficiencies. Before the end of the seventeenth century most administrations were heavily in debt.

From time to time efforts were made to cope with the situation by economy drives of various kinds, but the preferred solution was usually to raise more revenue. Attempts to levy higher dues on the peasant, though made, were limited in effect, because tax levels were already close to the point at which they would provoke resistance. Taxing merchants – apart from some small imposts on the guilds and on urban housing – was apparently beyond the regime's competence. This left two other financial devices. One was manipulation of the currency: debasement of the coinage by the Bakufu, which was undertaken several times, beginning in 1695, and the issue of paper money by domains. Since these measures tended to increase the instability of urban prices, they proved no more than palliatives. So did the second recourse open to officialdom, which was to put pressure on merchants to subscribe to 'loans' (*goyōkin*). There was little expectation that subscribers to them would get their money back, but they carried inducements in the form of social dignities, such as minor samurai rank, to encourage generosity. The practice was becoming so widespread by the end of the period as to come close to being a tax on commercial wealth.

Of more significance for the future was the creation of monopolies, especially by domains, in which government not only provided a framework of authority, but also took a major share of the gains. Their basis was a partnership between the lord's treasury and the privileged merchants of the castle-town for the purpose of buying some specialized product of the region – not infrequently at fixed prices, paid in domain paper money – then 'exporting' it to Osaka or other commercial markets. There were cases, like Kagoshima's sugar crop, where the profits were enhanced by draconian rules against selling outside the monopoly and by seizing part of the crop by way of tax.

One result of this development, which reached its peak in the early decades of the nineteenth century, was to bequeath to post-Tokugawa Japan a modicum of commercial knowledge among samurai officials, together with a habit of intervention in the economy. For example, Mizuno Tadakuni, who was the Bakufu's senior councillor between 1841 and 1843, carried out a reform programme which included sumptuary laws, limitation of interest rates on loans, and controls on commodity prices (reinforced by the abolition of merchant monopolies in Edo, which he believed were keeping prices high). His measures proved too ambitious for the administrative machinery at his disposal for enforcing them. Others, setting their sights lower, achieved more. Between 1833 and 1848 Zusho Hiromichi restored Satsuma's finances by reducing waste and reorganizing the sugar monopoly. Murata Seifu did much the same for Choshu between 1838 and 1844, though he took a different line, putting an end to the domain's monopolies (apparently because of the hostility they had aroused among rural producers), and seeking to stimulate agricultural production.

Despite the existence of reformers and monopolists, men with any kind of commercial or financial skill were in a minority among samurai, many of whom got their household finances into disarray through a simple inability to cope with the urban economy in which they lived. Those who received stipends in rice – the great majority – had to turn them into cash in order to pay their living expenses. They usually did this by making a regular arrangement with a merchant, who served as agent but also made advances against future income in case of need. There were all sorts of reasons why such advances proved difficult to repay: high interest rates; the fact that samurai always had the worst of the market (large numbers, all selling at the same time, drove prices down); and rising expectations, that is, the temptations offered to families which were in effect on fixed incomes by an ever greater availability of goods. Unlike their lords, samurai who fell into debt could not use the domain's authority to extricate themselves. This left few options. They could form ties through marriage or adoption with a well-to-do merchant house, so marketing their rank. They could abandon their samurai status, by withdrawing from their duties in the castle-town and taking up agriculture or trade. Or they could decline into genteel poverty, as many of them did.

Yet the social disorder to which these circumstances gave rise among samurai was certainly no greater than that to be found in the countryside. Commercial agriculture and the spread of a money economy to the village offered opportunities for poverty, as well as wealth. Those who already had plots larger than the average were likely to grow richer, simply because they had the resources to open up new land and pay for improvements in technology. In addition, as urban markets developed, some lesser farmers turned to raising the cash crops for which rising standards of living in the towns created a demand: silk, cotton, paper, wax, rape seed, and indigo. These became ancillary crops for many, main crops for some. For the successful they were very profitable. On the other hand, those who failed in this new economic environment, squeezed between penal taxation and rising costs, had recourse to the money lender, often losing their land because of it. Many formerly independent cultivators became tenants or even landless labourers. Some made their way to the towns. Others remained, forming a pool of workers for the industries which began to spring up in rural areas, like cotton-spinning and weaving, dyeing, the brewing of saké, or the manufacture of paper.

These developments were at their height during the last quarter of the eighteenth century and the first quarter of the nineteenth, a period which saw the emergence of a class of rural entrepreneurs whose wealth was not based exclusively on land. These were farmers who had seized the opportunities which commerce presented and had been able to extend their operations into retailing, money lending or manufacture – or even all of them – keeping an interest in the soil as landlords but devoting relatively little of their time to its management. Such men were to be found in almost every village in the more economically advanced regions of central and west Japan. In food, dress, education, and entertainment they lived like samurai of middle rank or better. Despite this, it was not easy for them to break through formal status barriers, except by marrying into the families of minor officials, or by subscribing heavily to domain loans in order to acquire the right to bear a family name and wear the two swords of the samurai.

If the nature of Tokugawa government bequeathed to modern Japan the makings of a bureaucracy, social change in the village provided both the elements of a non-agricultural work-force and the nucleus of an élite concerned with commerce and industry. It also prompted forms of unrest which were to remain important through much of modern history. There had always been occasions when tyrannical lords or unjust officials had driven peasants to the point of desperation. After about 1800, however, there were two new causes of discontent. One was the exploitation of poor peasants by rich peasants, especially those who acted as money lenders. The other was the entry of feudal authority into the business of monopolies, depressing the profits of those farmers who had most to gain from commercial crops. There has been much debate among scholars about which of these factors was 'characteristic' of peasant revolt in the late Tokugawa period; but the fact is that all were present – sometimes in the same area at the same time – and contributed to outbreaks which grew rapidly in scale and frequency. In January 1823, for example, a mob said to be 70,000 strong stormed the town of Miyazu, a little north-west of Kyoto, in protest against an additional tax imposed by the lord. In the summer of 1831 anti-monopoly demonstrations near the town of Mitajiri in Choshu touched off riots, which then spread into mountainous districts of the domain, where they took the form of protests against tax levels and usury. This rising was one of a series in Choshu, continuing to 1837. For Japan as a whole it has been estimated that there were about 400 such incidents between 1813 and 1868 (though many would be better described as demonstrations or riotous assemblies than as rebellions in the full sense).

Like other phenomena prompted by economic change, they had political implications of lasting consequence. The tensions within village society, exacerbated by the modernizing policies of the Meiji period, were to remain a problem for Japan well into the twentieth century, as landlord–tenant disputes succeeded peasant revolt. More immediately, they raised among Tokugawa lords and samurai a sense of instability and crisis, a doubt about the durability of their way of life, which was being more and more reflected in contemporary debate.

CULTURE AND IDEAS

Much of traditional Japanese culture derived from China. Buddhism had first reached Japan in Chinese form; Confucianism was the country's only fully fledged philosophy; and a good deal of art was specifically Chinese in style, as were the more elegant pursuits of the upper classes. Chinese was Japan's classical language. Yet over the centuries most of these things had been so thoroughly naturalized, sometimes in symbiosis with indigenous ideas and practices, that by 1850 Japanese had come to accept them as their own.

Until 1550 Buddhism had been Japan's most powerful religion, both temporally and spiritually, but in the next hundred years the emerging *daimyō*, in the course of imposing their own authority within their domains, had deprived it of many lands and almost all its independence. Nevertheless, many sects, once they had bowed to the inevitable, received a measure of political patronage which enabled them to claim the formal allegiance of the greater part of the population. That allegiance was not exclusive, however. At the popular level Shinto rituals, especially those which concerned crops and marriage, continued to be observed alongside Buddhist ones in every village and household, forming part of an eclecticism which explained Shinto deities as manifestations of the Buddha and located Shinto shrines in Buddhist temple grounds. Confucian ideas, which had entered Japan from China along with Buddhist ones, provided as their contribution a simplified code of behaviour, applying to this world, which matched Buddhism's preoccupation with the next.

Allowing for variations in emphasis between one generation and another, this situation has persisted for most of modern times, so far as it applies to the mass of the population. Yet for élites, both intellectual and political, the composition of the eclecticism has changed a good deal. In the Tokugawa period Confucianism was very much more the philosophy of the educated samurai than of anyone else. Its prevalent form was Neo-Confucianism, as elaborated by Chu Hsi and other Chinese scholars of the Sung dynasty: one which gave the Confucian ethical concern with human behaviour in society a bias towards the maintenance of order and authority. It derived from a definition of the relationships between man and man, that is, what the seventeenth-century scholar Hayashi Razan described as 'the moral obligations between sovereign and subject, father and child, husband and wife, elder and younger brother, and friend and friend'.[3] These, except the last, were relations of inequality, reflecting the nature of the universe: 'heaven remains above and earth remains below'. In China they were used to justify the dominant place of the scholar-official in society. In Japan some adjustment was required to take account of the fact that samurai possessed status by circumstance of birth, but they were nevertheless applicable to his role as civil bureaucrat. Generations of samurai were accordingly brought up on the Confucian classics.

Some of what they learnt was simply a modification of Chineseness. There was, for example, an ethnocentric sense of cultural superiority, asserted not against China, the parent civilization, but against all other peoples in the world: the 'barbarians'. There was also an idealization of agriculture, partly signifying the ethical primacy of production over profit, partly the dependence of rulers – in Japan, as in China – on the farmer for revenue. Both were to be enduring elements in the Japanese value system. More specifically, Confucianism had its place in a reformulation of the samurai's code, Bushido. As stated by medieval writers this had identified the warrior virtues as obedience to lord and parent, respect for the gods (both Shinto and Buddhist), courage and self-discipline, plus a range of qualities appropriate to the officer and man of breeding. In the seventeenth century Yamaga Soko, one of Hayashi Razan's pupils, put these things into the context of the Confucian ethic, turning back for this purpose to the age of Confucius himself, which had been feudal, rather than that of the absolutist dynasties of later date. The central duties remained for Yamaga those of loyalty and filial piety. The samurai, however, was not just to observe them, but also to be mentor and moral exemplar to the people as a whole, undertaking 'personal cultivation, the guidance of others, the maintaining of peace and order in the world, and the winning of honor and fame . . .'[4] In other words, as the samurai's function changed from that of soldier to official, so he was encouraged to think of himself in terms that had been devised for the Chinese scholar-mandarin.

Yamaga Soko went further. Late in life, when attacks by Neo-Confucian rivals had driven him into provincial exile, he began to claim that the teachings of Confucius had first been divinely revealed in Japan's sage-emperors, so that historically it had been Japan, more than China, which had been the true repository of Confucian wisdom. This was the beginning, not only of a chain of argument that led some of his successors to identify Japan, not China, as the 'central kingdom', that is, the heartland of Asian culture, but also of an accommodation between Shinto and Confucianism that was to characterize much of late Tokugawa thought.

One aspect of it was a religious revival, intended to free Shinto from Buddhist domination. Another was the rejection of Confucianism as universal truth. The greatest of the Shinto scholars, Motoori Norinaga, writing in the eighteenth century, proposed a specifically Japanese view of good and evil, stemming not from imported beliefs but from Japan's own experience and tradition. It rested, he said, on divine revelation, transmitted by the sun goddess, Amaterasu, through her descendants, Japan's imperial line: 'Our Imperial Land . . . is superior to the rest of the world in its possession of the correct transmission of the ancient Way, which is that of the great goddess who casts her light all over the world.'[5] Though this can be dismissed as cultural chauvinism, much like China's, it was put in a conceptual framework different from the Confucian one. The specific components of the ethic Motoori outlines were much the same as those of Confucianism –Shinto had none of its own which might replace them – but it was given a validation uniquely Japanese.

The Shinto revival performed a similar service for notions of political authority. In Chinese terms, a ruler's right to require obedience from his subjects depended, at least in part, on his own observance of the Confucian ethic. Principle was superior to naked power. In Japan, such a doctrine had sometimes been applied to the Shogun; but the emperor, as Motoori and his colleagues saw it, ruled by prescriptive right, acting 'in perfect harmony of thought and feeling' with his ancestress, the sun goddess, and by that very fact entitled to unquestioning obedience. That made the emperor's authority independent of his virtue, or lack of it.

By 1900 such ideas were to be orthodox in Japan, but under the Tokugawa they were dangerously subversive. Motoori avoided Bakufu censure by asserting that things were as they were by will of the gods, so had to be accepted, even when the emperor's prerogatives were being exercised – improperly, in theory – by a Shogun. In the next generation Confucian scholars serving the Tokugawa branch house of Mito, of whom Aizawa Seishisai was the most famous, took a different route to a very similar conclusion. They reconciled feudal duty with imperial absolutism by arguing that loyalty was hierarchical: the samurai owed it to his lord, the lord to Shogun, Shogun to emperor. This enabled them to bring together several diverse elements into a new political philosophy. One was the Shinto concept of imperial divinity, which they used to validate the feudal order. Another was Confucian agrarianism, made into an argument for condemning all those developments in town and countryside which were putting the samurai's way of life at risk. A third was the Confucian ethic, detached from the Chinese cosmogony, so as to become simply a code of personal behaviour, conducive of social discipline. These were the essentials of what was called 'national learning' (*kokugaku*).

They were not by any means acceptable to everyone in late Tokugawa Japan. Quite apart from any objections that might be made on religious or philosophical grounds, a view of the social order which put samurai at the top and merchants at the bottom was unlikely to be welcome to the latter, no matter how it was justified. Many merchants, seeing the Shinto revival as an indirect attack on samurai ideology, gave their allegiance to Motoori and his successor, Hirata Atsutane, rather than to the Mito school. This was true in the countryside as well as in the towns. Yet most of those below the crucial dividing line between samurai and commoner preferred, except when driven by specific grievances, to avoid any political commitment that might attract the hostility of the Bakufu's police and censors. Ishida Baigan, for example, who in the eighteenth century argued that the merchant was worthy of greater respect, did so on the grounds that trade was a proper form of service to the state, entitled to recognition. This was an affirmation, not a denial, of the dominant values of society, capable of coexisting with a samurai-type code of loyalty, frugality and filial piety.

The fact was that town life under the Tokugawa, at least for the well-to-do, was one of extravagant costume, exotic foods and elaborate pastimes, which constituted an escape from political thought, not a stimulus to it. It contributed a new element to Japanese culture, one of noise and turbulence and colour, quite unlike the restraint thought proper to the classical and aristocratic traditions established by Buddhism and the Imperial Court. To cater to the whims of those merchants and others who could afford it, as well as some who could not, there emerged what contemporaries called *ukiyo*, 'the floating world'. In the words of a modern historian, it was a world 'of fugitive pleasures, of theatres and restaurants, wrestling-booths and houses of assignation, with their permanent population of actors, dancers, singers, story-tellers, jesters, courtesans, bath-girls and itinerant purveyors, among whom mingled the profligate sons of rich merchants, dissolute samurai and naughty apprentices'.[6] This was hardly the material for a political revolution, but it provided the subject-matter for an art and literature that had the makings of a social one. Colour prints depicted actors and famous *geisha*, as well as street scenes in busy commercial quarters. The theatre, especially the puppet drama, found its themes in subjects which the townsmen relished: the clash between feudal or family loyalty and personal inclination, or the fortunes, good and bad, of rich merchants and poor artisans, of their mistresses and wives. Novels and short stories, often bawdy, took the same line. It was not a literature for the prudish, but it was bursting with life.

It is possible to draw two conclusions from all this. One is that economic change was creating an 'alternative' society alongside the feudal one, but had not yet given rise to a political philosophy appropriate to it. The other is that Japan was moving away from cultural Chineseness in the direction of something more obviously indigenous and less completely the prerogative of an élite. Both statements have substance. One must bear in mind, however, that samurai, or men of samurai origin, were to provide the country's political leadership at least until the end of the Meiji emperor's reign (1912); and while they did so, their cultural preferences continued to determine norms. Samurai values remain a significant part of modern Japanese life.

2

WESTERN CHALLENGE, JAPANESE RESPONSE

There is a Chinese phrase, rendered in Japanese as *naiyū-gaikan*, 'troubles at home, dangers from abroad', which describes a state of affairs likely to bring about the downfall of a dynasty. The Japanese were reminded of it by their situation in the middle of the nineteenth century. Feudal reformers had increasingly shown themselves to be concerned about 'troubles at home', whether in the form of financial crises or of peasant revolt. Samurai intellectuals – principally the Confucian scholars employed by the Bakufu and domains – wrote books and pamphlets setting out their own prescriptions for a cure. It would be wrong to say because of this that Japan was in ferment; but there was a prevailing sense of unease, and it became acute when 'dangers from abroad' also materialized, signalled first by reports of what was happening in China, then by visits of foreign warships to Japanese harbours.

In this and the following chapter we shall be examining the manner in which the Japanese reacted when their way of life seemed to be threatened by what was taking place. Many saw the foreign threat as a problem which could only be solved by making significant political changes within Japan, or by adopting methods, such as the use of Western military science and industrial technology, which would have profound implications for the nature of Japanese culture and society. The slogans of the age reflected such concerns: *sonnō-jōi*, 'honour the emperor, expel the barbarian'; *fukoku-kyōhei*, 'enrich the country, strengthen the military'. Each implied a causal relationship, in which action to be taken at home was a condition of success abroad. For this reason the story of foreign relations and that of domestic politics cannot readily be disentangled.

THE CLOSED COUNTRY

In the 1620s and 1630s the Tokugawa rulers had come to the conclusion that Japan's existing relations with Europeans should be discontinued, partly because they gave Japanese dissidents the possibility of alliance with a military force outside Bakufu control, partly because they had opened Japan to 'corruption' by the ideas of Christianity. Christianity was savagely persecuted. Once it had been suppressed, regulations were issued to ensure that it would not be revived. Soon foreign trade was also brought to an end, except in so far as it was allowed to continue on a small scale through Chinese junks coming to Nagasaki and through a Dutch trading post established within that port at Deshima.

These decisions inaugurated the policy of the 'closed country' (*sakoku*), which was to last until 1854. Such trade as survived was closely supervised by Bakufu officials; Dutch merchants were only permitted to travel within Japan under escort for approved purposes; and Japanese people were forbidden to go abroad on pain of death. Hence contact with the outside world was very limited. Dutch and Chinese were required to report from time to time on what was happening in Europe and Asia, though the information they gave was restricted as a rule to the Edo government. In addition, they imported books (carefully scrutinized for signs of Christian influence) and a few artefacts, like clocks, which gave those Japanese with access to them some notion of changes in Western science and technology. The Dutch establishment at Deshima also served an interested public as a specimen of European life – there are Japanese pictures of its residents sitting on chairs, eating with knives and forks, playing billiards – and in later years the physicians attached to it were able to impart the rudiments of their profession to Japanese doctors. Nevertheless, national seclusion, as it is called, meant that Japan was substantially cut off from a knowledge of what was happening beyond East Asia.

That, at least, was true for the first hundred years or so. Thereafter, hostility towards knowledge of the West slowly declined, as curiosity overcame suspicion, and anti-Christian sentiment was dulled by time. Censorship did not come to an end by any means, but in relation to matters that were politically neutral, like art, or useful, like medicine and cartography, it was relaxed. Late in the eighteenth century, for example, Ino Tadataka produced under Bakufu patronage an accurate map of the Japanese islands, using Western-style instruments and techniques. His contemporary, Shiba Kokan, experimented with oil painting and copperplate etching.

These developments came at a time when Western countries showed signs of renewing their interest in Japan. During the Napoleonic wars a British frigate visited Nagasaki on a commerce-raiding mission, seizing hostages and holding them until provided with stores. In 1813 and 1814, when Java was occupied by Britain, the lieutenant-governor, Thomas Stamford Raffles, tried to initiate a British trade with Nagasaki under the Dutch flag, though without success. More ominously, Russians began to appear in the north, setting up fishing and hunting posts in the Kuril islands from their territories round the Sea of Okhotsk. In 1792, and again in 1804, they sent representatives to seek access to Japanese ports. When the second of these was turned away –with scant courtesy – Russian officers carried out raids on Japanese settlements in the islands. The Bakufu responded by seizing the captain of a Russian surveying vessel in 1811.

The British and Russian approaches were made on local initiative, not as a result of policy in London and St Petersburg, but Japanese officials were not in a position to know that this was so. Consequently there was a hardening of Bakufu attitudes towards the West in the early nineteenth century. There was also a shift of emphasis in studies of it. English and Russian were added to the languages acquired by the handful of Bakufu interpreters. Military science and technology began to figure more prominently in the writings of the 'Dutch scholars' – so called because they based their work on books which Deshima imported – and in Edo a translation bureau was established with those subjects very much in mind. One official in Nagasaki, Takahashi Shuhan, learnt gunnery from the Dutch in 1823–7 and became an advocate of Western military drill. Another, Egawa Tarozaemon, who studied under Takahashi, began to construct a reverberatory furnace in 1853 and succeeded in casting cannon. The remains of his furnace can still be seen near the village of Nirayama in the Izu peninsula. There were similar ventures in a few of the large domains, notably Saga (Hizen) and Kagoshima (Satsuma).

Simultaneously, the external threat, and what should be done about it, became topics of public discussion among samurai. The prevailing tone – and much of the vocabulary of the debate – was set out in a book called *Shinron* (New Proposals), written by the Mito scholar Aizawa Seishisai in 1825. Its argument ran as follows. In order to defend Japan, that is, to expel the barbarian (*jōi*), it was necessary that the country's ruling class be united through a structure of loyalty, of which the highest level was loyalty to the emperor (*sonnō*). Unity was also a condition for successfully promoting national wealth and strength: first, by restoring health to agriculture, so as to enrich the country (*fukoku*); second, by reviving samurai discipline and morale, in order to increase military potential (*kyōhei*).

These slogans were in time to be given a different meaning, related to Western military science and industry, but Aizawa himself remained in these matters a traditionalist. In the West, he said, 'every country upholds the law of Jesus and attempts therewith to subdue other countries', employing religion 'to deceive and delude the people' as a preliminary to attack. It was necessary, therefore, for Japan to guard against subversion from within, especially in view of what the Dutch scholars were doing. Many of them had been 'taken in by the vaunted theories of the Western foreigners', writing books 'in the hope of transforming our civilized way of life into that of the barbarians'. In the end, if such delusions were to spread, the Japanese would be suborned by 'novel gadgets and rare medicines, which delight the eye and enthrall the heart', to the point where they would cease to resist attack.[7]

Many other Confucian scholars echoed this kind of language, but their Shinto colleagues took a rather different line. For one thing, they identified Japan's special qualities with divine descent, not Confucian civilization. As Hirata Atsutane put it in 1811, because 'Japan is the land of the gods and we their descendants . . . Japanese differ completely from and are superior to the peoples of China, India, Russia, Holland, Siam, Cambodia, and all other countries of the world'.[8] By the same token, Japanese learning encompassed all the rest, including Confucianism and Buddhism. This left room for Dutch studies, especially scientific ones, to be assimilated, not rejected.

Such ideas bring us closer to the position of men like Takahashi and Egawa, whose interest in the West was to acquire technological skills, which might be used on Japan's behalf. Sakuma Shozan, military expert and Edo official, was their most famous spokesman. As a samurai, whose lord was appointed to the Tokugawa council in Mizuno Tadakuni's time and put in charge of coastal defence, Sakuma was led by circumstance to the study of Dutch and of Western gunnery. In the 1840s he built on this experience in a number of memorials, in which he argued that Japan must prepare for attack, both by purchasing modern armaments and by learning to make them, too. He himself studied the technique of casting cannon. In 1849 he sought his domain's help in the preparation of a Dutch–Japanese dictionary and in the translation of appropriate Dutch books, on the grounds that it was necessary 'to know one's enemy'. The following year he put the case to the Bakufu in even stronger terms. Western countries, he said, had been able to achieve overwhelming material strength 'because foreign learning is rational and Chinese learning is not'.[9] It was China's failure to recognize this which had been responsible for its defeat by Britain in the Opium War. Therefore, if Japan were to avoid China's fate, her people must study what the West had to teach in a variety of fields, not merely those which were of direct application to war.

Sakuma's reward for his efforts was assassination at the hands of an anti-foreign fanatic in 1864, though he left a number of students to carry his thinking forward into Meiji Japan. He also bequeathed to posterity yet another slogan: 'Eastern ethics, Western science' (*Tōyō no dōtoku, Seiyō no gakugei*). At its simplest this could be taken to mean no more than retaining traditional values while introducing technological innovation to Japan. In reality, however, there was rather more to Sakuma's ideas than that: he was moving away from the concept of defending a culture towards that of defending a country (as, indeed, the Shinto scholars were doing, except that they defined it in terms of race). He saw in the policies of Peter the Great a model for what needed to be done in Japan, that is, to ensure political unity, introduce Western technology, build a fleet, and so win international recognition.

There were others in the early nineteenth century who made a much more fundamental critique of existing society in this context. Sato Nobuhiro, for instance, who came from a non-samurai family in northern Japan, had learnt Dutch while serving as an adviser on agriculture, forestry, and mining to a number of feudal lords, then applied it to the study of Western geography, history, navigation and military science. From his reading and experience he evolved a mercantilist plan for reinforcing Japanese strength, which envisaged an expansion of foreign trade and the acquisition of colonies on the Asian mainland. China's defeat in the Opium War in 1842 persuaded him that in the short term this was unrealistic, but he continued to believe in economic and military preparedness as a national goal. In one of his books he described the sort of Japan he would wish to see created in order to achieve it: a government conducted through six specialist departments, two for army and navy, the rest economic; a population divided into hereditary classes, defined by function and subordinate to appropriate ministries; an education service, training children from the age of eight to be of service to the state; and a national university to provide the privileged and talented with a higher level of instruction in law, foreign languages and Western science, as well as in Japanese philosophy and religion. The pattern has more in common with the policies followed after 1868 than it had with those of the Tokugawa Bakufu.

THE UNEQUAL TREATIES

The alarm aroused by British and Russian activities at the beginning of the nineteenth century was kept alive within Japan by occasional incidents thereafter, mostly involving whaling vessels, but for over a generation fears of something on a larger scale were to prove unfounded. In fact, it was not until Britain became engaged in war with China in 1840 that the possibility of moves against Japan became a real one. The Opium War, by opening Chinese ports to foreign trade as far north as the

Yangtse, increased the number of merchant ships employed there, as well as the size of the naval squadrons sent to guard them; and it therefore provided the powers most concerned with the region – Britain, France, Russia, and the United States – with the means to intervene in Japan if they wished to do so. The Dutch representative at Deshima warned the Bakufu in 1844 that in these new circumstances it would not long be able to maintain seclusion, and would be wise to take the initiative in ending it. His advice was rejected: *sakoku* was 'ancestral law'.

Some foreigners did make their way to Japan in the 1840s in an official capacity. British surveying vessels, for example, went to Nagasaki in 1845 and Edo Bay in 1849. French warships visited the Ryukyu Islands. An American sloop called at Nagasaki in 1849 to repatriate shipwrecked sailors from a whaler. These were all routine occasions, testing Japanese resolution, perhaps, but lacking serious diplomatic purpose. Nor were diplomatic overtures, when devised, ever pressed home. Sir John Davis, Britain's senior representative in China, made plans to secure a treaty with Japan in 1845, but dropped them when he failed to raise 'a respectable force' to back his negotiations. London accepted his decision without demur. Commodore James Biddle, commanding the United States Pacific squadron, went to Edo Bay in 1846, only to withdraw again when his request for trade was refused unceremoniously. Opinion on the China coast was that his acceptance of the rebuff made matters worse, not better.

There was nevertheless more substance to American interest in Japan than there was to British or Russian. Britain wanted trade with Japan, but was willing to leave others to take the risk of arranging it. Russia was chiefly concerned to consolidate her position on the Amur, not to get access to Japan or settle the question of sovereignty over the islands to the north. The United States, by contrast, was in the process of becoming a Pacific power. Oregon and California were being added to her territory. There was talk of a transcontinental railway, linked to China by a trans-Pacific steamer route, which would make Japanese coastal waters into an American shipping lane. Japan itself was a potential coaling station. These were issues which were likely to be of greater moment than Japan's notorious lack of hospitality to whalers.

In consequence, the next American approach was carried

through with more determination. Washington announced in 1852 that an expedition was to be sent to Japan, commanded by Commodore Matthew C. Perry, who would have at his disposal a substantial naval force for the purpose of negotiating an agreement. The whole world, including the Tokugawa government, was told of this, making it plain that Perry would not lightly turn away. Indeed, if one is to believe the journals of Europe and America, it was generally thought that this time the closed door must open, or it would be broken down. The *Edinburgh Review* commented:

> 'The compulsory seclusion of the Japanese is a wrong not only to themselves, but to the civilised world. . . . The Japanese undoubtedly have an exclusive right to the possession of their territory; but they must not abuse that right to the extent of debarring all other nations from a participation in its riches and virtues.'[10]

Perry, who reached Uraga in July 1853, showed just as much care for his country's dignity as the press had been led to expect, but rather less for trade. True, the letter which he brought from the American President, delivered with great ceremony at Kurihama under the squadron's guns, referred to commerce, as well as to the treatment of shipwrecked sailors and the provision of ports of refuge for vessels needing coal and stores, but Perry's own, handed over at the same time, was narrower in scope. It was also more minatory. The United States, it said, wanted to live in peace and friendship with Japan, 'but no friendship can long exist, unless Japan ceases to act toward Americans as if they were her enemies'. Accordingly, it was to be hoped that the Japanese government would respond favourably to the President's letter, when the commodore returned for an answer to it next year. He would, he added, bring with him on that occasion 'a much larger force'.[11]

He did: eight ships instead of four, entering Edo Bay in February 1854. The Bakufu, recognizing that its defences were inadequate, instructed its negotiators that their task was to persuade Perry to go away without giving a direct answer to the American requests or precipitating a confrontation. This was contradictory, as the commodore's reactions soon made clear. On the other hand, Perry's own reluctance to make trade a *sine qua non* of any agreement left room for manoeuvre. After detailed talks, requiring constant reference back to Edo, a convention was signed on 31 March at Kanagawa, opening Shimoda and Hakodate as ports of call, where American ships could obtain stores from Japanese officials; authorizing the appointment of consuls at a later date; and making no unambiguous provision for trade. For the Bakufu, this was to make the best of a bad job. To Perry it was a foundation on which others could build.

Perry's achievement, though dismissed as inconsiderable by the merchants of Europe, America and the China coast, was quickly emulated by the British and Russian admirals, who were not interested in trade so much as in the fact that their countries had just declared war over the Crimea. Sir James Stirling went to Nagasaki in September 1854 in an attempt to obtain a declaration denying Japanese ports to Russian warships, except on terms such as would obtain in Europe during a period of hostilities. He failed completely to make himself understood in this, since he had no efficient interpreter, not least because the context of his statements was unintelligible to Japanese officials who had no knowledge of international law; but when the latter, in despair, offered him the same terms as had been granted Perry, he accepted, in the belief that a foothold in Japan, no matter how limited, was worth having. His Russian rival, Putiatin, did rather better. Having played hide-and-seek with Stirling up and down the coasts of East Asia for several months, he finally reached Shimoda to open talks with the Japanese in December. There, despite the destruction of his flagship in a tidal wave the following month, he was able to secure a convention that gave him more than Perry: it included a clause dividing the Kuril Islands between Russia and Japan at a point between Uruppu and Etorofu.

Perry and Stirling were right to claim that they had laid foundations, for the American and British governments, having been presented with agreements which their merchants criticized, were not likely to let matters rest until they had secured something better. Neither, however, showed signs of acting with enthusiasm or despatch. Britain (in alliance with France) was at war with Russia until 1856, then almost at once at war with China over the *Arrow* incident, so was inclined in these years still to leave the initiative to the United States, save for occasional forays into naval diplomacy. America, though free from such distractions, was reluctant to become too much involved in a country which was remote and not of immediate commercial value. As a result, Townsend Harris, who arrived at Shimoda as American consul in August 1856 with instructions to conclude a proper commercial treaty, was given very little help in carrying his orders out. In May 1857 he recorded in his journal that he had not seen an American warship since he came to Japan. This not only left him with no instructions from Washington, but also without means of leverage on the Japanese, who 'yielded nothing except from fear'.[12]

Ingeniously, he was able to find an alternative form of leverage in the shape of the war being fought by Britain and France in China. Late in 1856 Bakufu officials, under a new senior councillor, Hotta Masayoshi, began to reconsider Japan's position in the light of what was happening on the mainland. They quickly came to the conclusion that a trade agreement of some kind would be necessary in order to prevent the powers from attacking Japan. The problem to which they chiefly addressed themselves, therefore, was to identify the minimum level of concession which would bring it about.

What seemed to be an acceptable compromise was worked out in the course of negotiating treaties with the Dutch and Russians, signed at Nagasaki in October 1857. These removed the restrictions formerly imposed on the total annual value of Dutch trade, but retained official supervision of it, together with substantial customs dues; provided that Nagasaki and Hakodate were to be open ports, plus another to be added instead of Shimoda (which was held to be unsuitable commercially); and imposed a mass of detailed regulations on the conduct of the trade and the persons taking part in it. In other words, they revealed that what Edo envisaged was a modest liberalization of the way things had been done in Deshima in the past, not a fresh start.

For this reason, when offered something similar, Townsend Harris would have none of it. Such terms, he said, were 'disgraceful to all parties engaged in making them'.[13] They could by no means be considered an alternative to the kind of treaty which he sought. Nor would they be acceptable to Britain. Against a background of renewed hostilities between Britain and China, this comment was persuasive, with the result that Harris was allowed to go to Edo and open the whole issue again. He arrived there early in December, had an audience with the Shogun on the seventh, and began his diplomatic business five days later. In a long meeting with Hotta he pointed out the advantages of making concessions by agreement with an American ambassador, 'unattended by military force', rather than a British one, 'who should bring fifty men-of-war to these shores'.[14]

Given that the officials to whom he spoke were already conditioned by their own earlier discussions to accept something like this view of things (and were confirmed in their opinion almost immediately after by news that the British had captured Canton), Harris had little difficulty in securing acceptance of the main drift of his proposals. Turning them into a treaty proved more difficult, however. The Japanese negotiators, having little with which to bargain, resisted stubbornly on points of detail, so that matters like the number and choice of open ports, rights of travel in the interior, the place at which an American representative should reside, all became subjects of interminable debate. Harris often became exasperated by it. Nevertheless, he eventually got his way on all important questions. As agreed in the middle of February 1858, his draft treaty provided that the American minister was to be in Edo, not away from the centre of events in Kanagawa or Shimoda, as the Japanese had wished; that trade was to be entirely free of official intervention and subject to low tariffs (which were to be specified in the agreement); that Americans in Japan were to remain under American law, administered in consular courts (the privilege known as extraterritoriality); and that five ports were to be opened. These were to be Nagasaki and Kanagawa (Yokohama) from 1859, Niigata from 1860, and Hyogo (Kobe) from 1863, in addition to the existing ones of Shimoda and Hakodate. Foreigners were also to be admitted to the cities of Edo from 1862 and Osaka from 1863.

Harris might reasonably have assumed that his mission had now come to a successful end. On 17 February, however, when no points of substance remained in dispute, he was told that the Bakufu was not yet ready to sign. The proposals, it was explained, were causing great contention among the feudal lords, so much so that Edo had determined to seek the emperor's approval for the treaty. Once this had been obtained – and there was no doubt that it would be, the officials assured him – all objections would be silenced. It was just a matter of waiting for a while.

The statement was more than a little disingenuous. What had happened was that the Bakufu's policy-makers, much better informed than other Japanese about their country's true position, had become more and more divorced from the realities of Japanese opinion. Outside their circle there were deep divisions about what ought to be done, dating from as far back as Perry's arrival in 1853. The senior councillor at that time, Abe Masahiro, aware that the feudal lords were much at odds over foreign policy, had decided to circulate the American letters and ask for comment on them, in the hope of establishing a consensus. What he had achieved in practice was to underline the fact of discord. Replies from the great majority of lords merely repeated time-worn clichés, critical of Christianity and trade, while calling – unrealistically – for the preservation of both peace and seclusion. The minority was sharply divided in a manner which the Bakufu found embarrassing. Tokugawa Nariaki of Mito, head of one of the three senior Tokugawa branch houses, recapitulated the arguments put forward thirty years earlier by his retainer, Aizawa Seishisai, and concluded that Edo's proper course was to issue a clarion call for war, even if it had no intention of acting on it. Only in this way, he maintained, would it be possible to preserve morale and offer resistance to the West. A number of other powerful lords agreed with him. By contrast, the leading *fudai* lord, Ii Naosuke, also with significant support, argued that what was needed was to increase Japan's real strength by engaging in overseas trade and creating a Western-style navy (Sato Nobuhiro's argument, but without its social concomitants). This implied that a treaty would first have to be signed, in order to win time for implementing the rest of the policy.

Between the winter of 1853–4 and that of 1857–8, when Hotta consulted the lords about the Harris negotiations, there were two shifts in opinion. The majority became convinced of the inevitability of permitting trade, as had the Bakufu's officials (though only as a means of avoiding conflict with the powers). The politically active minority – we are talking of perhaps ten or a dozen *daimyō* out of nearly three hundred – began to direct their criticism at the Bakufu's leadership, rather than its foreign policy as such. Typically, Matsudaira Shungaku of Echizen, another Tokugawa relative, brought together Ii Naosuke's recommendations in favour of trade with Mito-style plans for reform at home: 'the services of capable men must be enlisted from the entire country; peacetime extravagance must be cut down and the military system revised; the evil practices by which the *daimyō* and lesser lords have been impoverished must be discontinued; preparations must be made both on land and sea, not only in the main islands but also in Ezo [Hokkaido]; the daily livelihood of the whole people must be fostered; and schools for the various arts and crafts must be established.'[15] Coupled as it was with demands for new appointments in Edo, and the choice of a man of ability to be the childless Shogun's heir – Hitotsubashi Keiki (Yoshinobu), one of Tokugawa Nariaki's sons, was the candidate Shungaku and his allies had in mind – this was a programme far more sweeping than any Bakufu official dared to contemplate.

Hotta's optimistic belief that the prestige of the Imperial Court could be called upon to bolster Edo's authority in this situation proved ill-founded. The emperor himself and most of his courtiers were personally in favour of seclusion. They even showed themselves willing to insist on it in the face of Bakufu 'advice' (their courage bolstered by secret messages from Nariaki and the other lords). So when Hotta went to Kyoto in March 1858, the best he could get after a month's hard bargaining was a draft decree which recognized that decisions on foreign policy were for the Bakufu to take, not the Court; and even this compromise broke down when the emperor, Komei, let it be known in confidence that he had been pressed into approving it against his will. In the furore which followed, the decree was revised and Hotta had to leave with what was in effect a command to reconsider his plans.

Edo took the affront seriously. Almost at once a decision was taken to appoint a Regent (*Tairō*) with a standing greater than that of the regular councillors. The choice fell on Ii Naosuke, who as the senior *fudai* was assumed to owe his first loyalty to the Tokugawa establishment, whatever his views on foreign affairs.

It was several weeks later that Townsend Harris received news of a peace settlement in China (the Treaty of Tientsin), which would free British and French forces to mount an expedition against Japan, if they so wished. He promptly travelled back to

Kanagawa to press for his own draft treaty to be signed. In a council in Edo, summoned within hours, Ii Naosuke accepted the recommendation, in the belief that this was the only way of avoiding the harsher terms that Britain would demand. Signatures were put to the document on 29 July. During August the Dutch and Russian representatives made similar agreements. So did Lord Elgin for Britain (arriving without the threatened fleet, but marking his claim to superior status by sweeping past Kanagawa to an anchorage off Edo). With the help of Harris' secretary as interpreter, his talks took only two days. The French envoy, Baron Gros, arrived in September and completed a treaty early in October.

Elgin did in one particular amplify what Harris had done, that is, by adding a most-favoured-nation clause to guarantee that Britain would automatically share in any privileges secured thereafter by the rest of the powers. In due course others did the same. This completed the application to Japan of the pattern which the West had worked out for its treaties with China. As a consequence, the treaty port system, when it came into operation in 1859, bore virtually no resemblance to the rules under which the Dutch had traded at Nagasaki for over two hundred years. Foreigners were to be permitted to trade at the specified ports free of official interference, save for the imposition of a low level of customs dues, which were fixed by treaty; they could establish commercial and residential premises in designated foreign settlements in those ports; and they were to live there under the laws of their own countries, administered, if at all, through consular courts. Thus despite the Bakufu's diplomatic rearguard action and the strong criticism coming from many influential Japanese, Japan had at last been brought – in a subordinate condition – into the world of what scholars now call Free Trade Imperialism.

TERRORISM

Ii Naosuke was well aware that having signed the treaties in direct contravention of the emperor's stated wishes he was taking a political risk. He therefore moved quickly to suppress opposition. Early in August he removed Hotta and other Edo officials who might question what he had done. At the same time he announced a decision about the Shogun's succession, choosing a candidate from the Kii branch of the Tokugawa, who was closest by blood to the incumbent, Iesada, but still only twelve years old. The boy became Shogun under the name of Iemochi ten days later. Those lords who had supported the Hitotsubashi claim and voiced public complaints about the quality of Bakufu leadership, including Tokugawa Nariaki, were ordered into retirement or house arrest. A number of their retainers, who had acted as agents for them, especially in the intrigues at Court, were sentenced to prison, exile or execution. The purge was even extended to some of the courtiers in Kyoto.

Having thus ensured compliance where it mattered, the Regent took up the issue of imperial approval for the treaties, sending one of the Edo councillors, Manabe Akikatsu, to Kyoto in October with orders to regularize the Bakufu's position. Having failed in long discussions to shift the emperor's personal views, Manabe turned to threats: a hint about the risks being run by those imperial advisers who opposed his mission; and a direct statement that Edo would feel duty bound to disregard the Court's objections, on grounds of national interest, if they were not modified. This brought compromise, embodied in a decree of 2 February 1859. The emperor promised 'forbearance'; the Bakufu undertook somehow to prevent the opening of Hyogo and Osaka, despite their inclusion in the treaties; and both parties committed themselves to revoking the treaties altogether at some unspecified future date, that is, to 'revert to the sound rule of seclusion as formerly laid down in our national laws'.[16]

The outcome, however, was not to silence the Bakufu's critics, but to alienate them further, because of the pressure Manabe was known to have put upon the Court. Many samurai from the politically active domains were already hostile, angered by the punishments inflicted on their lords or on their friends. Many more resented the manner in which the treaties had been signed, which, they held, had shown an attitude of subservience towards the foreigners. When to this was added a Bakufu attempt to browbeat the Court into accepting all that it had done, Ii Naosuke found himself pilloried for one of the worst of samurai sins, namely, being complaisant to the strong, tyrannical to the weak. As a consequence, 'honour the emperor' and 'expel the barbarian' took on new meaning, becoming radical slogans directed against the Shogun's government.

What is more, they were slogans which appealed to a much wider circle of samurai than those who had participated in the earlier debates over opening the country or choosing the Shogun's heir. Many of those who used them after 1858 were men of middle or lower rank, brought into politics by their seniors in the recent crisis, or infected by the atmosphere of danger and excitement occasioned by the coming of foreign ships and envoys to Japan. Many were students at the schools of gunnery and swordmanship in Edo, vying with each other to achieve a name as monarchist or anti-foreign zealots. In Kyoto, which was again becoming a centre of politics, as it had not been for centuries, such self-styled activists found a refuge and an opportunity. The patronage of Court nobles gave them some kind of protection. It also held out the prospect of influencing political decisions, something which men of low rank could hardly hope to do in Edo or the domains. Samurai began to flock there in considerable numbers, abandoning families and fiefs or stipends without their lord's consent, and so risking loss of rank or still severer punishments. A few were revolutionaries, dedicated to overthrowing the regime. The majority were simple fanatics, sincere but ill-organized, or mere youths, attracted by the expectation of adventure. All, since they had renounced their status and their loyalties, were ripe for violence. Politics in Japan therefore entered a new phase, characterized more by action than by memorials, and worked out as much in the streets of the cities and the open ports as in the council chambers of the Shogun or feudal lords. Its chief instrument was terror.

Often the men involved in it looked for inspiration to a young teacher and samurai from Yamaguchi (Choshu), called Yoshida Shoin. Born in 1830, he had studied under Sakuma Shozan and established connections with the Mito scholars. In 1854 he had tried to stow away in one of Perry's ships with the intention of studying abroad, in order to acquire the knowledge needed to defend Japan, but Perry handed him over to Bakufu officials and he was briefly imprisoned. Sent back to Choshu for punishment, he was then sentenced to house arrest, though permitted to continue teaching. To his students (who included several future leaders of Meiji Japan) he expounded during the next few years a doctrine based on the premise that Japan's existing rulers, lords as well as Shogun, had sacrificed their claim to authority by the weakness and incompetence they had shown in the face of foreign threats: the only chance of salvation for Japan, he believed, was an uprising of men untainted by wealth or office, led by a resolute minority of the samurai class, and united by their loyalty to the emperor. He did not appear to mean by this a co-ordinated attempt to seize power and substitute some new social and political order for that of Bakufu and domains. Rather, he wanted exemplary action by 'men of spirit' (*shishi*), putting conscience before calculation. They must be ready to sacrifice themselves to bring about a situation that would force their superiors to think again. They must even be willing to put their country in obvious jeopardy in order to rally the population to its defence (on Sun Tzu's principle that an army put in a position of 'inevitable death' will fight with desperation and success).

Yoshida chose to demonstrate what he believed to be required by planning the assassination of Manabe Akikatsu, symbol of the Bakufu's contempt for the Imperial Court. That he was detected, brought to trial, and executed greatly enhanced his reputation among the dissidents. His example was followed. On 24 March 1860 a group of samurai, mostly from Mito, cut down Ii Naosuke outside one of the gates of Edo castle, publicly declaring him accountable for 'the dishonour of our divine land'. This removed the Bakufu's one strong man. It also inaugurated a decade in which assassination was to be the common currency of Japanese politics. Lords and senior officials soon became better guarded, as one would expect, though another member of the Edo council was wounded early in 1862. Their subordinates were more at risk; and activists were easily convinced that those who determined policy, if hostile to the cause, might be influenced in their judgement by receiving the head or ears of one of their retainers. What is more, it was reasoned that attacks on foreigners had a double purpose in this situation: to deter them from implementing the treaties they had signed; and to provoke them into taking action which Edo would have to resist. Thus the Bakufu began the last decade of its history facing turbulence at home, the threat of still more abroad. The Chinese phrase about the downfall of dynasties began to look uncomfortably apposite.

3

THE OVERTHROW OF THE TOKUGAWA, 1860–1868

Japanese politics until 1858 were essentially feudal. That is to say, struggles for power operated within a structure comprising Bakufu and domains, which was not expected to be fundamentally changed by success or failure; the participants were Edo officials, feudal lords and their senior retainers, who accorded only a minor role to samurai of lesser rank; and the domestic issues in contention were those of Bakufu hegemony and baronial rights. The early disputes over opening the ports did not materially alter this state of affairs.

The crisis in the summer of 1858, however, prepared the way for a different kind of politics. By appealing to the Imperial Court to sanction their respective positions on the treaties and the Tokugawa succession, Hotta Masayoshi and the lords of the Hitotsubashi party brought the emperor into current controversies. By signing the treaties without the emperor's approval, Ii Naosuke provoked an explosion of anger that spread political activity to the lower levels of the samurai class. Both changes proved irreversible. What is more, the new participants in politics were less bound to the existing feudal framework than their predecessors had been. Yoshida Shoin, for example, writing just before his execution, argued not only that the Bakufu and the lords had proved themselves incapable of acting as the times demanded, leaving the task to be shouldered by men of humbler rank, but also that Japan could only be saved by a transformation of society, 'replacing the rotten pillars, discarding worn-out rafters, and adding new wood'.[17] It is not entirely clear what he meant by this – like the other 'men of spirit' who came after him, he never expounded a coherent social philosophy – but his teachings and his example undoubtedly helped to introduce a new variable into Japanese politics. Much of the story of the 1860s concerns the way in which the Bakufu and the lords responded to it.

FOREIGN POLICY AND DOMESTIC OPPOSITION

In the first few years after the opening of the ports there was a good deal of violence directed against foreigners in Japan. Two Russians were killed in Yokohama in 1859 and a Dutch merchant captain in February 1860. Townsend Harris' secretary was murdered in January 1861. There was an organized night attack on the British legation at Tozenji in July 1861, followed by another smaller one a year later. These incidents led to diplomatic protests – at rising levels of indignation – and the transfer of part of Britain's China squadron to Japanese waters.

Nor was it only foreigners who suffered from such attacks. They were also made on Japanese employed by foreigners and on officials who were thought to have contributed to the continued foreign presence in Japan. And in some cases they had objectives which went a good way beyond a mere desire to cause conflict and disruption. For example, the assassination of Ii Naosuke in 1860 had been part of a much wider plot, involving plans for an assault on the foreign settlement at Yokohama and the seizure of Kyoto by a force from Satsuma, which had been intended to make the Bakufu revoke the treaties and to give its opponents command of the Imperial Court. Neither object was achieved. Carrying out so complex an operation proved to be beyond the capacity of the conspirators, while those from Satsuma were unable to deliver on their promises. Yet the idea lived on. In the spring of 1862 there was another attempt to bring Satsuma openly into an anti-Tokugawa posture, to be effected on this occasion by a rising of *shishi*, the 'men of spirit', coupled with the assassination of senior Court and Bakufu officials in Kyoto; but again the Satsuma establishment refused to move. Indeed, several of the activists were killed in a hair-raising fracas in the dark, when the *daimyō* sent guards to bring them to order.

Projects of much the same kind were to recur in 1863 and 1864. They had a common pattern: first, steps by the disaffected to dominate the Imperial Court, relying partly on terrorism, partly on the emperor's known anti-foreign sympathies; second, use of the Court to persuade one or more of the feudal lords to co-operate; third, a threat of military action to force Edo to abandon the treaties and show greater deference to the emperor's wishes. There seems to have been no intention at this stage to do more than replace the Shogun with an emperor-centred feudalism, in which the head of the Tokugawa house would be merely one of the great lords. Even so, the concept was enough to alarm *daimyō*, as well as Bakufu. The lords of Satsuma, Choshu, and a few other domains were ready enough to seek ways of weakening the Shogun's hold over themselves, but they recognized nevertheless that the existence of the Bakufu had in the past served to confirm their own position within their feudal territories. To the extent that what was happening in the emperor's capital posed a threat to the social order, not just Bakufu authority, they viewed it with distrust.

These plots and the violence which accompanied them triggered a complex struggle for power, lasting several years, between a multiplicity of groups with widely differing aims. At one extreme stood the members of the anti-foreign movement, a body of men much too diffuse in their purposes and organization to be called a party, but broadly agreed on their attitudes to recent events. A list of some of their acknowledged leaders will give an idea of the movement's social character. Among the oldest was Maki Izumi of Kurume, a Shinto official of samurai status, who had been born in 1813. Arima Shinshichi of Satsuma, born in 1825, was a full samurai by adoption, but a lower-ranking rural samurai (*gōshi*) by birth. Hirano Kuniomi of Chikuzen, born in 1828, was another full samurai, while Takechi Zuizan of Tosa, a year younger, was a *gōshi*. Youngest of the famous ones was Kusaka Genzui of Choshu, a samurai doctor, brother-in-law to Yoshida Shoin, who was born in 1840. All five were to be killed because of their political activities between 1862 and 1865.

Their followers were, like themselves, men from the lower levels of the samurai class, or just outside it – they included a number from the families of village headmen – drawn from the domains of western and south-western Japan. In years, too, they were much like those who led them, except that there were more of Kusaka's age. On the other hand, they had sympathizers, sometimes allies, among the middle and higher samurai ranks, through whom they might hope to get their lords to approve their plans. A few of these were samurai whose background and opinions might easily have made them rebels themselves, had they not chosen otherwise. For example, Saigo Takamori (1827–77) and Okubo Toshimichi (1830–78), both of Satsuma, and Kido Koin (1833–77) of Choshu, who belonged to the same generation as the extremist leadership, opted for careers in the bureaucracy of their domains. From this vantage-point they were able to play a key part in the Bakufu's overthrow.

A separate segment of the opposition to the Bakufu was manifest in the re-emergence into politics of the lords of the Hitotsubashi party, or those who were left of them, in 1862. Tokugawa Nariaki was by that time dead, so his son, Hitotsubashi Keiki (Yoshinobu), became a principal, rather than a figurehead. Satsuma was represented by Shimazu Hisamitsu, brother of the former lord (who had died in 1858) and father to his successor. Yamauchi Yodo of Tosa and Matsudaira Shungaku of Echizen were the other leading members, as they had been earlier. They were supported on some issues by another Tokugawa relative, Matsudaira Katamori of Aizu. The *daimyō* of Choshu, Mori Yoshichika, was also willing to throw his weight against Edo from time to time, but a deep-rooted rivalry with Satsuma kept him from giving the group his full co-operation. All these lords stood for baronial privilege. On the other hand, they had no wish to change the fabric of society, or to precipitate a conflict with the West, and this prevented them from coming to terms with the 'men of spirit'. The three Tokugawa collaterals among them, Hitotsubashi and the two Matsudaira lords, were also ambivalent on the subject of the Shogun's authority. When the situation eventually clarified into a contest between the Bakufu and the rest after 1864, they were more often to be found on the side of the Edo officials than on that of Satsuma or Choshu.

In dealing with these two very different threats to their customary power, Bakufu councillors and their subordinates, shaken by the killing of Ii Naosuke, proceeded at first with caution. The 'reforming lords' far outranked them and had access to the Imperial Court. They therefore had to be handled warily. The 'men of spirit', in so far as they represented a simple threat to law and order, would in the past have been firmly suppressed; but in the crisis atmosphere which then existed in Japan it was by no means certain how the domains would respond to any use of force against them. Accordingly, Edo temporized, seeking a settlement with the *daimyō* and the Court before attempting anything more incisive. In 1860 a marriage was arranged between the young Shogun, Iemochi, and the emperor's sister, Kazunomiya. In June 1862, when Shimazu escorted an imperial envoy to Edo, the council gave way to his demand that Hitotsubashi and Echizen be appointed to high office there. The system of 'alternate attendance' was relaxed in October and the great lords were given the right to 'advise' the Shogun when they visited his castle.

What frustrated these efforts to win high-level harmony was the fact that the Bakufu was responsible for dealing with the foreign powers. The foreign representatives in Japan not only insisted on their countries' rights under the unequal treaties, but also possessed the military resources by which to resist any step that was likely to undermine them. Edo recognized, as it had done in 1858, that *force majeure* left it little choice in this matter. Against that, the Court had exacted as its price for the Kazunomiya marriage a promise that the treaties would be revoked within ten years, reflecting in part a fear of the 'men of spirit', who were strident in their calls for the foreigners to be expelled. To complicate the situation further, the great lords were divided on the issue. Shimazu was against expulsion. He was ready, if need be, to use force against the extremists who demanded it. Hitotsubashi and Echizen, by contrast, believed that national unity required at almost any cost a rapprochement between Court and Bakufu, which would not be available without some gesture from Edo towards the closing of the ports.

These considerations made foreign policy the principal focus of Japanese politics between 1862 and 1864. In the first of these years, the Bakufu tried to turn the growing turbulence to its advantage by using it as an argument to win concessions from the powers, hoping that these in turn might serve to reduce the hostility it faced at home. Trade, it explained to the Western diplomats in Edo, had brought a rise in commodity prices, which pressed particularly hard on samurai families (because of their fixed income from stipends). The unrest this prompted could be contained, given time. It would be exacerbated, however, if Edo, Osaka and Hyogo (Kobe) were opened during 1862 and 1863, as the treaties required. It would be better to amend the agreements in this respect. Rutherford Alcock, the British minister, whose response was central to any decision on such a matter, was sceptical; but he was ultimately persuaded of the logic of the argument – by an unsuccessful attempt to assassinate another member of the Shogun's council – and lent his support to a Japanese mission which was sent to London in 1862. On 6 June of that year it signed a protocol to postpone the opening of any further ports or cities until 1868, subject to the treaties being fully implemented at the ports already open. The other powers made similar concessions during the next few months.

News of the London agreement had barely reached Japan before there was another anti-foreign incident. In September 1862 a British party from Yokohama, riding through the nearby village of Namamugi, failed to give way on the road to Shimazu Hisamitsu's entourage, which was on its way back to Kyoto from Edo. The escorting samurai killed Charles Richardson, a visitor from Shanghai, and wounded two of his companions. British residents demanded the landing of troops to take revenge. The British chargé – Alcock was in England – lodged vigorous protests, which caused Edo to call on Satsuma to surrender those who had made the attack. It refused. They had, the domain's officials argued, acted in accordance with feudal custom and did not merit punishment. Indeed, the affair was the Bakufu's fault for signing treaties which paid so little heed to Japanese tradition.

The dispute obviously put the Bakufu's recent diplomatic gains in peril, though it was not until the following spring that the full effects became apparent, because of the long time it took for the news to reach London and for instructions to come in reply. In the interval, Shimazu withdrew to his domain in case of British attack, while Hitotsubashi and Echizen set out to mend fences in Kyoto. They arrived there early in 1863, only to find that the situation was very much worse than they had thought. Faced by fresh outbreaks of terrorism (and without the stiffening which Shimazu's presence might have given them) they ended by accepting a 'compromise' which put Japan's foreign relations into total disorder. In the name of 'Court–Bakufu unity' they agreed to set a date – 25 June was eventually chosen – on which action would be taken to 'exclude' the foreigners from Japan. A decree was issued to this effect. By those who spoke for the Bakufu it was read as an instruction to open negotiations with the powers to close the treaty ports, or at least the most important of them, Yokohama. In Choshu, however, loyalists took it to be the long-awaited signal to sweep the foreigners from their land. Since their feudal superiors saw it as a chance to become the emperor's favoured ally, in place of Satsuma, when the appointed day came Choshu steamers attacked an American vessel in the Shimonoseki Straits. Early in July the shore batteries there fired on French and Dutch ships, inflicting damage and casualties. By the end of that month, despite local intervention by the French and American naval commanders in Japan, the Straits, which formed part of the shortest sea route between Yokohama and Shanghai, were closed to foreign shipping.

British reactions to the Namamugi incident added to the turmoil. In December 1862 the British Foreign Secretary, Earl Russell, had drawn up instructions, which reached Japan in March 1863, requiring his representative to demand from the Bakufu a formal apology and an indemnity of £100,000. Satsuma was to be required to execute the offending samurai and pay compensation of £25,000. Failing this, the Royal Navy was to carry out such measures 'of reprisal or blockade, or both', as seemed appropriate. On receipt of the dispatch the chargé promptly communicated its contents to the Bakufu, using language which was notably immoderate: Japan had committed a 'barbarous outrage'; reparation for it was 'peremptorily demanded'; and if it were to be refused, making necessary a resort to arms, 'the penalty imposed . . . now computed in thousands, will inevitably expand into millions'.[18]

Since Hitotsubashi and Echizen were still in Kyoto at this time, negotiating with the Court, officials in Edo did their best to delay a reply to the British note. They succeeded in doing so for some weeks, but the news from the capital eventually led them to conclude that there could be no prospect of discussing the closing of Yokohama, which was their preferred interpretation of 'repelling' the barbarians, until this issue had been settled. In June 1863, only a day or two before the first of Choshu's attacks on foreign ships at Shimonoseki, the first instalment of the Bakufu indemnity was therefore handed over. That left the question of what to do about Satsuma, though the domain's continuing silence on the matter made naval action by Britain well-nigh unavoidable in the circumstances. It took a few weeks to complete the arrangements for it, but in August a British squadron, which had been assembled at Yokohama, left for Kagoshima Bay with orders to secure compliance with London's ultimatum. On arrival there its commanding officer, meeting with little readiness on Satsuma's part to meet his terms, decided to seize three steamers in the harbour as a pledge for the compensation Russell had required. He thereby precipitated a general engagement with shore batteries along the Kagoshima waterfront, during which much of the city was destroyed (almost certainly by intent, though London later denied it). The squadron itself suffered considerable damage, especially the flagship, which strayed across the practice range used by the Satsuma guns. So when the action was broken off and the British ships withdrew, both sides were able to claim a victory. Later in the year a settlement of the affair was reached at Yokohama. Satsuma paid compensation (or rather, arranged for the Bakufu to do so on its behalf), while promising to punish the murderers, if and when they were caught. Nothing more was said of them thereafter, though their identity and whereabouts were widely known.

These events left Shimazu Hisamitsu free once again to turn his attention to domestic politics. The 'expulsion decree', as it was called, together with Choshu's attacks on foreign ships, had given an enormous stimulus to the Kyoto activists, whose ambitions reached new heights in the summer of 1863. A number of the samurai among them received nominal Court appointments. In September they planned for the emperor in person to put himself at the head of the anti-foreign movement by making an official progress to the shrines at Ise, ostensibly to make his intentions known to his ancestors, in reality to provide the occasion for 'men of spirit' to form themselves into a loyalist army round the throne. Shimazu moved quickly to forestall the move when he learnt of it. Working with contingents from Aizu, which provided the Shogun's garrison in the city, Satsuma units seized the palace gates on 30 September and ejected the Choshu guards who had been holding them. Several court nobles, who had been associated with the samurai loyalists, fled with their allies to take refuge in Choshu. A handful of other survivors raised a short-lived rebellion in nearby Yamato.

The change this brought about in the balance of power in Kyoto was chiefly Shimazu's doing, and he lost no time in showing that he knew it. In November he arrived from Kagoshima with 15,000 men. Having thus secured an unchallenged position at Court – it was even rumoured that one of his retainers was drafting the emperor's correspondence – he now had in his own estimation a claim to leadership in the making of policy. Hence when the Shogun was brought to Kyoto a few months later to consolidate the Bakufu–Satsuma success, Shimazu made it plain that the time for talk of expulsion or the closing of ports was in his opinion past. Hitotsubashi, who was becoming more and more a Bakufu man, did not agree. As he saw it, for the Shogun's government to blow hot and cold on the subject of foreign affairs at the bidding of whoever happened to dominate the Imperial Court would destroy what little prestige was left to it. He therefore proposed that Edo should resume its efforts to negotiate the closing of Yokohama as a demonstration of sincerity in submitting to the emperor's will. At this, Shimazu, the older man, showed contempt for what he clearly thought to be shilly-shallying; Hitotsubashi waxed indignant at Satsuma presumption; and in an emotional scene on 23 March 1864 the two quarrelled violently. Hitotsubashi won his point, but broke up the *daimyō* coalition in the process.

The quarrel marked the beginning of a political realignment. During the next few months Hitotsubashi and Shimazu became regular spokesmen for pro-Bakufu and anti-Bakufu points of view, respectively. Simultaneously there was a shift in the attitudes of Choshu and its friends among the loyalist samurai, which was directly attributable to the actions of the Western powers. By May 1864 the foreign representatives in Japan had received instructions from their governments to take such action to secure the re-opening of the Shimonoseki Straits as seemed to them appropriate. Prompted by Rutherford Alcock, now back at his post, they decided that this meant making an example of Choshu, in order to put an end to anti-foreign demonstrations in Japan. There was some delay in putting the decision into effect, however: first there had to be talks with the Bakufu, which came to nothing; then two Choshu samurai, Ito Hirobumi and Inoue Kaoru, came back from London, where they had been studying – they had read about their domain's danger in the *Times* – and offered to mediate; finally, when their efforts, too, were unsuccessful, a Bakufu mission returned from Paris, having signed (without authority) a convention by which Edo agreed to open the Straits on its own account, accepting naval help from France, if needed. It was not until this agreement was disavowed on 24 August that the foreign envoys at last felt free to act.

A combined Western fleet of seventeen ships (nine British, three French, four Dutch and one American) carried out a bombardment of shore batteries in the Shimonoseki Straits on 5 September 1864. During the next two days men were landed to capture the emplacements and dismantle their equipment, seizing a number of guns and destroying others. Choshu came to terms. A truce was agreed, providing in principle for uninterrupted passage of the Straits in future and for the payment of an indemnity. The talks were then transferred to Yokohama and Edo, where the Bakufu accepted responsibility for the costs of the expedition (an indemnity of three million dollars, payable in six instalments), and a convention setting out the arrangements was signed.

In domestic politics these events had the effect of transforming expulsion from a genuine aspiration to a tactical device. What had happened at Kagoshima in August 1863 and at Shimonoseki in September 1864, no matter how earnestly it was represented as a victory for patriotism and resolution, persuaded most samurai that something much more was required for Japan's defence than reckless attacks on foreigners. A new leadership began to emerge – Saigo and Okubo in Satsuma, Kido and Takasugi Shinsaku in Choshu – committed to a different definition of the Mito slogan about 'wealth and strength'. Wealth was to be sought through trade, not agriculture; strength was to be found in Western-style ships and guns and military organization. A corollary was that action had to be taken by officialdom, that is, by domains, not through individual acts of fanaticism, or by warrior bands seeking to terrorize Kyoto. The 'man of spirit', in fact, would have to yield pride of place to the bureaucrat and the politician.

Rallying samurai opinion behind this proposition was made

easier by the failure of the radicals' last desperate throw in Kyoto. In August 1864, as the foreign fleet was preparing to sail for Shimonoseki, some 2,000 men from Choshu, backed by rebels from other domains, launched an attempt to seize the emperor's palace, in order to regain the position they had lost the year before. Bakufu and Satsuma forces drove them back after bitter street fighting, in which many of the most famous loyalists, including Maki Izumi and Kusaka Genzui, lost their lives. Others suffered imprisonment and execution in the weeks that followed, as Bakufu and lords took their chance to punish indiscipline. Those who escaped, apart from a few who remained a danger to foreigners in the streets, gradually came round to the view that loyalty to their domains, provided they were led by men sympathetic to the anti-foreign cause, was the only effective way left open to them of defending Japan against the powers.

THE END OF THE BAKUFU

The events of 1863 and 1864 had done much to simplify the struggle for power within Japan, since they had eliminated the samurai dissidents as an independent variable. In Satsuma, Choshu and Tosa, where loyalist influence had always been strong, samurai of middle rank were beginning to take over the direction of affairs at the head of a more formidable anti-Tokugawa combination than any that had existed previously. It embraced the surviving 'men of spirit' and a handful of their refugee allies from the Court, plus the *tozama* members of the old Hitotsubashi party, along with their own supporters: *daimyō*, domain officials, Court nobles, renegade samurai, even a few commoners. Their object was to challenge, not the treaties, but the Bakufu; the point at issue, not what should be done, but who should do it. In other words, once the debate on expulsion was set aside, because of the West's demonstration of strength, what remained was the question of whether the Shogun could survive as national hegemon.

There were those in Edo who thought he could. The years of caution and indecision were coming to an end, as Hitotsubashi gathered round himself an able group of officials determined to preserve the Bakufu's prerogatives. As a means to that end they chose, like the Manchus in China, to reach agreement with those who represented 'dangers from abroad', in order to devote their energies to suppressing 'troubles at home'.

The first public evidence of this came in the autumn of 1865, when the Bakufu experienced difficulty in meeting the deadline for the second instalment of the Shimonoseki indemnity, and Alcock's successor, Harry Parkes, used this as grounds for making fresh demands upon it. In November he offered to waive all further payments in return for other concessions: a more favourable tariff agreement; the immediate opening of Hyogo; and an acknowledgement by the emperor that the treaties had his consent. Since the Shogun and most of his council were in Osaka at this time, the negotiations took place there (in the presence of a sizeable foreign squadron). The Bakufu recommended to the Court that it agree to the proposal. The Court, true to form, refused. Thereupon the Shogun threatened to resign, making it plain in his submission to the emperor that it was now Bakufu policy to abandon seclusion and employ the profits from foreign trade, 'to construct many ships and guns' with a view to 'using the barbarian to subdue the barbarian'.[19] Armed with this forthright statement, Hitotsubashi overbore Kyoto's objections, securing sanction for the 1858 treaties (though not for the early opening of Hyogo). This made it no longer possible for dissidents to claim that expulsion was the emperor's personal wish.

Working out the implications of what had been decided involved not only a new tariff convention (June 1866), but also following up the hint which France had given to the Bakufu mission in 1864 about the possibility of foreign help against domestic enemies. It was clear to Edo that direct French military intervention in Japanese politics would be a disaster. However, the French minister in Japan, Léon Roches, was in fact offering something more acceptable. During 1865 he arranged French technical assistance to establish a small shipyard and iron foundry at Yokohama, then a dockyard at Yokosuka, both to be financed by the profits from a Franco-Japanese trading company, dealing mostly in silk. A further agreement in November 1866 provided for the dispatch of a French military mission to advise on modernizing the Shogun's army.

In January 1867 Hitotsubashi became Shogun as Yoshinobu, succeeding Iemochi. In March he had a meeting with Roches in his new capacity, at which plans were discussed for a complete reorganization of the Bakufu on Western lines. They envisaged a remodelling of the central bureaucracy, which was to have specialist departments of army, navy, finance and foreign affairs; military reform, especially an increase in the number of French-trained rifle units; the imposition of tighter controls on the domains, which would be required to provide cash in place of other forms of service; and steps to promote industry, mining and commerce. This was a blueprint for 'wealth and strength' on the lines which the Meiji government was later to follow; and even such parts of it as the Bakufu was immediately able to carry out – chiefly those which could be effected on its own lands and with respect to its own vassals – were calculated to restore its dominance within Japan.

The main problem about achieving this was that results were a long time working through. Following the unsuccessful attack on Kyoto by the extremists in August 1864, it had been decided that the first move towards re-asserting the Shogun's authority must be made against Choshu. At the Bakufu's urging, the Court authorized a punitive expedition against the domain, in which the great lords would be expected to participate. Troops assembled at Osaka for the purpose during the autumn, only to disperse again without having undertaken any fighting in January 1865, when the Choshu council agreed to accept exemplary punishment. Before the truce terms could be carried out, Takasugi Shinsaku and Kido Koin, aided by irregular units which they had raised for action against the foreigners at Shimonoseki, overthrew what they called the 'pro-Bakufu' party in the domain and made the *daimyō* their prisoner. Edo thereupon announced a second expedition in May 1865, this time to be commanded by the Shogun personally.

While it was in preparation there were important changes in Satsuma, where Okubo Toshimichi and Saigo Takamori were assuming control. Satsuma's policy was not unlike the Bakufu's in these years: it sought better relations with the powers, especially Britain; sent students and a diplomatic mission to Europe, where a trade-for-arms deal was negotiated with Belgian interests; and accelerated the Westernization of its military forces. Simultaneously, however, it was drawing closer to Choshu, not least by acting as intermediary in the purchase of foreign arms. In March 1866 this co-operation led to a secret alliance, concluded by Kido and Saigo at Osaka, which was dedicated to the overthrow of the Tokugawa. It gave the anti-Bakufu movement for the first time a solid core of organized armed force.

It also made Choshu confident enough to ignore a Bakufu ultimatum calling for the domain's submission. Accordingly, military operations against it began in July, land attacks being launched from the north (along the Japan Sea coast) and east (from Hiroshima), while a sea-borne invasion was attempted from the west (across the straits from northern Kyushu). The initial assaults were all held or repulsed. The Bakufu had superior numbers, despite the refusal of Satsuma and several other domains to send contingents, but this advantage was balanced by Choshu's greater military proficiency, which was largely the product of Takasugi's skills in organization and training. By the end of the summer the Bakufu's armies were being driven back on every front and in September, when news came of the Shogun Iemochi's death, Edo gratefully accepted it as a pretext for bringing the campaign to an end.

The defeat instilled greater urgency into Yoshinobu's dealings with Roches; confirmed Parkes in his view that Britain should move closer to Satsuma and Choshu, in case there were to be a change of regime; and temporarily gave the anti-Tokugawa movement greater confidence. Yet in May and June 1867 the Shogun demonstrated that he still had a firm hold on the Imperial Court, when he blocked a Satsuma attempt to win pardon for Choshu as the price of approval for the opening of Hyogo. This turned the thoughts of Saigo, Okubo and Kido towards mounting a coup d'état, especially since it was evident – Ernest Satow, Parkes' interpreter, went out of his way to warn them of it – that the longer they waited the stronger the Bakufu would get.

Tosa, along with other less committed domains, like Echizen and Owari, found the prospect of a coup frightening because, win or lose, it would put power into the hands of irreconcilables. In July, therefore, the Tosa leaders drafted a set of proposals, emanating mostly from one of the domain's own loyalists, Sakamoto Ryoma, designed to give the moderates a continuing voice in affairs. The Shogun should step down from office to join the ranks of the great lords, the document argued, being replaced by a council responsible to the emperor. This body would be bicameral, consisting of an upper chamber of *daimyō* and selected Court nobles, a lower one of samurai and even commoners. It would 'conduct affairs in line with the desires of the people' and negotiate fresh treaties with the West 'on the basis of reason and manifest justice', while such practices and institutions of the Imperial Court as were found to be 'no longer appropriate' to current needs would be revised 'in the light of customs elsewhere in the world'.[20]

This proposition, which foreshadowed early Meiji policy statements, was originally put forward as the basis of an alliance between Tosa and Satsuma, but in September Yamauchi Yodo used its recommendations in a memorial urging Yoshinobu to resign. The idea was not altogether anathema to a man who had for most of his adult life been a defender of baronial privilege. After all, though resignation would deprive him of hereditary office and the rights it carried, it would leave him with the Tokugawa lands, hence the country's largest military force, and perhaps a role as senior executive. That seemed to Yoshinobu a reasonable price to pay for averting a civil war at a time when Japan was still under threat from Western imperialism. On 9 November 1867, therefore, he put his prerogatives at the emperor's disposal. Ten days later he resigned as Shogun.

The argument which made this gesture acceptable to Yoshinobu's entourage, namely, that it was a device for retaining the realities of power, was precisely that which reinforced the suspicions of Satsuma and Choshu. Saigo and Okubo, in particular, were willing to have a baronial council, but not to risk having Yoshinobu as its president, especially if he were to keep his vast estates. Consequently, as debates and lobbying about the matter continued at the Court, they set about moving troops to the vicinity of Kyoto. At the end of December they let it be known to the representatives of four other domains (Owari, Echizen, Tosa and Hiroshima) that they planned to seize the palace within the next few days; and since, having little choice, these all agreed to join the undertaking (though Echizen sent a warning to the Shogun), troops under the command of Saigo Takamori took over the palace gates on the morning of 3 January 1868. An imperial council was immediately summoned, from which known opponents of the coup were excluded, and a decree was issued stripping Yoshinobu of his power. The text made it clear that responsibility for governing the country was to revert to the emperor. It was this which has given the event its English-language name: the Meiji Restoration, that is, the restoration to the young Meiji emperor (Mutsuhito), who had succeeded his father Komei earlier in the year, of the administrative authority which heads of the Tokugawa house had for several centuries exercised.

The coup d'état did not immediately settle all the arguments. Yoshinobu withdrew to Osaka, but his relatives, Owari and Echizen, continued to urge that he be made a member of the new council and allowed to keep most of his lands. Towards the end of January some of his collaterals and *fudai*, notably Matsudaira of Aizu, moved a substantial force towards the capital, apparently in an effort to give substance to this plea; but outside the city they clashed with 'imperial' units from Satsuma and Choshu, who drove them back in heavy fighting round Toba and Fushimi. The ex-Shogun fled to Edo. The Court this time declared him rebel, as it had done in similar circumstances to Choshu, just over three years earlier.

During the weeks that followed, an imperial army, made up of contingents from a number of 'loyal' domains, moved steadily eastward in what was more a procession than a campaign. Most *daimyō* along the route submitted before even the advance-guard reached them. Finally, Yoshinobu issued orders forbidding all resistance, with the result that Edo was occupied early in April and surrender terms were negotiated shortly after. The ex-Shogun was to go into retirement. His successor as head of the Tokugawa house was to retain lands of 700,000 *koku* around Shizuoka, that is, a little less than Satsuma's. Aizu rejected the settlement, fighting stubbornly in the mountains surrounding Wakamatsu for another six months; but when its lord yielded with his castle and its garrison at the beginning of November, the rest of the north surrendered, too. Thereafter the only Tokugawa adherents who continued to resist were a thousand or so who had escaped by sea to Hokkaido, where they held out until June 1869.

4

BUILDING A MODERN STATE, 1868–1894

Japan had no tradition of political theory in the European sense. Having taken over Confucianism from China as a ready-made doctrine concerning the ethical character of the state, the Japanese did not seek thereafter to enter into comparisons of different kinds of body politic – monarchy, oligarchy, democracy – or to examine Confucianism in the light of alternative concepts of the way in which individuals might relate to society. At most, attempts were made to modify Confucian thought, so as to reconcile it with the distinctive types of political and social institutions that developed in Japan. In particular, they had to take account of the existence of an emperor of supposedly divine descent and of feudal rulers whose office, like their status, was hereditary.

As a consequence, the Meiji Restoration was not preceded, as were the revolutions in seventeenth-century England and eighteenth-century France, by public debates about social justice or the desirability of a new political order. There existed a variety of discontents, sometimes expressed in writing, sometimes in action, but proposals for overcoming them tended to focus on the familiar issue of substituting rule by emperor for rule by Shogun, which had for centuries been the only significant point of constitutional contention in Japan. The new leadership after 1868 did not therefore inherit a blueprint for reform – except, perhaps, that which the Bakufu had bequeathed to it from its final years – so much as a preoccupation with the regime's viability. This prompted a period of largely administrative experiments, which only gradually took coherent shape.

When they did so, it was as what is now called 'the emperor system' (*tennō-sei*). One aspect of this was that the emperor's theoretically absolute powers were to be exercised in his name by appointed officials, that is, bureaucrats, not feudal retainers or hereditary nobles. Another is that they acted through a governmental machinery that was increasingly of Western provenance. The way in which the structure took shape is the main theme of this chapter.

IMPERIAL RULE

The men who were the victors in the confrontation of January 1868 were popularly supposed to advocate a policy of 'honour the emperor, expel the barbarian' (*sonnō-jōi*). Neither component in the slogan proved immediately practicable. As the Bakufu had discovered – and as the bombardments of Kagoshima and Shimonoseki had demonstrated to a wider audience – provoking the West in the name of expulsion was a dangerous thing to do. Yet the early weeks of 1868 saw fresh examples of anti-foreign violence, which left the Court and its advisers facing the same kind of crisis as the Bakufu had formerly done: foreign protests, coinciding with civil strife at home. They had little choice but to follow the Bakufu's example in handling it. The attackers were punished. A promise was made that treaties signed by the Bakufu would be scrupulously observed. What is more, the emperor approved a memorial from the leading *daimyō*, urging that expulsion be disavowed. Since the document recommended that Japan abandon the attitude of 'the frog looking at the world from the bottom of a well', and resolve instead to learn from foreigners, 'adopting their best points and making good our own deficiencies',[21] it seemed to herald something much more sweeping than an acceptance of *force majeure*.

Honouring the emperor also posed problems, for the Court still had prestige without power: no lands and no officials outside the immediate area of the capital; no state revenue; no military force of its own. Decrees issued in the emperor's name could be enforced only at the pleasure of the feudal lords, or where the imperial army, furnished by loyal lords, happened to be fighting. Since the Bakufu's administration was already at a standstill, it is fair to say that at this stage Japan had no central government at all.

During 1867 there had been some discussion of what institutional arrangements might replace the Bakufu, but it had not been carried very far. Those who were most concerned about such things – notably Iwakura Tomomi – were clear about two points: that there should be no new line of Shogun; and that there must be some resurrection of ancient Court offices, dating from a pre-feudal past, instead of those which had been unduly under Tokugawa influence. This much was quickly given effect. Room was also found within the system for a wide array of appointments, designed to give a measure of satisfaction to every group that had played a part in the movement to overthrow the Tokugawa. At the head of the administration was an imperial prince. As deputies he had the two Court nobles who had been most prominent in loyalist politics, Sanjo Sanetomi and Iwakura Tomomi. Senior councillors (Gijo) included several other representatives of the Court, plus the five lords whose troops had taken over the palace gates (Satsuma, Tosa, Hiroshima, Owari and Echizen). They were later joined by Choshu. As junior councillors (Sanyo) were a number of Court nobles of lesser rank, together with three samurai from each of the same domains; but as more *daimyō* declared allegiance, so the numbers of Sanyo grew, reaching over one hundred by June. In theory, the Gijo and Sanyo controlled administrative departments. In practice, since the offices had almost nothing of significance to do, appointments to them were principally meant to cultivate goodwill.

So was the period's most famous state document, a declaration in the emperor's name, known as the Charter Oath, which set out the government's broad intentions. Issued on 6 April 1868, it promised that policy would be decided only after wide consultation, taking account of the interests of all Japanese, 'high and low'; that 'base customs of former times' would be abandoned; and that in the pursuit of national strength 'knowledge shall be sought throughout the world'.[22] Implicit in this was a hint of reconciliation with the defeated Tokugawa and the trained officials in their service, whose help was certainly going to be needed if the country's administration were to function smoothly.

Once Edo surrendered and there was a prospect that Kyoto would have most of the Tokugawa lands to govern, the central machinery was reorganized with a view to greater efficiency. This meant having fewer nonentities in high office. At the level of junior councillor and vice-minister the representation of Court nobles was reduced from over forty to just three. Only nineteen samurai were now included with them, chosen from several domains: Owari was omitted from the six which had taken part in the January coup; the Kyushu domains of Hizen and Kumamoto were added. Thirteen of the nineteen were samurai of middle rank. Nearly all had held office in the governments of their domains.

The concentration of power was taken further in August 1869, when the fighting was over. This time the institutions of government were put into a form which was to last with little alteration until the introduction of a Western-style cabinet in 1885. Sanjo Sanetomi, as Minister of the Right (Udaijin), became the senior member of the Executive Council (Dajokan); but real power rested with the two groups of advisers and councillors immediately below him, who also served as ministers and vice-ministers of the six departments, namely, Civil Affairs (re-organized as Home Affairs in November 1873), Finance, War (divided into Army and Navy separately at the beginning of 1872), Justice, Imperial Household, and Foreign Affairs. Samurai from Satsuma, Choshu, Tosa and Hizen practically monopolized the post of vice-minister in these departments. After the summer of 1871 they gradually emerged as ministers, too, ousting all but a handful of the Court nobles and *daimyō* who had managed to survive in office until that time.

Of the men who ran this structure, Sanjo Sanetomi (1837–91) and Iwakura Tomomi (1825–83) were Court nobles, having close ties with Choshu and Satsuma, respectively. Sanjo had the higher personal rank, Iwakura the greater political capacity and influence over the emperor. Saigo Takamori of Satsuma was the most famous of the samurai and the hardest to understand: widely acclaimed as a model of samurai virtue; a social conservative become revolutionary against his will; at the end a rebel under arms against his monarch and his former friends. His boyhood companion, Okubo Toshimichi, was in complete contrast, a ruthless politician with an instinct for governing. As Home Minister after November 1873 he emerged as the key man of the ruling group, a fact which cost him his life by assassination. Less incisive, but more flexible and open to new ideas, was Kido Koin, virtually unchallenged as the representative of Choshu after the premature death of Takasugi Shinsaku in 1867.

Saigo, Okubo and Kido, who have already appeared in our account of the Bakufu's fall, were from families of full samurai rank, though with little pretension to wealth. Most of their close colleagues were men much like themselves, young, able, usually with some experience of office as well as loyalist politics. Those whose only claim to consideration rested on radical views and a record of anti-Tokugawa or anti-foreign violence did not reach this level; while some who had served the Bakufu found even this stain on their record no disability once a year or two had passed and wounds had healed. Katsu Awa (1823–99) is a good example. A samurai of modest rank, well known as Edo's chief naval expert before 1868, he was the only councillor (Sangi) appointed between 1869 and 1885 who did not come from one of the four paramount domains.

There were others, a few years younger, who were to comprise the next generation of the Meiji leadership. They included Matsukata Masayoshi (1837–1924), a Satsuma man of semi-samurai status, who as Finance Minister after 1881 checked inflation and opened the way for the first stage of industrial growth. From Hizen there was Okuma Shigenobu (1838–1922), a middle samurai, student of Dutch and English under the Tokugawa, who reached cabinet rank in the fields of finance and foreign affairs, became a party politician, and also founded Waseda University. Two Choshu men, both something less than samurai by birth, achieved even greater distinction. Yamagata Aritomo (1838–1922) was soldier more than politician, at least until his middle years, whereas Ito Hirobumi (1841–1909) was a modernizer with more than average knowledge of the West. Each was to be prime minister, elder statesman, prince. Ito, with Iwakura's help, succeeded Okubo as the government's leading figure after 1880. Yamagata was his principal rival by the end of the century.

These were not the kind of bureaucrats one can call 'faceless'.

Indeed, they were men of initiative, even idiosyncrasy, who had risked their lives and in some cases an established position in society to break free from the trammels of upbringing and tradition. Their actions in government reflected this. In the sixteenth century they might well have become feudal lords. In the nineteenth they were to be the architects of a powerful, Western-style Japanese state, which they made authoritarian as well as modern.

Their first concern, as we have seen, had been to set up a central machinery for decision-making. This done – it took more than a year – there remained the question of how their decisions were to be made effective, other than by persuading a large number of nominally independent feudal lords to act on them, each for his own territories and in his own way. A preliminary step in that direction had been to transfer the emperor to the Shogun's former castle in Edo and to rename the city Tokyo, 'eastern capital', implying that the emperor's government was to have a role much more like that of the Bakufu than its own in the recent past. Another was to make provision for samurai representatives to be attached to it, partly to improve the processes of consultation, partly to provide a channel of communication with loyalists in the rest of the country.

None of this went far enough to ensure that Japan's political life was directed from the centre. Accordingly, voices began to be heard arguing that for the country's sake – always in the background was a consciousness of the foreign threat – government must be centralized by abolishing the domains. Such a proposal was bound to face obstacles on account of inherited prejudice and divided loyalties. On the other hand, these counted least among the men who mattered most, that is, the samurai on the Executive Council. By accepting office they had already begun to separate themselves from their lords; they had received rewards in cash and promotion which helped to confirm their choice; and they more than any others felt the frustrations of the existing mode of doing things. As Ito put it in a later reminiscence, 'obsolete shackles and formalities hindered us at every step'.[23]

It was Kido who made most of the running. During the summer of 1868 he persuaded Choshu to offer to surrender its territory to the emperor, provided Satsuma did the same. Later in the year he won over a doubtful Okubo and the leading samurai from Tosa and Hizen. As a result, on 5 March 1869 these four domains submitted a joint memorial putting their lands and people at the emperor's disposal. Its wording was ambiguous, capable of being read either as a surrender of feudal rights, or as a request for the confirmation of feudal privilege: the Court, it said, should dispose of the lands at will, 'bestowing that which should be bestowed, taking away that which should be taken away'.[24] In this it fairly represented the uncertainties that still existed within the ruling group. Okubo, in particular, questioned whether feudal opinion could yet be brought to accept a really radical change. Hence in July, when the memorial was approved and all other *daimyō* were ordered to follow the example set by Choshu, Satsuma, Tosa and Hizen, there was an element of compromise. The lords were appointed governors of the lands they had surrendered. In principle they became imperial officials, but in practice their position seemed likely to be much what it had been before.

Despite this, the government did not mean the gesture to be an empty one, as was made apparent by the orders which it issued shortly after. Domain revenues were to be divided, a distinction being made between the expenses of the former *daimyō*'s household and those of administration; reports were to be made on population, military force, and tax; samurai stipends were to be reviewed. Such ominous signs of a willingness to intervene in local matters provoked stirrings of discontent. Yet it was also clear that in many parts of Japan the lords and their senior retainers, who were finding the old ways difficult to operate, would not be unwilling to see responsibility in someone else's hands. Within a year of the surrender of domain registers (*hanseki-hōkan*) in 1869, Okubo had come round to the view that a determined push would bring the process of dismantling the feudal structure to a successful end.

Preparing for it took time. First there had to be a reconciliation with Saigo and Shimazu Hisamitsu, who had recently held disapprovingly aloof. Then troops had to be moved into Tokyo, in case the decision was resisted. Finally, it was necessary to redistribute central government posts, in order to ensure that the key ones were held by men who had strong nerves and solid backing. It was August 1871 before all this was done. On the 29th of that month the emperor summoned to his palace those former feudal lords who were present in the city and told them that the domains were at last to be abolished. They would be replaced by prefectures, administered directly from the capital (on the Chinese model). Giving substance to the change, another decree a month later ordered domain armies to disband, except for those which were already part of the imperial forces.

LAND TAX AND MILITARY REFORM

In their first three years the Meiji leaders had done a good deal to give the slogan 'honour the emperor' an institutional reality. Councils and ministries in the capital had taken the names and functions of those which had existed before Court nobles and Shogun had usurped the emperor's authority. Administration of the country and its people had been brought within their competence by the abolition of domains. Even so, there were things yet to do if Japan was to have a viable central government. Above all, it was necessary to create an efficient tax system and a disciplined military force.

Since each of the *daimyō* territories, now under central control, had long had its own tax rates and tax exemptions, tax-collecting was complex and burdensome. Variations in market prices made revenue unpredictable, because most dues were still paid in kind. Moreover, much of what was received was already mortgaged to the payment of samurai stipends. This state of affairs made tax reform an early topic of concern to the administration, though its exact nature was a matter on which different offices found it difficult to agree. The Finance Ministry, for example, was anxious to maximize receipts, because of the heavy demands that were being made on its expenditure. As a result, Kanda Kohei, one of its senior officials, put forward proposals in 1869–70 for collecting tax in cash on the basis of a valuation of the land, which would, he claimed, provide a revenue which was both stable and predictable. By contrast, prefectural officials, who had to deal with a renewal of peasant revolt – 177 outbreaks between 1868 and 1873 – were in favour of any measure which would reduce unrest. Matsukata Masayoshi, then a provincial governor, called for tax relief and the standardization of tax rates in all regions and localities as a means to this end.

Matsukata's appointment to a post in the Finance Ministry in 1871 put him in a position to draw these different threads together, though it was still some time before details could be agreed, because a balance had somehow to be struck between the requirements of the tax office, on the one hand, and those of landlord, tenant, and owner-cultivator, on the other. A start was made in the spring of 1872, when the Tokugawa ban on land sales was abolished and certificates of ownership were introduced. In order to value holdings which had not been subject to sale, a draft tax law in the autumn of that year proposed a system of local consultation, subject, however, to a mean of ten times the annual crop. By this estimate, a tax level of 3 per cent of value would set the tax at 30 per cent of yield, which officials believed to be on average what was being paid by way of feudal dues across the country as a whole.

This arrangement is broadly what the Finance Ministry secured in the final version of the tax law, announced in July 1873. Such changes as were made in various drafts before that date, apart from the addition of an extra 1 per cent of tax (equalling 10 per cent of yield) for local government purposes, tended to favour landlords against tenants rather than farmers against the tax-collector. So did the long series of consultations, which then began in the villages (lasting until 1876 for arable, 1881 for forest). Inevitably, landlords were better able to influence the committees set up for this purpose than were their tenants or the poorer owner-farmers. The outcome, therefore, was that the government got the reliable cash revenue it wanted, while landlordism became legal (as it had not been under the Tokugawa), and much more profitable.

A significant feature of these reforms was that they did not provide for former lords or samurai to retain a direct interest in the land on the basis of hereditary feudal rights. In 1871, both groups had been offered financial inducements to accept with good grace the abolition of domains: for *daimyō*, one tenth of the revenue from the area they had governed, received now as private income; for samurai, a continuation of their stipends without corresponding obligations to service, though only at the reduced rates established since 1868. This soon turned out to be a greater weight of debt than the government was able or willing to carry. At the end of 1871 members of the feudal class were granted permission to supplement their incomes by taking up farming, commerce, and other occupations, which status rules in the past had forbidden them to do; and when many got into difficulties as a result, they were told in 1873–4 that they could commute their stipends for cash. Not many chose to do so.

On 5 August 1876 what had been optional for some was made compulsory for all. A scale was published showing the amount in government bonds which would be distributed as a once-for-all payment in place of annual allowances. For the very largest pensions, those of the great lords, bonds would be issued at a value of five years' income, bearing interest at 5 per cent; for the very smallest, the calculation would be based on fourteen years and 7 per cent. There would be a series of gradations in between. The result was to provide ex-*daimyō* with substantial capital, enough to ensure that they continued to enjoy comfort and social dignity, while the poorest ex-samurai received a good deal less than would support their families in even modest style. The government for its part – at some cost to its reputation for good faith – had achieved a major economy, reducing its annual budget for this item by approximately 30 per cent.

Samurai without land or stipends usually had to look for jobs. One career open to them was the bureaucracy, of course, but not all had the qualifications for it. Another, one might have thought, was the army, in view of their upbringing. However, those responsible for organizing Japan's modern armed forces were none too sure about wanting them, at least as rank-and-file, since there was doubt whether samurai would accept the necessary rules of discipline and promotion, which had to be imposed without regard for personal status. Commanders – themselves ex-samurai, but a minority among them – who had had some experience with non-samurai troops, especially in Choshu, expressed a preference for a conscript army; and although Omura Masujiro, who put the idea forward in 1868–9, was murdered for his pains, he found successors in Yamagata Aritomo and Saigo Tsugumichi (Takamori's younger brother). The two men went to Europe for a year in 1869–70 to study what was done in France and Germany. On their return they became officials of the Ministry of Military Affairs and put what they had learnt to use, drafting plans for conscription which were brought forward for discussion when the domains were abolished. Despite opposition from conservatives, who held that samurai should form the core of any military élite, in December 1872 and January 1873 an imperial edict, followed by a Conscription Law, provided that the army was in future to comprise men called to the colours at age twenty, serving for three years, then four years in the reserve. This was calculated to provide a peacetime force over 30,000 strong.

Following the Bakufu's example, the Meiji government had arranged for the training of its army to be supervised by a French mission, which also gave advice about military organization. By 1875 Japan had an officer training school, an arsenal employing 2,500 workers, a gunpowder factory, an ordnance yard, and a practice range for artillery. The assumption at this time was that the force existed primarily to supplement the work of the police in keeping order within Japan. There was recurrent peasant unrest to be suppressed. Occasionally after 1873 there were samurai revolts, undertaken as protest at loss of stipends and other privileges, or simply at the direction which national policy was taking. The largest took place in Satsuma in 1877 under the leadership of Saigo Takamori. Though the rebels were outnumbered, defeating them tested the resources of army and police to the limit, revealing weaknesses in command structure, logistics, and planning which led to the creation of an Army General Staff in 1878 to take responsibility for these functions. A staff college for the training of senior officers was added in 1883.

Much of the detail for these later changes was worked out by two of the younger military commanders, Katsura Taro and Kawakami Soroku, who had spent several years in Germany and looked to that country for their models. Hence while training at the lower levels remained French in character, staff work and command became largely German. Major Klemens Meckel was recruited from Germany to teach at the staff college and advise the General Staff. Specialist schools were set up for artillery and engineering branches. At the same time, the army acquired a new strategic role. As Japan became involved in disputes on the Asian mainland in the 1880s (see chapter 9), its forces were required to develop a capacity to operate overseas. A revision of the conscription law in 1883, providing for three years with the colours and nine with the reserves, raised the peacetime establishment to 73,000 men and wartime strength to 200,000 more, which seemed sufficient for this purpose. All were equipped by 1894 with modern rifles and artillery, mostly of Japanese manufacture.

The navy received less attention in this period. For one thing, maritime defence was a less vital issue once Japan had resolved to operate within the framework of the treaties. For another, the navy was expensive, especially in terms of foreign currency, which was always in short supply. Naval officers required a long and technical training, much of it not available at home, and warships had still to be bought abroad, if they were to be of acceptable quality. These circumstances help to explain why there was no naval officers' training school until 1888, while the Naval General Staff was established as late as 1891. The fleet, though efficient, remained small by European standards – only 28 modern ships in 1894, aggregating 57,000 tons, plus 24 torpedo boats – though dockyard facilities were sufficient to provide it with all the repairs it needed.

The cost of the army and navy together took up a third of the national budget on the eve of Japan's first foreign war, becoming the largest single charge on revenue. The services had also acquired a distinctive place in political society. Because the army, in particular, had a crucial part to play in preserving order, it was accorded a special relationship with the imperial house, designed to ensure its independence and loyalty. The emperor became commander-in-chief. He attended parades, manoeuvres, military and naval reviews. Members of his family regularly took up military careers. As a corollary, the Chiefs of the Army and Navy General Staffs, removed from the control of their respective ministries, were given direct access to the emperor in all matters concerning the command prerogative. Though the step was devised as a safeguard against political interference with the services, in the event, as we shall see, it enabled the services to intervene in politics.

THE MACHINERY OF GOVERNMENT

The abolition of the domains in 1871 did not directly prompt any changes in the central administration of Japan, except in so far as it concerned the nature and control of local government. The domains were renamed prefectures (*ken*), their number being reduced to 72 when boundaries were redrawn in 1872, later to 43. In addition, the three cities (*fu*) of Tokyo, Kyoto, and Osaka were given equivalent status. In 1878 all these were subdivided into districts, called *ku* in cities and *gun* in prefectures, each under an appointed official, while the lower subdivisions – villages (*mura*) and city wards (*chō*) – were under elected headmen. To replace the former domain and Bakufu officialdom a new system of local bureaucracy was gradually created, codified in November 1875 by regulations defining the titles, functions, and authority of its members. At its head in each area was the prefectural or city governor (*chiji*), who controlled the police and was responsible for public order. He and his subordinates also carried out or supervised a wide range of other functions, which included maintenance of schools and public buildings, tax reassessment in the event of local calamities, reclamation of forest land, river and harbour works, repair of roads and bridges, census returns, and land registration. Effectively, they replaced feudal lords.

The principal difference was that they were tied to central government through their subordination to the Home Ministry (Naimusho), which was established in November 1873. Under Okubo, it taught provincial authorities to look to Tokyo for tenure and reward. They thus became part of a bureaucracy which depended on national, not local, connections, and drew its personnel from a variety of sources: former samurai officials of the domains and Tokugawa estates; Japanese of less privileged background who had acquired special knowledge by travel or study abroad; and some, though they were few as yet, who qualified by possession of a measure of economic expertise. That most were ex-samurai reflected the limited opportunities to gain experience in the old order as much as it did the prejudices of the new. Moreover, for senior posts, whether in prefectures or ministries, the record suggests that evidence of political reliability, in the form of past loyalist activities or of domain origins, affording a link with members of the Executive Council, also had a part to play. It was this which gave the Meiji government the reputation of being dominated in the 1870s and 1880s by men from Satsuma and Choshu, though the charge did not by any means hold true at the lower levels.

After Okubo's death in 1878 it was Ito Hirobumi who assumed the task of giving the bureaucracy a modern, Western character.

In December 1880 regulations were issued for the conduct of official business in the central government, defining the powers and duties of ministers and their staffs and listing those matters in which they required the Council's authority before taking action. However, this did not eliminate all administrative abuses. Indeed, government business was soon widely held to be losing its way in a sea of paperwork and memoranda, reflecting a lack of confidence and initiative on the part of juniors. In December 1885, therefore, Ito sent a circular to departmental heads, calling on them to remedy these faults and impose proper discipline. Two months later came a new set of civil service regulations. They envisaged a system of examinations to decide appointments and promotions (not actually implemented until 1887); prescribed the limits of departmental budgets; laid down with precision the number of posts to be filled; and dealt with a host of details concerning archives and accounts. One may question whether this was the best way of restoring a sense of responsibility to individual members of the government machine, but there is no doubt that it took Japan a step nearer to being a modern state. From this time on, civil servants were to be recruited on the basis of their attainments in a Western-style education system and promoted in accordance with formal tests. Those at the highest levels came mostly from the newly-established university in Tokyo, whose graduates were exempted from the entrance examination until 1893 and provided much the largest proportion of successful candidates thereafter. By 1910 one third of the bureaucrats who held the post of bureau chief or higher had been admitted by examination. By 1920 the proportion was four-fifths, including most vice-ministers. Nearly all were men whose family circumstances had been such as to enable them to pay for the relevant training: sons of samurai, often enough, but also sons of landlords and merchants.

Those who won their way to the very top, whether or not they did so by examination, received due recognition of their achievement. In July 1884 the emperor announced his wish to create a new peerage, honouring two groups: the 'high-born descendants of illustrious ancestors', and men who had shown merit 'in the restoration of my rule'. There were to be five ranks, those of prince (or duke), marquis, count, viscount, and baron. Of the 500 titles first created, all but about thirty went to families of the old

Court and feudal nobility. Some were promoted. Sanjo and Iwakura were made princes, for example, the latter posthumously, since he had died the previous year. The rewards for more recent service included elevation to marquis for Okubo and Kido, also posthumously, plus fourteen counts, chosen from men (mostly ex-samurai) in government office. Among them were Ito and Yamagata. The viscounts included twelve who were generals and admirals of the new armed forces. This highly selective approach was relaxed in the course of time, as is the way of such things, making titles the norm for a large number of senior bureaucrats. By the same token, they were regularly refused to the government's opponents. Setting the tone, Goto Shojiro and Itagaki Taisuke of Tosa and Okuma Shigenobu of Hizen, all of whom were linked with the popular rights movement in the 1880s, were pointedly omitted from the original list, despite having done as much as any in the regime's early days.

Another step, taken in December 1885, was the substitution of a cabinet (Naikaku) on European lines for the Executive Council (Dajokan). Its members, as ministers, were each to be responsible for policy within their own departments, while the Prime Minister (Sori Daijin) handled co-ordination between them, together with the making of general recommendations to the emperor. Since the cabinet itself largely replaced two separate boards within the Dajokan, this represented a significant simplification of the policy-making process. Moreover, Ito, as the first Prime Minister, wielded a lot more power than his predecessors in the Council had done (or, indeed, than most of his successors were to do).

The coping-stone was set on the edifice in April 1888 by the creation of a Privy Council (Sumitsu-in) to provide the emperor with a body of senior advisers who would be in some degree independent of the cabinet without undermining its authority. They were to be consulted on the interpretation and any revision of the written constitution (then in draft; see chapter 5), on major reforms of the law, and on foreign treaties, but they had no right to initiate action. Specifically, the regulations stated, the Privy Council 'shall not interfere with the executive'.

Taken together, these changes had the effect of shifting the emphasis in Japanese political institutions from ancient Chinese to recent Western models. They had two obvious motives. First, for a country which was trying to persuade the West to revise the unequal treaties, there was much to be said for presenting an appearance which would be acceptable because it was familiar. This was especially true of law and judicial practice (see chapter 6). Second, it seemed logical that the administration of a tax system, armed forces, and industrial structure on Western lines –the elements of 'wealth and strength' – should be entrusted to a Western-style government. By the 1880s, after all, a high proportion of Japanese officials were already being trained in the appropriate Western skills.

5

THE MEIJI EMPEROR AND THE MEIJI CONSTITUTION, 1873–1904

A concept which most Japanese historians of recent years have used in one form or another is that of Meiji 'absolutism' (*zettaishugi*). It starts from the proposition that the leaders who emerged as a result of the Restoration did so as bureaucrats, serving, but also controlling, an emperor whose authority had never in theory been limited, whether by recognition of an overriding ethic, as in China, or by the assertion of rights on the part of his subjects, as in Europe. It explains the success of those leaders in terms, not of a rising social class, which they might be said to have represented, but of an incomplete revolution: a feudalism undermined but not wholly destroyed; an emergent bourgeoisie, still not strong enough to assume power; commoners whose discontents were reflected in unrest, but not in meaningful organization. One purpose of the Meiji reforms, it is argued, was to maintain that state of balance and therefore the perquisites of those who profited from it.

As a Marxist interpretation of Japanese history in the late nineteenth century, this set of ideas has focused on the potential for moving society from feudalism through bourgeois democracy to socialism. It is not necessary to accept the Marxist framework, however, in order to find the interpretation valuable. In particular, it has directed the attention of scholars more closely towards the nature of opposition in Meiji Japan and its significance as a commentary on the 'modernizing' view of what took place. Because the new leaders had come to power without any advance commitment to specific programmes of reform, many Japanese at the time had expectations of them which were destined to be disappointed. Anti-foreign fanatics who found their country still bound by unequal treaties, imperial loyalists shut out from office and influence by ex-samurai bureaucrats, peasants whose way of life became different, but not in the short run noticeably better, all found much to complain about. Many of them, moreover, had been conditioned in the decade before 1868 to express themselves through violence. Controlling them, or reconciling them, was therefore one of the regime's urgent tasks. One way in which it sought to do so we have already described, that is, by creating a strong government machine. Another was to provide an outlet for grievances through the workings of a carefully drafted constitution. A third was by devising, or at least fostering, an appropriate ideology, propagated through the state education system and a variety of official or semi-official organizations.

THE CONSTITUTIONAL MOVEMENT

The opposition which set the constitutional movement in train was that which came from samurai, who had much to protest about and a position in society from which the more easily to do it. The Restoration and the abolition of the domains had dislocated many feudal loyalties. Samurai had lost the right to wear swords, their stipends had been cut, then cut again, and finally abolished in return for what were in many cases derisory sums of capital. It is not surprising that there were revolts in Choshu in 1869–70, in Hizen early in 1874, and in Choshu again in 1876. The largest of all was in Satsuma in 1877, when several thousand men with Saigo Takamori at their head set out to take their complaints to Tokyo. Checked at Kumamoto, their rebellion was in the event confined to southern Kyushu, but it took the whole of the standing army and its reserves six months to suppress it. Saigo and his principal followers died by their own hands at Kagoshima in September 1877 in the face of overwhelming odds.

This proved to be the last of the feudal uprisings against the Meiji government, but not the end of samurai opposition.

Although samurai in other areas had not been sufficiently at one with Saigo to rally behind him, he had many sympathizers among them and these continued to advocate his policies. Especially was this so of his plans for Japanese expansion in Korea (see chapter 9). They were taken up by men who formed the first patriotic societies of the period, who were not averse to using force in domestic politics, much as their predecessors, the 'men of spirit', had done. Okubo himself was a victim, killed in May 1878. A bomb was thrown at Okuma Shigenobu, then Foreign Minister, because of his concessions on treaty revision in 1889. The Education Minister, Mori Arinori, well known for his commitment to Western-style reform, had died at the hands of a 'patriot' earlier in the same year.

A different type of samurai political activity was equally a product of the crisis over Korea in 1873. Itagaki Taisuke and Goto Shojiro of Tosa had been members of the Executive Council at that time and had supported Saigo's proposals for a military expedition, partly in the belief that it would provide opportunities to rehabilitate many distressed samurai; and when they resigned, having been defeated on this issue, they decided to continue to pursue their aims through political pressure. Early in 1874 they petitioned for the creation of an elected legislature. In one respect this was to look back to the ideas their domain had put forward in 1867 for a constitutional structure to replace the Tokugawa. In another it was an attempt to rally the disaffected, that is, all those who were disappointed with what had happened since. It was these for whom the two men claimed to speak: 'the samurai and the richer farmers and merchants . . . who produced the leaders of the revolution of 1868'.[25]

Itagaki and Goto had a factional as well as a public motive for what they did, which was to challenge the near-monopoly of high office that the men from Satsuma and Choshu were in the process of establishing. But those who backed their demand for 'freedom and popular rights' (*jiyū-minken*) reflected a much wider spectrum. Indeed, the movement they initiated resembled in its composition and complexity that of the pre-Restoration loyalists, shorn of those who had achieved success in later years. It included surviving advocates of the policy of 'honour the emperor, expel the barbarian', who argued that a constitutional assembly was needed for the sake of national unity in the face of foreign threat. There were others who believed that a parliament's function would be to control the emperor's advisers, not limit the emperor's authority, in much the same way that moderates in the 1860s had called for restraints upon the Bakufu. In addition, the more radically minded – not least, as we shall see, men from the countryside – saw the issue as one of social justice within Japan.

Of the government's leaders, Kido had more sympathy than most with what was being said on the subject. On his return from Europe in 1873 he had published a long article stating the case for a constitution as a means by which Japan could gain respectability abroad and reduce disunity at home. Okubo and Iwakura were more cautious, especially about making concessions to those who attacked their power. Nevertheless, they had always recognized that some measure of popular participation would contribute to stability. Early in 1875, therefore, they established an assembly of prefectural governors – replacing an earlier consultative body of samurai, which had proved too argumentative – to serve as a sounding-board of local opinion. Above it was to be a Senate (Genro-in), also advisory, but composed of nobles, senior bureaucrats and specialists in law. To the latter body was entrusted the task of drafting a constitution.

Before it could report, major changes had taken place in the personnel of government. Kido died in May 1877, Saigo and Okubo within the year thereafter, leaving only Iwakura of the original power-brokers. Three younger men now joined him in the inner circle: Okuma Shigenobu of Hizen, Finance Minister since 1873, who had been largely responsible for putting the land tax into operation; Ito Hirobumi of Choshu, who had been in charge of the Ministry of Public Works during the same period and hence much of the economic modernization programme; and Yamagata Aritomo, also of Choshu, chief architect of Japan's new army. It was these three, together with Iwakura, who were to play the central role in decisions about the constitution.

The least controversial part of what they did was to introduce an electoral element into local government. Assemblies were established in urban areas (*fu*) and prefectures (*ken*) in 1878 to supervise the spending of that portion of the land tax designated for local use and to discuss any matters put to them by the governor. He retained a veto on such action as they might recommend. The electorate for these bodies was limited to males over twenty-five, paying a specified sum in national taxes. The assembly men served for four years, half retiring after every two. Decisions were by simple majority vote. In April 1880 similar assemblies were created in towns and villages, later also in cities (*shi*) and districts (*gun*). The whole structure was then more closely co-ordinated in 1889–90, when revised regulations, produced under Yamagata's direction, increased the degree of central supervision through appointed officials. Eligibility for voting and election remained closely tied to tax-paying, as they were also to be in the national context until 1925.

Meanwhile, in June 1878, the Genro-in had produced a draft for a national constitution, under which, it was proposed, some legislative powers should be entrusted to an assembly elected under rules much like those being used in prefectures. The principle was criticized by leaders of the Executive Council as being altogether too progressive. Iwakura and Ito, in particular, wanted greater emphasis on the emperor's prerogatives. As Ito saw it, the object was to disarm critics, not to cede real power. Yamagata for his part urged that the legislature consist of appointees, or persons elected indirectly by the prefectural assemblies. Only Okuma disagreed, apparently because he saw in the issue an opportunity to gain an advantage over his rivals from Satsuma and Choshu. In March 1881 he produced a memorandum demanding not only an elected assembly, but also party government and a cabinet responsible to parliament in the English manner. Moreover, he called for early action: framing of a constitution during 1881, an announcement of it in 1882, the first elections in 1883.

If Okuma expected by this, as seems likely, to get himself swept to power on a wave of popular support, he was disappointed. His proposals were formally rejected by his colleagues in June, and when he responded by associating himself with public criticism of scandals in the sale of government undertakings in Hokkaido, he was pushed out of office. Simultaneously, in a move to disarm such opposition as he might be able to organize, the cabinet announced that the decision to establish a constitution had already been taken and would be implemented in nine years' time. The imperial edict making this promise (October 1881) warned that any who in the interval 'may advocate sudden and violent changes, thus disturbing the peace of Our realm, will fall under Our displeasure'.[26]

It transpired that a good many people were prepared to run that risk. Within a few days Itagaki and Goto had formed the Jiyuto, or Liberal Party, which they hoped would influence the drafting of a constitution and stand ready for the day when they could benefit from its provisions. The party was linked regionally with Tosa, ideologically with French radicalism, and socially in large part with rural areas. Okuma followed suit with the Progressive Party (Kaishinto), which looked to Hizen, English liberalism, and city businessmen. Both soon found that the government's threats were seriously meant.

Japan already had a Press Law, dating from 1875, largely because the Western-style newspapers which were emerging at that time had shown themselves to be anti-government in their observations on events. It required that owner, editor, and printer be registered; that all comment be signed; and that the editor be held responsible for subversive or slanderous articles, including any material that 'reviles existing laws, or confuses the sense of duty of the people to observe them'.[27] A revision of July 1877 gave the Home Minister the right to prohibit or delay publication of any offending paper. Then in April 1880 the range of controls was extended to include the activities of political parties and similar organizations. Political meetings were put under police supervision; members of the armed forces, teachers, and students were denied the right to attend them; and associations formed for political ends were forbidden to advertise meetings, to solicit membership, or to correspond with any such groups in other parts of the country. The Peace Preservation Law, issued in December 1887, strengthened the hands of the authorities still further. It empowered the police to ban from the immediate vicinity of the capital any person plotting or inciting a disturbance, 'or who is judged to be scheming something detrimental to public tranquillity'.[28]

Regulations of this kind were ostensibly of general application, but in practice they were directed against the advocates of parliamentary rule. Arrests, both of editors and politicians, were frequent. Against the movement's original nucleus of ex-sumurai and intellectuals, mostly town-dwellers, who had been educated to a knowledge of Western political thought, such action was frequently effective, because they had a good deal to lose. On the other hand, the Liberal Party also had a following in the countryside, not only among rural élites, but also quite widely among farmers in parts of the country where unrest had been endemic for a generation or more. These farmers often showed a remarkable degree of political awareness and understanding. They had also come to see in the idea of a constitution a means of redressing specific grievances, such as arose from land tax reform or the impact on farm prices of government financial policy. Consequently, they were less willing than their urban partners to submit without demur to government repression. Some even turned to violence, as their fathers had done before the domains were abolished. In 1882–4 there were outbreaks in the inland provinces to the north and east of Tokyo, claiming the Jiyuto as parent, but similar in character and social composition to the peasant revolts of the late Tokugawa period. They were put down easily enough by the police and the army; but they signalled the danger, which was not overlooked by those who made Meiji policy, that traditional forms of protest, not yet removed, could be given political direction by modern ideologies.

THE CONSTITUTION

The government's response to the constitutional movement was not wholly negative. In the summer of 1881 Ito and Iwakura had worked out an outline of the constitutional provisions they thought to be acceptable, including a cabinet clearly responsible to the emperor (which was established first, as we have seen); a bicameral assembly with an elected lower house, having no power to initiate legislation or in the last resort to deny the government money; and an electorate based on a property qualification, such as already existed in the prefectures. The proposals were not published, but the inner council approved them in October.

In March 1882 Ito left for a visit to Europe on a constitutional fact-finding mission which was to last eighteen months. Since he knew broadly what he was looking for, he went straight to Berlin and Vienna, where he expected to find it, and only later paid visits to Paris and London, where the political traditions were alien to his purpose. Most of his time was spent seeking advice from Rudolph Gneist and Lorenz von Stein, whose ideas were later injected directly into the drafting of the constitution by two Germans employed by the Meiji government, Alfred Mosse and Hermann Roesler. A brief excursus into the theory of parliamentary government under the guidance of Herbert Spencer did little to change the overall character of the expedition.

For some time after his return to Japan Ito was preoccupied with plans for the peerage, cabinet, and civil service. Once work started on the constitution itself, which was not until 1886, it was carried out in secret under Ito's personal supervision. The pace was leisurely, little affected by public agitation or debate. It is not surprising in these circumstances that the nature of what was done did not differ fundamentally from the principles laid down in 1881. Indeed, the document put before the Privy Council in May 1888, and proclaimed at a short ceremony in the palace on 11 February 1889, might well be described as little more than an amplification of points originally made by Iwakura, who had always been more alert than most of his colleagues to constitutional questions.

Much of its philosophical framework nevertheless derived from Lorenz von Stein's concept of 'social monarchy'. As Stein envisaged it, such a monarchy existed to arbitrate the competing interests of different groups in society, that is, to personify the general will and remain 'transcendentally' above the class struggle, preventing the exploitation of the weak by the strong. When expounded by Roesler and interpreted to Ito by Inoue Kowashi, some of the social purpose disappeared from this argument; but an emphasis on social harmony remained, appealing greatly to men who saw what they were doing in the tradition of Confucian thought and in the context of national strength. To the Meiji leaders, political dissent was seditious, because it weakened the state. In Ito's words, 'the onslaught of extremely democratic ideas' had to be resisted, because 'in a country such as ours, it was evident that it would be necessary to compensate for its smallness of size and population by a compact solidity of organization'.[29]

In consequence of this approach, many powers were reserved to the emperor, including declaration of war, conclusion of treaties, and supreme command of the armed forces. In addition, the emperor had extensive ordinance rights and could freely adjourn or prorogue the national assembly, the Diet. As regards finance, some important items of regular expenditure were excluded from the Diet's considerations altogether. More significant, it was laid down that should the assembly fail to pass the budget, that of the previous year might be repeated. Thus parliamentary control went no farther than the right to deny new taxes; and though this could be a potent weapon in harassing a cabinet, as the next few years were to show, it did not provide a sufficient lever to give the Diet control of national policy. Nor was it by any means certain that the elected lower house, the House of Representatives, could determine the actions of the Diet. The House of Peers, after all, had equal authority with it, and a membership, appointed as well as hereditary, that tended naturally to support the regime.

Because of these limitations, the House of Representatives, when it first met in 1890, became the scene of a struggle, not so much between parties debating policies and interests – though that existed, too – as between parliamentarians and government, each seeking to dominate the other (see chapter 8). In that struggle the cabinet enjoyed a number of advantages. It was not itself responsible to the Diet. Moreover, any constitutional reform sought by the parties to better their position had to be initiated by the emperor and approved by the Privy Council. Neither was likely to be easily persuaded. The alternative, which was to secure a share in power by the use of spoiling tactics, tended not only to bring the politicians into public disrepute, but also to cost them money by causing frequent elections. In these respects, the Meiji constitution cannot be said to have promoted harmony. It also had restricted value as a charter of personal liberties. The rights of subjects, as stated in it, were in all cases described as 'within the limits of the law', or 'within limits not prejudicial to peace and order'.

Where it concerned the monarchy, however, the constitution departed from the Prussian model, to which in other matters Japan's German advisers tended to defer. Roesler, when he drafted the section of the document relating to the emperor, had followed the norms with which he was familiar, whereby the ruler was held both to possess and to wield authority. The emperor, he wrote, 'presides over the Cabinet and decides its proposals',[30] subject only to the proviso that the documents embodying his decisions were to be countersigned by ministers. This was not at all what Ito and his colleagues had in mind.

The emperor's importance as a source of legitimacy for the Meiji leadership had never been in doubt. Nor had his value in the business of rallying popular support. It was for this reason that announcements like the Charter Oath had been made in his name, not that of his council; that rescripts were issued in which he admonished his subjects on a variety of topics; and that he was encouraged to make public appearances, not only on state occasions, but also by way of imperial progresses to different parts of the country. Yet among officials there had been much disagreement in previous years about what the monarch's role should be in the actual government of Japan. Some who took their Shinto doctrine seriously, especially those who had found a place in the palace, close to the emperor's person, argued that he should be trained to be in reality what he had always been in theory, an absolute ruler. The corollary was that he should take a full part in the decisions of the Executive Council or cabinet. The most powerful figures of the Meiji government did not accept this view. To them, the emperor was more useful as a symbol – and occasionally as a weapon of last resort, to be invoked against opponents – if he were detached from everyday politics. Iwakura put their preferences succinctly in 1875. When the councillors as a whole were in agreement about a measure, it was to be submitted to the throne for approval; when they were not, the emperor's senior political advisers – not his personal ones – must try to find a recommendation they could make collectively; only if this failed, too, was the emperor to be asked for a decision. Making due allowance for occasional changes in context and application, the principle underlying this statement held good for the next fifty or sixty years.

Ito observed it when he compiled the cabinet regulations in 1885. He made the point again in an address to the Privy Council in 1888, in which he argued that the emperor's function was not to rule, but to define and preserve by his superior authority the framework within which government worked. This was achieved in Europe by Christianity and constitutional theory, he pointed out. In Japan, neither Shinto nor Buddhism could in this sense provide a religious sanction. Nor did Japan have a relevant constitutional tradition of her own. It followed that 'the one institution which can become the cornerstone of our country is the Imperial House'; 'the first principle of our constitution is the respect for the sovereign rights of the emperor'; 'European ideas of separation of powers or . . . joint rule of the king and the people' must in Japan be set aside.[31]

This being so, Ito removed from Roesler's draft the reference to the emperor's governmental duties and replaced it with a section which laid emphasis on the 'national polity' (*kokutai*), that is, the emperor's divine descent, by virtue of which he reigned, together with the unique relationship which existed because of it between sovereign and subject. The constitution accordingly gave this concept legal standing. Its first chapter described the emperor as 'sacred and inviolable'. It also asserted that his sovereignty rested, not on a personal divinity, but on the fact that he belonged to 'a line of Emperors unbroken for ages eternal'. In other words, he came before his people, not principally as ruler, but as a symbol of the imperial lineage, stretching back beyond the state itself to the time of the world's creation. It was from this set of ideas that Japan's dominant ideology in the first decades of the twentieth century was to spring.

THE EMPEROR AND POLITICAL IDEOLOGY

Ito's approach to the theory of the constitution, justifying imperial authority by reference to *kokutai*, had in effect signalled that the emperor was to be put 'above the clouds' again, as he had been before the Restoration. It also contributed to the working out of a body of mystical beliefs by which the Japanese could be induced to give unquestioning loyalty to the human ministers who spoke in their sovereign's name. One element in it, to which political philosophy gave great attention after 1889, was the concept of the family-state. For example, Hozumi Yatsuka, professor of law at Tokyo's imperial university, equated obedience to the emperor with a quasi-religious obedience to the head of the nation-family. 'To be obedient to the family head is to be obedient to the spirits of the ancestors', he wrote; and since 'the present emperor sits on the throne in the place of the imperial ancestors', obedience to him was obedience to them.[32]

Hozumi was German-trained. He was therefore influenced by

late nineteenth-century German ideas of *staatsrecht*, giving priority to the state over the individual, and to organic law over natural rights or the social contract. In his discussion of the emperor, however, he was also reflecting the more prominent position which Shinto had been accorded within Japan's religious and philosophical eclecticism during the Meiji period. Buddhism had lost much of its standing as a public creed, though it was still the most widely recognized private one. Attacks made on it in the early Meiji years, ostensibly for the purpose of separating it from Shinto, but involving image-breaking and other forms of violence, had led to the closure of nearly 18,000 temples in less than a decade. Buddhist ceremonies were discontinued in the imperial household in 1871 and many temple lands were confiscated. Confucianism had fared better, because influential figures regarded its ethical code as a necessary element in the training of the young; but the cosmology from which the ethic nominally derived was undermined by the findings of modern science, so Confucianism came to be treated as a branch of secular philosophy, rather than a religion, notwithstanding its link with ancestor worship. Shinto, by contrast, coming more closely into relation with Confucianism as it was separated from Buddhism – a shift already heralded in the late Tokugawa period – secured as early as 1868 the open patronage of the state. Immediately after the Restoration the Council of Religion (Jingikan), which was concerned with Shinto ritual, had been made in theory the highest organ of the central administration. Even when this arrangement came to an end in 1871, the main Shinto shrines continued to be organized into a hierarchy, approved by government. Moreover, their special status was confirmed in 1882, when the more popular varieties of Shinto – the sects, whose activities included shamanism, fire-walking, and the reading of oracles – were given separate recognition as religious organizations, like any other, while being forbidden to receive help from official funds, such as was given to the 'national' shrines.

In 1872, the Bureau of Rites, successor to the Jingikan, inaugurated a campaign to propagate ideas which it called the Great Teaching (*taikyō*). Drawn from all three branches of Japan's religio-philosophical tradition, they included injunctions to respect the gods and to revere the emperor, as well as to love one's country and to obey the rules of moral behaviour, amounting to a code in which civic duty and support for the aims of government played at least as important a part as ethical and religious belief. In practice, the campaign to promote this teaching was confused and ineffective, but it established a precedent for later attempts to devise some kind of official ideology.

The first was a rescript issued in 1885 and addressed to the country's soldiers and sailors. Its emphasis, as one would expect, was on obligations to the nation and its monarch: 'neither be led astray by current opinions nor meddle in politics, but with single heart fulfil your essential duty of loyalty'. At the same time, loyalty was put into a context of ethical behaviour. It was to include 'sound discrimination of right and wrong', 'faithfulness and righteousness', and the avoidance of 'luxurious and extravagant ways', much as the samurai code had done. These qualities were together described as 'the Grand Way of heaven and earth and the universal law of humanity'.[33]

The equally famous Education Rescript of 1890, manifesting the influence of the emperor's Confucian tutor, Motoda Eifu, also put stress on the virtues of loyalty and filial piety, as did the regulations laid down from time to time about the teaching of ethics (*shūshin*) in schools (see chapter 6). In 1897 the Diet ruled that the textbooks to be used for this purpose must be official publications, not private ones. Starting with the edition of 1903, therefore, teachers were expected to expound a state-prescribed orthodoxy in their courses, comprising an 'absolutist' interpretation of the emperor's position in the state, deriving from Shinto; a 'family' concept of his relationship to his subjects; and a Confucian view of proper personal behaviour, modified by the assertion that loyalty took pride of place over filial piety. Copies of the emperor's portrait and the Education Rescript were placed in every school as objects of ritual reverence.

Although Christians, in particular, found these things difficult to accept, the situation in practice proved to be rather less consistent and authoritarian than such a statement of the facts implies. At the highest levels of abstraction, academic lawyers disagreed for many years to come about the theoretical nature of the emperor's authority. In the popular press, alternative ideologies, usually of Western derivation, continued to be canvassed. In the schools themselves teachers interpreted 'ethics' in the light of personal prejudice and intellectual fashion, not always in strict accordance with the textbooks. In consequence, all that one can say with certainty is that in most walks of Japanese life there was a prevailing insistence on duty and service, expressed in a variety of ways, which fell a long way short of being totalitarian.

Having entered that caveat, it might be helpful to take a particular example of how the threads were brought together. In 1904 Hibino Yutaka published a book called *Nippon Shindō Ron* (On the Way of the Subject in Japan), which was designed to serve as a commentary for teachers. He took as his starting-point – he was writing on the eve of the Russo-Japanese War – the fact that the country was beset on every side by enemies 'like raging tigers'. The danger could only be averted, he believed, if the Japanese held fast to their two central virtues, those of loyalty and filial piety. Authority and good government had a part to play as well, but in the last resort, he wrote, national safety rested on the willingness of the people to 'serve the emperor with their last breath'. It was this that would give the nation 'the combined strength of a bundle of arrows which cannot be broken'. And underpinning this loyalty, though secondary to it, was filial piety: 'filial piety in the child results in true loyalty in the subject'. Nor was either possible without the virtues associated with the Confucian family: 'The vigorous and unimpeded advance of our culture, the constant increment of our wealth and power, our supremacy in the east, our equality with the other great powers, our imposing part upon the stage of human affairs, all depend upon the establishment of a healthy home life, wherein husband determines and wife acquiesces.'[34]

Hibino's book was both influential and representative. Many of its ideas were inherited from late Tokugawa writers, but its view of the emperor, ostensibly traditional, had a great deal to do with the way in which political institutions had changed in the previous thirty years. His was a modern monarch, not an archaic one. The emperor was a figurehead, to be sure; but his role was to preside over the transformation of Japan in the name of 'wealth and strength', giving countenance and legitimacy to the men who evolved the appropriate policies.

6

CULTURAL BORROWING, 1860–1912

In 1894 a Japanese newspaper, *Yorozu Shimbun*, published a cartoon depicting the stages of Japan's relationship with the West during the previous twenty or thirty years. It consisted of three panel drawings. In the first, as the British minister in Tokyo explained, when sending a copy to London, Japan was 'a helpless child in the presence of an angry and overbearing foreign teacher'. In the second, the teacher slept while the boy grew up. In the last, he awoke to find his pupil vigorous and strong, 'able to avenge his former ill-treatment by dragging his frightened and thoroughly subject teacher by the beard'.

The cartoon exemplifies one strand in Japan's response to the West in the nineteenth century, that which gave priority to achieving Western-style national strength. Many Japanese, following the lead they had been given by the Tokugawa Shogun in 1865, saw their country's primary task as being to acquire the knowledge and skills by which 'to use the barbarian to control the barbarian'. There were other ways of looking at the relationship, however. One was Social Darwinist, manifested in a recognition that the West had climbed higher on the evolutionary ladder than Japan and implying that the purpose of study was to acquire 'civilization'. To do this involved learning about Western philosophy and law and patterns of behaviour, as well as science and industry. At a different level, there was the simple desire to satisfy curiosity. In two hundred years of national seclusion the Japanese had been starved of information about the mysterious occident. After 1860 they set out to make good that deficiency, celebrating their freedom to do so in a wave of fashion for what Aizawa Seishisai had called 'novel gadgets', now extended to include food, clothing, music, the arts, and almost every other aspect of Western life.

It is not surprising that this brought complaints from those who believed that Japan's own culture was thereby being undermined. Such sentiments had to be taken seriously by political leaders, because they could not afford to acquire a reputation for being unJapanese. In the eyes of government, indeed, political unity required a dash of cultural conservatism. We have already seen it expressed in the Meiji constitution and in state-sponsored ideology. During the closing years of the century it was also reflected in legal and educational reform, as well as in much contemporary writing.

LEARNING ABOUT THE WEST

Most of the envoys whom the Bakufu sent abroad before 1868 had been expected to bring back information on a variety of topics. In addition, they had the task of arranging suitable places of instruction for students whom the Bakufu had chosen or approved. There were no less than 68 of these between 1862 and 1867. Some domains followed the Bakufu's example, though the action was illegal until 1866: Choshu permitted Ito Hirobumi and Inoue Kaoru to go secretly to London in 1863; Satsuma sent a group of fourteen students to Europe in 1865, all travelling under false names. Other domains took similar steps as soon as it became permissible to do so, with the result that the number of students overseas before the Restoration, including those from the Bakufu, was as many as 150. Usually they were required to devote themselves to subjects which would make a direct contribution to national strength, such as military science, navigation, ship-building, and other aspects of technology, but a few were allowed to choose law or medicine or education, because these were also seen to have a practical value. Some, once abroad, extended the scope of their studies on their own initiative. Nishi Amane, for example, whom the Bakufu sent to

Holland in 1862 to study law and economics, spent a good deal of his time at Leiden learning about Western philosophy.

After 1868 the Meiji government enlarged the definition of what was to be considered useful, taking as its model Japan's approach to China in the sixth and seventh centuries, when the object had been to understand a culture, not just acquire selected skills. Conspicuously, this was a function of the Iwakura mission of 1871–3. There had been some talk as early as the time of the Bakufu's overthrow about sending a diplomatic mission to the West, both to seek recognition for the new regime and to examine those elements in Western civilization that could most profitably be borrowed by Japan. A preoccupation with domestic political reform prevented any immediate progress, but the proposal surfaced again once the domains had been abolished in 1871. Iwakura Tomomi, who had originally put the idea forward, was seen to be the logical man to lead the venture. Kido and Okubo made a claim to accompany him, because they wanted to learn more about the international problems which their country was likely to face. Together, the three formed an irresistible pressure group. Accordingly, in October 1871 plans were agreed for a formal mission to Western governments, headed by Iwakura, who was to take Kido and Okubo as his deputies. This powerful nucleus, representing Court, Choshu and Satsuma, respectively, was to be supported by nearly fifty officials, including Ito Hirobumi, and accompanied by 59 students, who were to be attached to schools and universities in various parts of the world.

Winning diplomatic recognition for the Meiji regime remained one of the mission's stated purposes. Another, that of giving an impetus to cultural borrowing, was linked with treaty revision. As the instructions given to the envoys put it, Japan had 'lost her rights and been made subject to the insults of others'. It was now necessary, therefore, to begin restoring her equality, a task that could only be carried out by remedying 'the faults in our laws and institutions', while convincing the powers that 'the arbitrary habits of the past' had been abandoned.[35] To this end the staff of the mission was organized into three sections, the first assigned to the study of constitutions and laws; the second to finance, trade, industry, and communications; and the third to education. Information on military equipment, training, and organization, such as might be 'of benefit to our country', was to be collected by all members of the mission as opportunity occurred.

The party left Yokohama by steamer in December 1871. It spent seven months in the United States, followed by four in Britain, then visited France, Belgium, and Holland more briefly before arriving in Germany in March 1873. From there some of its members returned to Japan via Russia, others via the Mediterranean countries. Everywhere Iwakura, Kido, and Okubo were received by heads of state and had talks with senior ministers (including Bismarck, though not Gladstone). They inspected government departments, military establishments, parliaments, law-courts, churches, museums, schools, banks, and factories of every kind. They and their assistants made copious notes. As a result, although they made little headway on the subject of treaty revision, they took home with them a body of facts and opinion which made their report, published in five volumes in 1878, a guide to Western-style modernization in all its aspects. What is more, the attitudes of the men who took part were profoundly influenced by their experiences. Kido came back a constitutional reformer. Okubo was for the rest of his life an advocate of industrialization. Iwakura, while remaining in most respects a conservative, accepted from that time on that the way forward would have to be in the Western manner.

The students who went with the Iwakura mission were by no means the only ones to go abroad at this time. It has been estimated that as many as 350 were overseas under government sponsorship in the years 1871–3. Of these, about two-fifths were in the United States, where they studied technology, mining, commerce, and agriculture. Those sent to Britain, amounting to roughly one-third, concentrated on engineering, industry, and trade, those in France on law, those in Germany on political science and medicine, extending later into the natural sciences. Regulations issued in January 1871 laid down rules about their selection, periods of stay, and the expenses they were allowed. The total cost of the arrangements came to approximately 10 per cent of the education budget for 1872–3.

Partly because of the expense, numbers were allowed to drop as Japan's own education system was developed. After 1875 the government was still prepared to pay for the advanced training of potential experts, who had already completed their basic education in Japan, but not for much else. On the other hand, this later period saw a steady increase in the number of students going to foreign countries at their own or their families' expense as an alternative to studying in Japan. About nine hundred went to the United States between 1868 and 1900. They studied the humanities and the social sciences, as well as the subjects which the Meiji government approved, thereby spreading a knowledge of Western civilization more widely through Japanese élites.

The learning process also included the hiring of foreign experts and advisers to serve in Japan. The Bakufu had employed about two hundred such persons in its closing years, apart from military missions. In the Meiji period as a whole (1868–1912) there may well have been as many as 4,000 *o-yatoi*, as they were called, of whom a little over 2,000 can be identified by name, job, and national origin. About half of those identifiable came from Britain in the early years, dropping to a third later. France, Germany, and the United States each provided on average one-fifth or a little less, the French proportion declining over time, the German and American ones rising. The great majority, especially in the 1870s, had a specific job to do: building railways, running the lighthouse service, commanding steamships, installing factory machinery, teaching in schools. In most cases it was assumed that they would also play a part in training Japanese to succeed them, though this was not their principal task. A minority were advisers, attached to a variety of government ministries as specialists in the Western way of doing things. Many of these were lawyers. All were on tightly drawn contracts, the terms for which were set out in 1870; were put unequivocally under the supervision of Japanese officials; and were dismissed as soon as there were Japanese people competent to replace them. They received salaries very much higher than those of any equivalent citizen of the country in which they worked. In other words, they were instruments of reform – Hazel Jones calls them 'live machines'[36] – expensive, valued, but not allowed themselves to become reformers.

The knowledge brought back by Japanese students returning from overseas or provided by foreigners working in Japan was disseminated through a growing range of translations, books about the West, and articles in the newspapers which emerged during the 1870s. One of the earliest examples was Fukuzawa

Yukichi's *Seiyō Jijō* (Conditions in the West), published in three parts between 1866 and 1870. Fukuzawa was a low-ranking samurai from Kyushu, who had first studied gunnery and Dutch, then English and medicine, before visiting both Europe and America as an interpreter attached to Bakufu missions after the opening of the ports. *Seiyō Jijō* was a compendium of the notes he made about Western governments, economies and social institutions, explaining as simply as possible how they worked. It was an immediate success. At one level, its sales provided the funds which enabled Fukuzawa to found Keio Gijuku, one of the two foremost Japanese private universities. At another, it contributed to a patriotic purpose. As Fukuzawa expounded it many years later in his autobiography, this was 'not only . . . to gather young men together and give them the benefit of foreign books, but to open this "closed" country of ours and bring it wholly into the light of Western civilization'.[37]

Another publication, which was also encyclopaedic in its manner and intent, was *Meiroku Zasshi*, the journal of Japan's first learned society, the Meirokusha, or 1873 Society. Its 43 issues, appearing in 1874–5, included contributions by most of the men who were regarded as Japan's leading commentators on the outside world. There were articles about tariffs and law reform and national character; summaries of well-known Western books and schools of thought; and a number of translations. Most of these arose from the society's lecture meetings and were expressed in simple prose. Occasionally they were controversial, causing problems with the censor after the government introduced the Press Law in 1875.

In addition, a wide range of complete or partial translations of Western works was published, sometimes separately, sometimes serially in newspapers and magazines. In 1871 Nakamura Keiu produced both Samuel Smiles' *Self-help* and J. S. Mill's *On Liberty*. Bulwer-Lytton's *Ernest Maltravers*, translated in 1878–9, was much imitated as a novel and valued as a source of information on Western manners. Jules Verne's *Round the World in Eighty Days* (1878) had great vogue as a sort of annotated handbook on foreign travel, while translations also appeared at about this time of *Robinson Crusoe*, Aesop's *Fables*, *The Arabian Nights*, and *Pilgrim's Progress*, to say nothing of More's *Utopia* and Rousseau's *Contrat Social*. A decade later attention turned to modern

European writers: Turgenev, Dostoevsky, Tolstoy, Ibsen, Victor Hugo. By the end of the century the Japanese student with no knowledge at all of European languages was nevertheless able to make the acquaintance of many of the world's great books.

The availability of such translations, coupled with visits to the West by individual authors, or contact with Western ideas through the medium of Christianity, produced a generation of Japanese novelists with a quite different concept of their craft from that of their Tokugawa predecessors. For the most part they used a straightforward modern prose. They also discovered a new interest in the individual as a subject whose life and thought should be explored, often in ways that were semi-autobiographical. Yet this is not to say that late Meiji writers were wholly Western in their literary conventions and techniques. One characteristic shared by many who were born at about the time of the Restoration of 1868 was that they had a much more vivid awareness of cultural change than those who came before or after them. They not uncommonly had a classical Sino-Japanese education in their early years, then a Western-style one at university or elsewhere, and earned their living as city intellectuals. Such experience made them exceptionally conscious of the discord between a Western and a Japanese cultural identity. Several made considerable efforts to maintain a link with their own country's literary and historical traditions: through poetry, for example, or the subject-matter of some of their novels.

There was an important visual side to the Japanese learning process, as one would expect, since images are usually easier to comprehend than words. Western art was taught in a special government school from 1876. Though it had long since influenced a number of notable Japanese artists, there is irony in the fact that it became fashionable just when Japan's own art forms were having their greatest impact in Europe. Western-style architecture was soon *de rigueur* for government offices, banks and railway-stations. Samurai hair-styles quickly disappeared – official approval for the change was given in 1871 – and Japanese began to appear in public in a variety of international clothing. In 1873, it is said, Satsuma samurai appearing in Tokyo in the old costume 'were as much stared at as foreigners had formerly been'.[38] Thereafter, the example of the Court, which adopted

Western ceremonial dress at the end of 1872, reinforced by that of frock-coated government officials and uniformed men of the armed forces and police, all helped to make the new types of clothing widely accepted. By 1900 they were used almost universally among the upper classes, at least on public and business occasions.

Western foods remained luxuries to the Japanese in this period, though eating beef in restaurants became a 'progressive' thing to do. Western music was performed in the 1880s at the Rokumeikan, a hall built in Tokyo to provide a place at which Japanese official society could meet diplomats and other foreign residents. Army and navy bands and Court musicians played there for ballroom dancing. Before long Western music became a polite accomplishment. It was studied at the Tokyo School of Music, founded in 1887, which in 1903 helped to put on the first opera in Japanese, a translation of Gluck's *Orpheus*. Popular taste ran more to martial music, also in the Western style, like the marches and songs that were taught in schools and performed at open-air concerts.

Clearly, what was happening in Japan in and after the 1870s was something more than a debate about how best to do things in the Western manner. Western habits and Western modes of thought had not yet penetrated much beyond the urban upper class – the countryside and the greater part of the population were little touched by them – but they were becoming influential enough to sound signals of alarm among those who valued tradition. As a result, the tide running in favour of 'civilization and enlightenment' (*bunmei-kaika*) soon lost some of its force.

LAW AND EDUCATION

The earliest forms of written Japanese law derived from China in the seventh and eighth centuries. Like China's, the codes in which the laws were embodied were statements of administrative practice, not rules to which governors and governed could equally appeal. Most legal disputes between subjects of the state, provided they did not touch on matters of tax or public order, fell outside them entirely. Much the same was true when Japan acquired a system of feudalism from the twelfth century onwards. The Chinese model had to be adjusted to a situation in which political authority was regionally fragmented and possessed by a military ruling class, but sections of it remained in use, alongside the emerging customary procedures which dealt with land and inheritance. Thus Japanese law, as it was transmitted to the Meiji government, was both feudal and Chinese. That is to say, it embodied much of China's imperial codes; it made little distinction between an official's duties as judge and as maintainer of order; and it varied in its provisions and machinery according to place (feudal territory) and personal status (lord, samurai, commoner).

Given that the first stage of Meiji political reform was ostensibly a reversion to eighth-century Chinese-style institutions, it is not surprising to find that law followed a similar course. The criminal law, for example, was codified on Chinese lines in 1871. However, neither the code itself, nor the machinery by which it was administered, met with the approval of the foreign powers. In both respects the law clearly needed to be modified if there were to be any hope of revising the unequal treaties, while other changes followed necessarily from the abolition of the domains.

Reform of the judicial process started in 1871 with the creation of local and regional courts, presided over by appointed judges, to replace those operated by former feudal lords. A Supreme Court was added in 1875, taking over from the Ministry of Justice as the highest court of appeal. The minister's power to remove or dismiss judges was restricted in 1886, and four years later it was decided that judges were to be appointed for life, subject to competitive examinations. Thus by the end of the century Japan had gone some way towards dissociating the judiciary from politics.

The laws it was to administer were also revised. Drafting a new criminal code was begun in 1875 under a French adviser, Gustave Boissonade de Fontarabie. He completed it at the end of 1877, though scrutiny by the Executive Council took several more years. It was 1882 before the final version was published and put into effect. Commercial law, by contrast, looked to Germany for precedent. Work on a full commercial code, starting in 1881, was carried out by Hermann Roesler, who was also engaged to advise Ito on the constitution; but his draft, ready by 1884, was not promulgated until 1890, following review by the ministries of

Justice and Foreign Affairs. Even then there were complaints that the result was too Western in character to provide a proper framework for the country's domestic commerce. As a result, full implementation of the code was not achieved until 1899.

The Civil Code was in some respects more difficult still. It had no direct relevance to consular jurisdiction and foreign trade, but arguments of consistency and international reputation suggested that it, too, should be Western in form. Nevertheless, to apply Western rules to matters like marriage and property, which were central to a whole range of traditional customs, seemed bound to cause disquiet and controversy. So indeed it proved. Drafting began in the 1870s on the basis of a translation of the French civil code. The first version produced was rejected by the government in 1878 as being altogether too 'foreign', like the Genro-in's draft of a constitution at about the same time. The next, prepared by Boissonade in 1886–8, met with objections from both political and academic circles, because it was held to strike an inappropriate balance between European and Japanese components. The ensuing debate delayed a final decision until 1898, though it did not make the published version very much more 'Japanese'.

As one would expect, the education of the young aroused feelings that were just as strong as those evoked by law, characterized by disagreements between those who saw the process as a necessary preparation for international competition and those who feared that inherited ways of life were being undermined. Japan began with the advantage of a pre-modern educational legacy which in both scale and quality was a good deal better than most modern societies have had: over two hundred official schools, run by the Bakufu and the large domains, at which samurai received a training in the military arts and some grounding in Confucian philosophy; more than 1,500 private schools and academies, similar in many ways, but substituting 'useful' skills for military ones, as befitted their lower-ranking pupils; and 10,000 or so 'temple' schools, where priests and other local dignitaries taught the children of commoners their letters and numbers, together with a modicum of moral precept. It has been estimated that by the 1860s these schools enrolled in all as many as a million students, ensuring that a high proportion of Japanese could read and write, albeit at minimum levels.

The Meiji government's attempts to build a national system of education owed a great deal to this inheritance from the past. Even so, they were remarkably ambitious. The Education Code of 1872 set out a vocational argument for education which was altogether recognizable to contemporaries in the West. It was to be the means whereby people in all walks of life could learn 'the cultivation of morals, the improvement of intellect and proficiency in arts', such as would enable the individual to 'raise himself, manage his property, and prosper in his business'; and it was to provide for every need 'from language, writing, and reckoning for daily use to knowledge necessary for officials, farmers, merchants, and artisans'.[39] Schools, it was said, must be available in every town and village. Consequently, Japan was to be divided into eight educational regions, in each of which there was to be one university and thirty-two secondary schools. Each secondary district, in turn, was to include 210 primary schools – one for every 600 of the population – where all children after reaching the age of six were to spend sixteen months under instruction.

The content of education, as was implied by its stated aims, was to be Western and utilitarian. Many of the schools themselves were former temple schools, put to new use, but Western advisers and teachers were brought in to key positions, while school texts (even those for reading lessons) were modelled on or directly translated from books published in the West. This was one source of complaint about the system: such books had few links with Japan's social or geographical environment. Nor did most of the teachers understand them very well, having had little training in anything but Japanese and Chinese studies. What is more, education, though compulsory, was not free. Despite makeshift accommodation and ill-paid staff, the cost of schooling was more than the poorest families could readily afford, making educational grievances one of the subjects about which the Japanese regularly protested, sometimes even rioted.

Despite this, by 1880 there were 28,000 primary schools with over two million pupils (about 40 per cent of the children of school age) and it had become possible to increase the compulsory period to three years. In 1886 attendance was 46 per cent and the period was increased by a further year. Thereafter numbers continued steadily to rise. Attendance was 60 per cent of the age group by 1895, 90 per cent by 1900. In the same period secondary education (which was not compulsory) was becoming specialized, as the government added normal schools (1872) to make good the deficiencies in teachers' training, middle schools (1881), higher middle schools (1886; renamed high schools in 1894), and high schools for girls (1889). To complete the pyramid, various institutions of higher learning, deriving from those of the Tokugawa Bakufu, were amalgamated in 1877 and reorganized as Tokyo Imperial University in 1886. A similar university was established in Kyoto in 1903.

A key part in the later stages of this development was played by Mori Arinori, a Satsuma man who had studied in Europe and America between 1865 and 1868, then served as envoy in the United States before becoming Minister of Education from 1885 to 1889. His ordinances gave the structure the shape it was to retain for twenty years, that is, an eight-year period of primary schooling, half of it compulsory; a middle school course of four years; then a range of higher education, reaching to the newly-created university. It had two general characteristics. One was close government control: the ministry prescribed all textbooks and exercised supervision of state schools through the workings of local government, while private foundations were subject to license and inspection. The other was the sharp distinction that was made between the lower and the upper levels. For the great majority of Japanese, education consisted of the acquisition of basic Western-style skills in the compulsory primary stage. Those who could afford to go on to middle school could qualify for jobs in the lower reaches of the bureaucracy, but there was no regular progression beyond that point. Entry to high schools was for a small minority destined to become an élite, that is, potential university students, trained to be members of the senior echelon of the bureaucracy, or experts in one of the branches of science, or intellectuals capable of exercising an influence on society through their writings. It was not a system that was privileged, in the sense of depending on birth, but the genuinely poor did not often get to Tokyo University, except, perhaps, through patronage.

To a generation not very far removed from the status system of feudal Japan, there was nothing remarkable about this. What many did feel to be unacceptable was the nature of what was being taught. Western skills were useful. Western ideas, however, were subversive, at least in the estimation of men who looked back with respect to the philosophy of Tokugawa scholars. A number of such men, including the emperor's Confucian tutor, Motoda Eifu, had posts in the palace from which they were able to exert a degree of pressure on ministers who would otherwise have paid them little heed. In 1879 they persuaded the emperor to issue a rescript condemning the 'indiscriminate emulation of Western ways' which was to be found in contemporary Japanese education. Teaching, it said, should put greater emphasis on 'the great principles governing the relations between ruler and subject, and father and son'. Loyalty and filial piety also formed the central theme of the 1890 Education Rescript, though the Japanese were then told to combine them with more ordinary civic duties, too: 'advance public good and promote common interests; always respect the Constitution and observe the laws; should emergency arise, offer yourselves courageously to the State'.[40]

Under the stimulus which these rescripts provided, conservatives were successful in winning greater prominence for the nexus of Japanese values in national education. After about 1890, textbooks, not only in ethics courses, were carefully scrutinized for evidence of undesirable kinds of foreign influence. Morals, patriotism, and 'the spirit of reverence for the emperor' were explicitly given some priority in the training of the nation's youth. As a result, the awareness of cultural dichotomy, which had been manifested in the constitution and in the debates about law, was also implanted in the minds of future generations.

ENLIGHTENMENT AND CULTURAL CONSERVATISM

Had the foreign residents in Kobe and Yokohama been asked in the 1880s what the West had to offer Japan, apart from the benefits of trade, a majority would certainly have answered, Christianity. In the nineteenth century evangelism was a mark of the West's self-confidence in every part of the world. Missionaries had entered the treaty ports as soon as the traders; and although they were nominally there to serve the foreign community, they took every opportunity to spread the gospel among the Japanese as well. In 1873 it became legal for them to do so, since diplomatic pressure at last brought an end to the Tokugawa ban on the 'evil sect'.

This did not remove anti-Christian prejudice, of course, but in the wave of enthusiasm for all things Western, which engulfed Japan in the 1870s, missionaries began to make headway. Some of their converts were mere 'kitchen Christians'. Some were students, who accepted the religion because it offered 'a window on the West', accessible to those who could not afford to travel overseas. Yet there were also many men and women of influence and standing – ex-samurai families, for example – capable of giving Christianity a more powerful voice in Japanese society than mere numbers might suggest. Numbers, in fact, were small. Despite a great outpouring of funds and human effort, there was an official total of no more than 140,000 converts by 1907. Of these, 60,000 were Roman Catholics, with an archbishop in Tokyo and bishops in Osaka, Sendai, and Nagasaki; just under 50,000 were Protestants of various kinds; and 29,000 were followers of the Greek Orthodox faith, which had been propagated with considerable success by a handful of priests from Russia. All these churches took steps to train a Japanese clergy. The Catholics and Protestants also engaged extensively in medicine and education, founding several schools which were later to be the nucleus of universities.

Nevertheless, there is no doubt that the West's religious beliefs were less attractive to the Japanese than its temporal ones. This was not just a matter of 'wealth and strength', to which the Meiji government gave priority. Among intellectuals, in particular, there was also a concern with 'civilization and enlightenment' (*bunmei-kaika*), reflecting a belief in the superiority of Western culture, which Japan, it was argued, had reason to emulate. The outstanding examples of this viewpoint in the middle and later Meiji years were afforded by Fukuzawa Yukichi (1835–1901) and Tokutomi Soho (1863–1957).

Fukuzawa's approach was most fully stated in a book he published in 1875, called *Bunmei-ron no Gairyaku* (An Outline of a Theory of Civilization). It identified Japan in Social Darwinist language as one of the semi-civilized countries of the world, together with China and Turkey; recognized that she was therefore inferior to those of the West 'in literature, the arts, commerce, or industry, from the biggest things to the least'; and argued that in order to move forward into the next higher stage of evolution she would need to acquire, not just technology and military strength, but also 'the spirit of civilization'. To this end, 'the first order of business', Fukuzawa claimed, 'lies in sweeping away blind attachment to past customs'.[41] Specifically, he meant by this the absolutist and authoritarian traditions of Confucianism. Because these were Chinese traditions, abandoning them did not in his view constitute a rejection of Japan's indigenous culture, so much as replacing the Chinese element in it by a better Western one. Arbitrary powers, which in accordance with Confucian precept were exercised by ruler over subject, by parent over child, by husband over wife, were, he believed, inconsistent with civilization, properly defined. Thus, while the imperial institution, which was unequivocally Japanese, ought to be preserved, it was necessary to erect below it a political structure that gave the population at large a voice in policy, together with a legal system that guaranteed them basic rights.

Tokutomi, too, envisaged a process of modernization different in kind from that which the Meiji government had chosen. In a book entitled *Shōrai no Nihon* (The Japan of the Future), issued in 1886, he took as his point of departure the ideas stated in Herbert Spencer's *Principles of Sociology*, especially its characterization of two types of society, a 'military' one (warlike, authoritarian, hostile to commerce), and an 'industrial' one (peace-loving, committed to individual liberties, economically laissez-faire). By identifying the first with the realities of Tokugawa and the second with his aspirations for Meiji, Tokutomi was able to evolve a critique of 'wealth and strength' from a progressive rather than a traditionalist viewpoint. As he saw it, what was needed in the world that had taken shape in the nineteenth century was the ability to compete economically. This in turn required a society much more geared to the interests of commerce and industry, and hence of commoners, who engaged in them, than the one which Japan was in the act of creating.

The Westernization of Japanese public life in the 1880s – the Cabinet, the Privy Council, the Army General Staff, the constitution, the civil service, the new codes of law are all examples of it – was not universally welcomed in the country. Men like Fukuzawa and Tokutomi for their part regarded much of it as a distortion of Western principles, contributing to the emergence of a powerful state rather than a civilized society. Traditionalists, of whom Motoda Eifu can be taken as typical, believed, by contrast, that Japan was in danger of losing rectitude in the pursuit of novelty. Somewhere between the two were members of a younger generation, brought up to accept the West as model, but concerned that it was being given too much prominence. One of their spokesmen, Kuga Katsunan, put the argument as follows in the newspaper *Nihon* (Japan) in 1889:

> 'We recognize the excellence of Western civilization. We value the Western theories of rights, liberty and equality; and we respect Western philosophy and morals. . . . Above all, we esteem Western science, economics and industry. These, however, ought not to be adopted simply because they are Western; they ought to be adopted only if they can contribute to Japan's welfare.'[42]

This more sceptical approach to Western civilization, insisting that Japanese traditions and culture had virtues of their own, was to be much more characteristic of the late 1880s and 1890s. Both Fukuzawa and Tokutomi, observing the spread of imperialism in Asia and Africa, were dismayed by the West's failure to practise what it preached, as they conceived it, and drew back to some extent from their earlier ideas. Tokutomi's resentment, indeed, acquired racist overtones. Neither peace nor tolerance marked a world under Western dominance, he wrote. Japan had made herself the 'most progressive, developed, civilized, and powerful nation in the Orient', but still had to endure 'the scorn of the white people'. He concluded that Asia was in danger, and that Japan could and should save it, by destroying 'the world-wide monopoly and . . . the special rights of the white races'.[43] This in turn had implications for the nature of Japanese society. What was needed, Tokutomi argued, was to emphasize Japan's own special qualities, rather than mere aping of the West; to encourage 'barbaric vigor' and 'the spirit of patriotic service'; to seek social equality and harmony through the expression of loyalty to a transcendental emperor.

Thus Tokutomi came in the end to a position not so very different from that of the Meiji government. Others travelled a different road. Okakura Tenshin, for instance, an art historian and critic, took it as his theme that Japan's past was a source of strength, not a cause for shame. In 1904 he wrote that the absorption of other Asian cultures over the centuries had given her own 'a freedom and virility unknown to India and China', in consequence of which 'we are able to comprehend and appreciate more easily than our neighbors those elements of Western civilization which it is desirable that we should acquire'.[44] Japan had always borrowed 'without violating her sense of tradition' and had successfully carried over part of her own traditions into modern life. For this very reason she had been able to save herself from the danger which was symbolized by Manchester and individualism.

The dilemma which Fukuzawa, Tokutomi and Okakura all faced in their different ways was not only that of controlling the political and psychological repercussions of Western-style modernization, but also that of asserting Japan's place in the world. Nakae Chomin (1847–1901), radical politician and translator of Rousseau's *Contrat Social*, dwelt on the relationship between the two problems in a book which he published in 1887. Entitled *Sansuijin Keirin Mondō* (A Discourse by Three Drunkards on Government), it was cast in the form of an inebriated discussion –a device for evading censorship – between three advocates of different points of view. One of them, the Gentleman of Western Learning, argued that Japan did not need weapons for her defence, only civilization and industry. 'If we adopt liberty as our army and navy, equality as our fortress, and fraternity as our sword and cannon, who in the world would dare to attack us?', he asked. Another, the Champion of the East, took the opposite stance, equating civilization with strength. For a backward country, he said, civilization had to be secured by purchase. Japan could only obtain the resources needed to finance it by expansion overseas, preferably in China, a neighbour weak enough to provide 'nourishment for small nations like us to fill our bellies with'. To the third member of the group, the Master, perhaps speaking for the author, it was not necessary to accept either extreme. Japan could preserve her independence with the help of merely defensive forces, he maintained, exploiting the balance of power between Western countries and cultivating China as her principal market.[45]

Nakae did not bring the debate to an agreed conclusion. Nor did the Japanese people. It was to continue in very similar terms throughout the country's modern history, feeding powerful emotions, not only on the subject of imperialist expansion, but also on that of the relationship between tradition and modernity.

7

INDUSTRIALIZATION: THE FIRST PHASE, 1860–1930

Industrialization was by no means the only significant feature of Japanese economic history after the opening of the ports, but it is the one which has attracted most attention. The country's industrial achievement was in scale and complexity unique outside Europe and North America before 1945. It is also central to an understanding of Japan in the twentieth century, since it not only settled the patterns of foreign trade and helped to decide the direction of territorial expansion, but also brought about the same kinds of social change and political unrest within Japan as occurred elsewhere in the world at similar stages of development. For these reasons it has been taken as the main thread of this chapter. Agriculture and commerce will be treated in a subordinate capacity.

There are a number of points of controversy about Japan's economic growth in these years which it will be necessary to touch upon. One is the extent to which Meiji developments were a natural, or even inevitable, sequel to what had already taken place under the Tokugawa, leaving aside entirely the changes caused by the coming of the West. Another is the role of official policy, that is, how far the state, not private enterprise, should be given the credit for the speed and effectiveness with which Japan industrialized. Indeed, the two questions are related to each other, in so far as the economic policies of the Meiji government were themselves in important respects a response to the dangers that were held to be inherent in Western imperialism. For that reason, the topics that are first taken up here are matters of political economy, rather than economics in the stricter sense.

FOUNDATIONS, 1860–1885

At the time of the opening of the ports Japan already possessed some of the attributes required for modern economic growth. In the more advanced regions of the country farmers were accustomed to operating in a money economy. There was a well-developed distribution system for goods, extending to rural as well as urban areas. Quite large numbers of Japanese had a measure of expertise in finance and commerce, though not so many in manufacturing, while a few members of the ruling class had some knowledge of Western science and technology, chiefly in its military and medical applications; a considerable proportion of the population had acquired a basic literacy, which facilitated the circulation of information and ideas; and there is evidence of small, but widely distributed accumulations of capital among commoners, together with indications of a rise in their standard of living in the later Tokugawa years. Japan had not yet entered the phase of modern growth, but was arguably moving in that direction.

In such a situation the unequal treaties had important consequences for Japan's economic future. By bringing her into the milieu of world trade they increased economic opportunity by providing access to foreign markets, technology, and institutional models. By posing a threat of colonial or semi-colonial dependency, they prompted military reform, the high cost of which put fiscal policy at the heart of government concerns. One of the perceived advantages of building a centralized state was that it increased the regime's ability not only to stimulate economic growth, but also to benefit from it by way of revenue.

The late Tokugawa practice of promoting industries which had a military purpose was continued after 1868, but it was not until 1874 that Okubo Toshimichi, who was by then the most influential member of the Meiji leadership, set out proposals for something broader in scope. Drawing on the experience he had gained with the Iwakura mission in America and Europe, and citing in particular the example of Britain, which he took to be comparable in size and resources with Japan, he argued that the country needed an increase in 'productive power' which could only be obtained through manufacturing industry. Given Japan's backwardness, he wrote, this was not likely to be developed as a result of individual initiatives alone. It required in addition 'the patronage and encouragement of the government and its officials.'[46] The task of providing this was in the event entrusted to the industrial section of Okubo's own Home Ministry, supported by the Ministry of Public Works under Ito Hirobumi.

A major part of their work was to improve transport and communications. As early as 1871 the government had instituted a postal service between Tokyo and Osaka, which was expanded to take in over 3,000 offices in its first three years. A domestic telegraph system was soon added. Railway-building was at first entirely under government control, though two-thirds of total mileage was to be privately owned by the end of the century. Tokyo, Osaka, and Kyoto had all been provided with rail links to their nearest deep-water ports (Yokohama or Kobe) by 1877; in 1889 the main trunk route connecting all three cities was completed; and two years later the line from Tokyo to Aomori in the north was opened.

Shipping services, both coastal and overseas, were made subject to government regulation, partly with a view to beating off foreign competition. One beneficiary was the former Tosa samurai, Iwasaki Yataro, founder of a firm which in 1873 became known as Mitsubishi. In 1871 he had taken over a few ships from his domain at its dissolution. He then acquired an existing shipping line which operated between Tokyo and Osaka, expanded his fleet by adding a number of military transports, bought by the government for use in an expedition to Taiwan in 1874, and finally opened routes to Hong Kong (1879) and Vladivostock (1881). In 1885, responding to official pressure, he allowed his shipping interests (though not his other concerns) to be amalgamated with some of its rivals to form the Nippon Yusen Kaisha (NYK), which had at its disposal 58 ships, totalling 65,000 tons. Dividends were guaranteed by the state at 8 per cent for fifteen years. In addition, the new company received subsidies, mail contracts, and other kinds of government help, accepting in return official supervision of its routes and operations.

Ministers were also concerned that Japan should have a financial system capable of funding foreign trade and modern enterprise. In 1872, while land tax reform was under discussion, regulations were issued providing for private banks on the American model, but no great advantage was taken of them because of the requirement that any notes they issued must be redeemable in gold. Once this restriction was removed in 1876, both banks and banknotes began to proliferate. The change coincided with a sharp increase in government expenditure, due to bond issues for samurai pensions (1876) and the cost of suppressing the Satsuma Rebellion (1877), with the result that inflation also grew, reaching a level at which yen paper money was worth no more than 55 per cent of its face value in silver by 1881. This was the main problem addressed by Matsukata Masayoshi when he became Finance Minister that October. During the next five years he set out to cut government spending and introduce additional taxes (on cigarettes and saké, for example), which enabled him to achieve a budget surplus and begin to redeem the large number of inconvertible notes in circulation. He also created central institutions of financial control: the Bank of Japan (1877), to regulate the banking system and the national currency; and a reorganized Yokohama Specie Bank to control foreign exchange. At the same time a post office savings scheme increased the funds at the Finance Ministry's disposal for channelling into approved investment.

By forcing down prices the Matsukata deflation caused bankruptcies and a good deal of rural distress, but it left Japan with a stable financial base for future industrial growth. Up to this point such growth as there had been in non-military industry had depended heavily on government initiative, undertaken in the context of foreign trade. During the 1860s Japan had developed an export trade, concentrating on tea and silk, much like China's (and in competition with it). To these commodities was later added coal, chiefly for use by Western ships calling at Shanghai, Hong Kong and Singapore, though sales were not achieved on any scale until production costs had been reduced by the adoption of Western mining methods and machinery. This apart, a small quantity of seafood continued to be sent to the Chinese market, as in the Tokugawa period. Imports were of two kinds. There were Western manufactured goods for the Japanese consumer, notably cotton textiles; and there were the machines and other equipment (including weapons) required for the modernization programme. The scale of the trade was small: at an annual value of under 55 million yen in 1875–9 it was worth less than a quarter of China's. The value of imports constantly exceeded that of exports.

Because the stipulations of the treaties made it impossible to employ tariffs as a means of regulating foreign trade, the Meiji government had to find other devices for redressing its unfavourable balance of payments. One was a drive to increase exports, involving not only greater production of silk and tea, but also improvements in standardization and quality. Regulations to control silk-reeling, introduced in 1873, were coupled with the setting up of government-financed filatures at Maebashi and Tomioka, which served to introduce Japanese entrepreneurs to Western manufacturing techniques and factory methods. Students were sent to acquire a knowledge of the European silk industry; pamphlets on sericulture were widely circulated; and instructors were sent out at government expense to silk-producing districts. Between 1868 and 1883 production of raw silk increased by 60 per cent, exports by over 100 per cent. More than half of the exports went by the end of that period to the United States, whose domestic silk market was growing rapidly during these same years.

Rather slower in its effects was import substitution. There were some government-sponsored attempts to introduce Western methods into the cotton textile industry, but little was achieved before 1885, so it is more appropriate to consider them in the next section of this chapter. Measures to reduce Japan's dependence on foreign machinery and building materials were even more contingent on official action, because more capital intensive. A machine factory, intended to be a training centre for students from the government training college, was established in 1871. Steam-powered factories for the production of cement (1875), glass (1876), and white bricks (1878) came shortly after. Shipbuilding was also important in this context, since the yards started in the Tokugawa period had not proved to be advanced enough in their technology to obviate the need for costly purchases abroad. The Bakufu yards at Nagasaki and Yokosuka, taken over by the Meiji government, were expanded. A new one was established at Hyogo (Kobe). While Yokosuka continued to be concerned entirely with naval construction, both Nagasaki and Kobe were producing small steamers for commercial use by 1885. All three yards had extensive machine shops.

Government spending on transport and industry totalled 130 million yen between 1868 and 1885, or about two years' ordinary tax revenue (at post-1873 levels) spread over the eighteen years. It is not surprising, therefore, that the cost of the programme was one of the targets of Matsukata's economy drive. In March 1882 he announced a plan to sell government plants to private buyers, explaining it as a withdrawal from businesses in which the state ought not to engage. The state's proper concern, he argued, was with 'education, armament, and the police', not trade and industry, since it would never be able to rival 'in shrewdness, foresight, and enterprise men who are actuated by immediate motives of self-interest'.[47] More practically, the policy was designed to rid the Finance Ministry of some loss-making factories and recoup the capital invested in them (though it was not until prices were reduced in 1884 that most were sold). The more important units went to companies which were to figure in the list of *zaibatsu* in the twentieth century: the Tomioka silk-reeling mill to Mitsui; the Nagasaki shipyard to Mitsubishi; cement and white brick factories to Furukawa; various mines to Asano and Kuhara.

Discussion of this period would not be complete without considering the significance of agriculture in the economy, not least because it provided a large proportion of the resources needed for modernization. Given the dominant place of primary products like tea and silk in Japanese exports, and the fact that government still drew half its revenue from land tax until the 1890s, it is clearly of the first importance that agricultural production expanded rapidly. The index (1921–5 = 100) rose from 28·6 in 1873 to 50·1 in 1890 and 65·3 in 1900. The staple crop was still rice, for which an annual average of about 30 million *koku* was recorded for 1880–4 and 40 million *koku* for 1890–4 (one *koku* equals approximately five bushels). This growth was partly a continuation of Tokugawa trends, but government also played a part in achieving it, just as it did with respect to trade and manufacturing. Some initiatives – encouraging farmers to raise sheep or grow olives, for example – were unsuccessful, but the main thrust of what officialdom did, which was to disseminate a knowledge of the best existing practices more widely throughout Japan, was very effective. Agricultural colleges were established in Sapporo (1875) and Komaba (1877); an experimental farm was set up (1885); and a national agricultural society (1881), sponsored by Tokyo, provided technical advice to local societies formed by landlords and farmers. As a result there was improvement in seed strains and planting techniques, pest control became more efficient, and fertilizer came to be used more generally and in greater variety (Hokkaido fish meal, Manchurian soybean cake, chemical phosphates). All these things contributed to better productivity. So did the extension of irrigation systems, for which funds were made available both publicly and privately.

It is important to recognize that these changes did not amount to an agrarian revolution in the European sense, involving major inputs of capital and the development of large estates. The area of taxed arable under cultivation (excluding Hokkaido) increased by approximately 13 per cent between 1880 and 1900, compared with a 30 per cent rise in yield per hectare. There was no significant consolidation of land holdings, and little change in the size of the farm labour force or in the use of farm machinery. In other words, Japanese agriculture continued to rely on the intensive cultivation of small plots – whether owned or rented – by family labour. A corollary was that population, when it began to move in greater numbers from country to town, did so because it was freed by improvements in farm technology, not driven out by rationalization or land enclosures.

INDUSTRIAL GROWTH AND FOREIGN TRADE, 1885–1930

In considering what happened to the Japanese economy after 1885 it is appropriate to place the emphasis less on government initiatives, more on the part played by private entrepreneurs and private capital. One example is to be found in the way foreign trade was conducted. Partly because of the advantages which foreign merchants enjoyed under the treaties, partly because Japanese merchants lacked experience of overseas markets and had no effective banking machinery at their disposal, exports and imports were handled almost entirely by foreigners in the first twenty-five years after the ports were opened. Japanese were similarly in control of the buying and selling of foreign trade commodities within Japan. Gradually, however, the latter began to realize how large a loss of potential profit this limitation implied, especially with respect to silk. Some therefore set out to establish their own links with markets in Europe and America. Sometimes they did so corporately – the Mitsui trading company, founded in 1876, was an outstanding example – sometimes individually, and by the closing years of the century they were showing a measure of success. It is estimated that as much as 90 per cent of the silk trade was still in foreign hands in 1887, only 60 per cent in 1900.

The domestic textile industry best exemplifies the use of private capital in manufacturing. Spinning, reeling, and weaving required less initial outlay and less technical know-how than heavy engineering; they were operations which could be carried out in small workshops; and they made use of a kind of labour which Japan's farm households could readily provide. Accordingly, they were something which Japan's existing entrepreneurs had the skills and resources to undertake, once they were convinced there was profit in them. From the mid-1880s they were no longer in doubt about this.

A steady rise in foreign demand, especially in the United States, ensured that silk production in Japan continued to expand throughout the period here being considered. By 1929 about 40 per cent of farm households had cocoon raising as their secondary employment. Some of the crop was still used for the domestic market, where traditional methods of reeling and weaving persisted into the twentieth century, but for the export trade, requiring better standardization and quality control, the trend was consistently towards factory organization and the use of powered machines. It was this sector that in the end determined the character of the industry. In 1893 Japan had 3,200 reeling factories employing ten persons or more. They were mostly small – only 124 of them had over a hundred basins – but by 1929 reeling was almost wholly a factory trade, carried out in fewer but larger filatures. The government's share in all this was to create a framework of regulations within which independent trade associations governed price and quality. The larger business firms, as well as banks, provided loans and advances, on which many small-scale producers relied, but they did not as a rule engage directly in manufacture.

The development of the cotton industry was no less rapid, but was geared from the start to rather larger units of production. Despite government moves in the early Meiji period, designed to promote import substitution, it was not until Shibusawa Ei'ichi founded the Osaka Cotton Spinning Company in 1882, using the less expensive varieties of Western technology, but compensating for its relative inefficiency by employing cheap labour on all-night shifts, that businessmen in the Osaka region were persuaded to change from traditional to modern methods and equipment. Prompted by the knowledge that Shibusawa was able to pay an 18 per cent dividend in 1884, many opened new mills, with the result that the number of spindles quadrupled and yarn output increased by a factor of seven between 1886 and 1890. Over-production then brought a temporary curtailment (organized by the Japan Cotton Spinners Association), but it was coupled with a drive to find new markets on the Asian mainland. In 1894 the government abolished export duty on cotton yarn. In 1896, as production rose again, it removed the import duty on raw cotton. Since victory over China in 1895 (see chapter 9) had given Japanese merchants privileged access to the Chinese and Korean markets, these measures contributed to a phase of export-led growth. The number of spindles in use rose from 382,000 in 1893 to 2·4 million in 1913 and to 6·6 million in 1929. There was a corresponding increase in the size of firms, seven of which owned over 50 per cent of the spindles by the latter date. Yarn output averaged 177 million lbs. in 1894–8 and nearly six times as much in 1925–9. What is more, after 1913 cotton was more and more being used to weave piece-goods, both for export and for the domestic market, rather than being sent abroad as yarn.

The importance of textiles in Japan's economic development is indicated by the fact that in 1930 they accounted for over 36 per cent by value added of the country's industrial production, the next largest sector being food and drink (16 per cent). Nevertheless, the most significant change in the direction of growth after 1900 was the shift towards large-scale heavy industry. According to the indices of manufacturing by physical volume (1910–14 = 100), textiles increased from 70 in 1905–9 to 270 in 1925–9, that is, they slightly less than quadrupled in twenty years. Metals and machinery (61 to 255) did just a little better, but chemicals and ceramics (53 to 453) grew twice as fast, while electricity and gas (27 to 653) had a growth rate which was six times that of textiles. The distribution of employment and the size of factories showed similar patterns, reflecting the transition to a more mature stage of industrial development.

Two special factors influenced the growth of heavy industry. One was war. By victories over China in 1894–5 and Russia in 1904–5 Japan became a world power, entering into rivalries which required a much larger military establishment than in the past. Increased spending on armaments and war-related industry had repercussions throughout the economy. Participation – at arm's length – in the world war of 1914–18 had two further effects: it provided an export demand for the products of Japanese heavy industry, despite inefficiencies of production which were reflected in high cost; and it reduced for a time the availability of foreign machinery of almost every kind, so increasing the opportunities enjoyed by Japanese manufacturers at home. Thus war made for faster growth in heavy industry than might otherwise have taken place. It also furnished government with additional reasons to intervene in that sector of the economy (as it no longer did in textiles, for example). At one level, the Finance Ministry, or the Industrial Bank (founded in 1900 under government sponsorship), put up capital where this was not sufficiently available from private sources: for the Yawata Iron and Steel Works, which began production in 1901; for nationalizing privately-owned main line railways in 1906; for overseas investment through concerns like the South Manchuria Railway Company, established in the same year. In addition, there were subsidies for ship-building and shipping, as well as indirect help in the form of official contracts.

Coal mining proved to be the least in need of government support among the heavy industries. Owned by some of Japan's largest companies – Mitsui, in particular, had a major stake – the mines raised their output from less than one million tons before 1885 to 21 million tons in 1914 and 34 million in 1929. In 1894 this left three million tons available for export, but the increase in industrial consumption – little was required for household use – had made Japan by 1929 a net importer. By contrast, home-produced iron and steel were never enough for Japanese needs before 1930. In 1914 output was about a quarter of a million tons each of pig-iron and steel, representing a half and a third of consumption, respectively. In the next fifteen years pig-iron production rose to just over a million tons (about 60 per cent of requirements) and steel to twice that amount (70 per cent). The greater part of the ore came at that time from Korea and China.

Ship-building was one of the more important customers for iron and steel, though by international standards the industry remained of modest size. By 1914 there were six yards capable of building vessels of a thousand tons or more, and the annual tonnage launched averaged about 50,000 tons. Completions fluctuated widely thereafter: over 600,000 tons in 1919; an annual average of 66,000 tons in the mid-1920s; 165,000 tons in 1929. However, this was enough to ensure that Japan's large merchant fleet, amounting to 1·5 million tons in 1914, nearly 4 million in 1929, was mostly Japanese-built.

In other fields of engineering progress was more patchy. The manufacture of steam locomotives and electrical equipment began just before the war with China in 1894–5 and made rapid headway thereafter, providing Japan with rolling-stock for 13,000 miles of railways in 1930, plus the plant needed to give more than four million kilowatts of electric generating capacity. She was also able to produce bicycles and certain types of textile machinery. In fact, machinery and vehicles accounted for 11·6 per cent of industrial output by value added in 1930. Even so, the country remained heavily dependent on imports for machine tools, automobiles and internal combustion engines.

Inevitably, changes of this magnitude had a major effect on the nature of foreign trade. Put simply, Japanese imports in 1894–8 included more manufactured goods (34 per cent) than they did raw materials (22·5 per cent), whereas in 1921–5 raw materials accounted for 49 per cent and manufactured goods for less than 18 per cent. The pattern of exports shifted in the opposite direction: raw materials were 10·7 per cent in 1894–8, only 6 per cent in 1921–5; manufactured goods rose from 26·5 per cent to 38·6 per cent; and semi-manufactured goods (which included silk) stayed more or less constant at close to 45 per cent. Over the same period trade expanded enormously in value. Exports more than trebled between 1890–4 and 1900–4, doubled again in the next ten years, then trebled again by 1920–4, rising from an annual average of 85 million yen at the beginning to 1,800 million at the end. Imports, which were always greater in value than exports, except in the war years 1915–19, increased from just under 86 million yen a year in 1890–4 to over 2,400 million in 1920–4.

Turning to the commodity composition of exports, tea, which had been as high as 26 per cent of the total in 1880, was down to 3 per cent in 1910 and continued to decline in following years. Silk thread remained the largest single item, varying little in its share: 30 per cent in 1880, 28 per cent in 1930. Cotton thread and cotton textiles were negligible export items in 1880. By 1910 thread amounted to 10 per cent of the whole, other cotton goods to 4 per cent. In the next twenty years, however, China's spinning industry, which brought together foreign capital and expertise, including that of Japanese investors, with cheap Chinese labour, became a major competitor, with the result that thread dropped to a mere 1 per cent of Japanese exports, while cotton cloth, mostly the coarser grades, rose to 18 per cent.

Among imports, raw cotton was of primary importance, rising from less than 1 per cent of the total in 1880 to 34 per cent in 1910. This proved to be a peak – the proportion was down to 23 per cent in 1930 – but the fall reflected the substitution of cheap thread from China for imported raw cotton, rather than a reduction in Japanese demand. From about the time of the Russo–Japanese War of 1904–5, when heavy industry was beginning to develop more rapidly, there was also a growth in the import of metals and chemicals: 100 million yen in 1904, eight times that figure in 1919. At first iron ore comprised a good deal of this, but as industrial output rose, pig-iron, scrap metal, and oil were added to the list. In 1930 metals and minerals accounted for 19 per cent of Japanese imports, compared with 30 per cent for cotton, wool, and rayon. Foodstuffs were also a significant item, since agricultural production failed to keep up with population growth after 1900, but a large proportion came from Japanese colonies – Korea's rice, Taiwan's rice and sugar – so did not appear statistically as part of 'foreign' trade.

The geographical spread of Japanese trade, or sections of it, has several times been referred to above, but a summary of it might be a useful way of concluding this discussion. Exports of silk went chiefly to the United States, comprising the principal element in a trade which took some 30 per cent of Japanese exports in the first quarter of the twentieth century. China's share of the exports – mostly cotton textiles at first, but diversifying into other consumer goods later – built up to a little over 20 per cent by 1914, and stayed at broadly that level, or a little higher. Japanese imports were more varied in both type and origin. The United States supplied 15 per cent or so before 1914, rising to about 25 per cent later, when oil, iron, and steel in considerable quantities were added to the machinery and cotton which had been typical of the Meiji period. By contrast, Britain, which had been the main supplier of both machinery and manufactures in the nineteenth century, saw its share fall sharply in the twentieth, dropping to less than 10 per cent in the 1920s. British India, as a source of cotton, and later of pig-iron, compensated for this to some extent, providing about 10 per cent of Japanese imports in 1890–4, 20 per cent in 1910–14, and rather more than 12 per cent in the following decade. China's contribution was usually between 12 and 15 per cent, except for the war years 1915–19, when it reached 18 per cent. This included cotton, and later cotton yarn; soybeans and bean products from Manchuria; and after 1905 raw materials for heavy industry, notably coal, iron ore, and pig-iron from Manchuria and northern China. China's ability to supply such materials was to be of increasing importance to Sino-Japanese relations as the century advanced. Indeed, of all the world's industrial nations Japan alone depended to this degree on imports to support its heavy industry, a fact which was to play a key part in foreign policy decisions during the 1930s.

THE ECONOMY IN THE 1920s

Japanese industrialization did not lead to quite the same kind of economic and social structures as had characterized modernization in the West, partly because of inherited differences, partly because Japan retained enough financial independence to resist the pressures making for conformity. Farming and commerce in the Tokugawa period had led to an accumulation of capital in private hands which proved sufficient to fund the first stages of growth, once government had provided an infrastructure and established the machinery by which to channel investment in appropriate directions. As a result, Japan did not require heavy capital inputs from abroad and had no considerable foreign debt before the Russo–Japanese War. The West provided technology, plus a knowledge of methods of business organization, introduced into Japan by foreign experts and advisers, but it had no great part in ownership or management. That increased the scope for modification of the Western model.

Yet this is not to say that Japanese industrialization was *sui generis*. If the preliminary stage of government-financed, defence-related industry is left aside, development followed the 'natural' sequence, by which light industry emerged first, heavy industry later. It was not until the 1920s that the process was reasonably complete. What is more, there had been a number of fluctuations and changes of pace before that state of maturity was reached, as there had been in the West some generations earlier. The 1880s and 1890s were phases of growth, explained in part by the Matsukata deflation. This was followed by a setback in the early years of the twentieth century, due to the strains imposed by higher military spending and the effect on export prices of adopting the gold standard in 1897; but progress was resumed after 1905 and continued, apart from a minor check in 1910–11, until 1918. At that point the end of the First World War brought a world-wide slump, in which Japan shared, since much of her industry lost its easy wartime markets overseas. Then a catastrophic earthquake struck the Kanto region in September 1923, destroying much of Tokyo and Yokohama. This impeded recovery by making necessary diversions of capital to reconstruction. In addition, Japan had now to face renewed trade competition from the West, while rising imports of colonial foodstuffs served to hold farm prices down, with the result that the 1920s, though recognized to be a decade in which commerce and industry had a more important place in Japanese life than they had ever had before, were not years in which the economy as a whole advanced to any remarkable degree. They do, however, afford a suitable occasion for considering the nature of Japan's industrial society, as it then existed.

National income at 1928–32 prices increased from 2,300 million yen in 1890 to 12,700 million in 1930. Of this, primary industry accounted for three-fifths at the beginning of the period and about one-fifth at the end of it, though it had grown by over 70 per cent in value. Secondary industry (mostly manufacturing) nearly trebled as a proportion (10 per cent to 28 per cent), tertiary industry (including commerce) rather less than doubled (28 per cent to 52 per cent). Within the manufacturing sector, heavy industry (chemicals, steel, non-ferrous metals, machinery) had a share of about one-sixth at the beginning of the century, rising to almost twice that during and after the 1914–18 war, while textiles stayed close to 30 per cent throughout. Food products, mostly traditional items like saké, soy sauce, and *miso* paste, took up much of the rest of manufacturing, that is, 35 per cent in 1900, 25 per cent in the 1920s.

These figures depict a state of affairs at or just before 1930 that would have been broadly appropriate to a country in Western Europe at that time. However, some of the structures underlying them are less familiar in Western terms. There was still an important segment of industry, for example, which was manufacturing consumer goods for a traditional lifestyle, not a modern one, even though it did so in factories, using powered machines. Moreover, industry's response to the low growth rates of the 1920s – cartels, rationalization, the adoption of improved technology – had the effect of emphasizing certain other features of the economy that were distinctive.

One was industrial dualism. Japan had at one extreme a very large number of small and medium concerns, competing fiercely with each other without much in the way of capital or technological resources. In contrast with them were a few much bigger firms, using advanced technology and substantial capital, which were able to achieve high levels of productivity, chiefly in such industries as iron and steel, engineering, mining, cement, and sugar-refining. They had commonly grown by a process of amalgamation over the years, and were, by virtue of their size, in a position to maintain prices and market share by a variety of restrictive practices. They also controlled a large proportion of Japanese industry. Companies capitalized at five million yen or more constituted 0·3 per cent by number and 36 per cent by capital of the national total in 1909, but 1·6 per cent by number and 65 per cent by capital twenty years later. Banking was equally concentrated. The Big Five (Mitsui, Mitsubishi, Yasuda, Sumitomo, and Dai Ichi), together capitalized at fifty million yen in 1914 and 280 million in 1927, controlled 19 per cent of private banking capital by the end of the period.

The outstanding examples of large-scale business were the great combines known as *zaibatsu*, each headed by a family holding company. Mitsui had been in existence since the seventeenth century, engaged in domestic retailing and finance. It was reorganized during the Meiji period by a group of able ex-samurai, who added a general overseas trading company and a bank in 1876, before branching out into coalmining, textiles, paper manufacture, sugar refining, and shipping. By the 1920s its ramifications extended to 120 separate concerns, either directly owned and managed, or controlled through stockholding and the appointment of directors. Next largest was Mitsubishi, which began in the Meiji period with Iwasaki Yataro's shipping interests, then added foreign trade, mining, shipbuilding, and a variety of other investments in heavy industry, which were eventually to include aircraft and automobiles. There was also a bank, founded in 1880. Sumitomo, which unlike the others was based in Osaka, not Tokyo, developed from a pre-modern firm engaged in copper-mining. Metals remained at the centre of its activities, though they gradually spread much wider, like those of other *zaibatsu*. Yasuda was the creation of yet another ex-samurai founder in early Meiji, who acquired his holdings in the modern sector of industry through an initial stake in trade and banking. In fact, banking was a crucial factor in the growth of all four of these concerns. It not only gave them access to scarce capital in their formative years, but also enabled them to exercise influence, if not control, over a spread of companies stretching well beyond their own groups. It has been estimated that by 1930 the Mitsui, Mitsubishi, Sumitomo, and Yasuda banks held 27 per cent of the bonds issued by non-*zaibatsu* firms.

The fact that enterprises of this kind – there were four or five others that one could add to those named above – were engaged in everything from domestic commerce to foreign trade, from textiles to heavy industry, from finance to armaments, gave them a resistance to economic downturns and hence an advantage over their competitors which put them in a class of their own in Japanese business. They always had close links with government, though by the 1920s it is doubtful whether one could properly call them its clients. Their tentacles spread more widely through the economy than even a description of their directly-managed operations would suggest, whether by way of loans to individual silk-producers, or through ties with sub-contractors, serving their manufacturing branches. Yet there were other, equally modern companies, which did not fall within this pattern. Construction firms, department stores, some producers of consumer goods, one or two innovators in the engineering field (Toyota, for example), often remained independent and of substantial size. Some were not even joint-stock companies. However, more characteristic of non-*zaibatsu* undertakings were the manufacturers of consumer goods like soap and hosiery, or non-export pottery and fabrics, working in small factories scattered throughout Japan. By 1930 there were over a million of them, often employing less than five workers, but in total accounting for more than half of that part of the labour force described as being engaged in manufacturing.

The differences between large and small concerns with respect to capital, technology, and organization were paralleled by differences in matters of management and labour. The smallest relied heavily on family members in both capacities. By contrast, the *zaibatsu* and other major employers began from about 1900 to look to the universities for management recruits, as did the bureaucracy. Both Mitsui and Mitsubishi took graduates from Fukuzawa's Keio Gijuku, later from Tokyo University as well. To provide a more specifically business training, Tokyo Higher Commercial School (now Hitotsubashi University) was founded in 1887. By the early twentieth century senior executives in the larger companies came frequently from these three institutions. In fact, a survey of top managers in 1924 identified just over half as having such a background. These above all were the men who introduced a professional approach into Japanese management: who had studied economics; who read books about American business methods; who made decisions about the introduction of new technology with a scrupulous care for returns on investment.

Employment in modern types of undertaking was still in this period for a minority of Japanese. In 1920, out of a total work force of 27 million over half were engaged in agriculture and forestry, only 16 per cent in manufacturing. A mere 6 per cent were recorded as being factory operatives. Improvements in farm productivity had released a good deal of labour to the towns, but much of it, despite the virtues of the education system, was unskilled or semi-skilled, aiming at best at jobs in commerce or the service industries. Managers of factories using advanced technology therefore faced two problems in this situation. They had to find workers who were skilled (preferably men, if they were in heavy industry), and also ways of keeping them, rather than see them drift away to other employment, or be poached by competitors. From this there developed, especially as industrial labour became more unionized (see chapter 8), the practice of offering not only higher wages in such conditions, but also other inducements, too: better job security; bonuses; seniority pay structures; and welfare benefits. Thus it was in these years that there began to take shape, though not yet in its complete form, the package of labour relations which has come to be regarded as typically Japanese. It applied to the major high-technology industries, spreading outwards, it would seem, from shipbuilding and the engineering trades, though even in those fields it benefited only part of the labour force. Unskilled and semi-skilled workers, who had no scarcity value, lacked the bargaining power to insist on comparable advantages, no matter who employed them. In other words, what was emerging was an élite among workers, similar to the one which the *zaibatsu* and a few other concerns comprised in the business world at large. This was a price the majority had to pay for rapid economic growth.

Farmers would have claimed that they were expected to pay an even greater one. Agricultural production had continued to increase after 1900, but more slowly, as Japanese farming approached the limits of what could be done without radical change in landholding and methods of cultivation. The index of agricultural production (1925–9 = 100) moved from 67 in 1900 to 110 in 1930, the rice crop from approximately 45 million *koku* to 60 million *koku* in the same period. Since the number of farm workers actually declined in these years (from 15·8 million to 13·7 million), there was a considerable rise in productivity per worker, due in part to the application of more scientific techniques to poor quality land. Despite this, agriculture was steadily losing its pride of place in the national economy. As population grew, farmers were becoming a smaller part of it. They produced much less of the national product than before, because commerce and manufacturing were expanding faster, even though some of them diversified into higher-value crops. Nor could they any longer feed the Japanese people without outside help. Japan became a net importer of rice soon after 1895, and by the end of the 1920s was importing as much as ten million *koku* a year, in addition to other foodstuffs.

Agriculture, indeed, was becoming recognized as a 'problem' in its own right. Since farm incomes failed to keep up with the increase in real wages that was achieved elsewhere in industry, cultivators were relatively disadvantaged. Nor was this all. Farm prices actually declined. They had risen substantially before 1918, protected to some extent from foreign competition by a duty on imported rice, imposed in 1905. At the end of the war boom, rice cost the Japanese consumer four times as much as it had at the beginning of the century. Then came recession, riots against high prices in the cities, the abolition of the duty on the import of rice from Korea and Taiwan. Rice prices halved in 1920–1. The crisis was short-lived, it is true, but recovery from it was never complete: despite direct government intervention and support, farm incomes had dropped by 50 per cent or more by the end of the decade, compared with a decline of about one quarter in costs. As a result, many farmers were in difficulties some time before the next world slump in international trade in 1929 and 1930, which compounded their problems by causing a sharp fall in the returns they could get from silk. Their resentments, like those of other underprivileged groups, had by then become a factor in national politics.

8

CAPITALISM AND DOMESTIC POLITICS, 1890–1930

Japan's leaders in the Meiji period set out to change the nature of their country's politics and economy, chiefly for the purpose of giving it the strength to resist the West. They succeeded in that object, as we shall see (chapter 9). Like other radical reformers, however, they also achieved results that were not part of their intentions. In founding a bureaucracy and shaping a governing élite they offended many who were left outside the newly-drawn boundaries of power and influence. In creating wealth they also redistributed it, giving political aspirations to some, leaving others in a state of disadvantage and discontent. The tensions which these things provoked were at the heart of early twentieth-century politics.

ECONOMIC DEVELOPMENT AND SOCIAL CHANGE

Japan's total population was approximately 35 million in 1873. Thirty years later it was 46 million, in 1925 it had risen to almost 60 million. At both the beginning and end of the period the numbers engaged in agriculture and forestry amounted to a little over fourteen million (though around 1900 they were higher). Thus the extra millions added in these years depended for their livelihood on commerce and industry. They also lived for the most part in cities and towns. The Meiji period had begun with something over ninety towns of 10,000 inhabitants or more, plus five cities of at least 100,000. By 1920 a little over 30 per cent of the population lived in communities of that size – that is, eighteen million people – while the six largest cities each held half a million. Indeed, Tokyo had 2·2 million in its central districts, another 1·2 million in its suburbs. Osaka, which had renewed itself in the middle of the Meiji period as a modern economic centre, doubling its population in the decade after 1887, had two million residents in the 1920s, second only to Tokyo. Most other important cities, like Nagoya, were former castle-towns, transformed by commercial and industrial development. Kyoto was an exception. So were a few others, whose functions had more recent origins: Yokohama (foreign trade), Yawata (steel), Sapporo (economic growth in Hokkaido).

Life within these cities was very different from that of Tokugawa times. Their very size meant that in many cases people could no longer live where they worked. The improvement in transport facilities made possible a life in fairly pleasant residential suburbs for those who could afford it, but the poorest found themselves condemned to industrial slums, unless they stayed in the narrow, dark shop-dwellings of the old commercial districts. City centres acquired paved roads, street lighting, and Western-style buildings for banks, office blocks and department stores. By contrast, homes remained small, single-storey, and mostly traditional, though some refinements, such as the use of straw-mat floors (*tatami*) and rice-paper partitions (*shōji*), which had once been the perquisites of samurai, spread gradually downward through society. Only after the end of Meiji did the well-to-do, as distinct from the rich, begin to add a Western-style room to their houses for entertaining.

The smaller towns and villages changed to nothing like the same extent. Modern transport meant a better supply of goods, including items for the home, like kerosene lamps, and a wider selection of foodstuffs. It also made it easier for Japanese in most parts of the country to indulge an apparently insatiable taste for travel. On the other hand, physical appearances, whether of houses or people, changed very slowly; the modernization of agriculture made more difference to output than it did to the rhythm of rural life; and social attitudes in the countryside remained much less 'enlightened' than those in the city.

Conservatives could still with some reason look to the village as an embodiment of the virtues of the past.

It is not easy to decide what all this meant in terms of standards of living. Between 1890 and 1925 there was a 10 per cent increase in the consumption of rice per head of population, plus greater use of items such as fish, sugar, and fruit. Perhaps 20 per cent more textiles were sold on the domestic market, mostly for clothing. Average per capita income increased by nearer 30 per cent, real wages by about the same in the period before 1914, rather faster in the next decade. All this suggests a gradual improvement in nutrition and comfort. Against that, it is clear that there were wide disparities between different occupational and social groups. One estimate puts the national average for per capita income at 170 yen a year in 1893–7, rising to 220 yen in 1918–22. The figures for industrial workers were above this average, rising from 316 yen to 444 yen in the same period – and there is not much doubt that those for skilled men in heavy industry were higher still – whereas incomes in agriculture and forestry rose only from 83 yen to 163 yen.

For farmers, improved yields and bigger profits, coupled with better job opportunities outside agriculture, certainly brought an increase in real disposable income. Even the greater incidence of tenancy in these years may be explained in part as a result of existing cultivators taking on more land, because it would yield a profit. Yet Meiji agricultural improvement had not extended to every region in the country: the northeast, in particular, remained backward and poor. Nor was growth constant over time. For example, competition from imported rice after 1920 made life exceptionally difficult for farmers, a condition all the harder to bear because it followed wartime years of some prosperity; and while producers in the more fertile and accessible areas could respond to hard times by diversifying crops or devoting more of their efforts to non-farm jobs, those elsewhere had no such option. In some parts of the country there were extremes of poverty, coupled with unremitting labour. It is significant that young men and women who went from villages into the army or textile factories not infrequently compared their new lot favourably with their old. The corollary is that those who stayed at home might well develop a sense of grievance. A foreign visitor to Japan just before 1920 was told in one village:

> 'In the old days the farmer did not complain; he thought his lot could not be changed. He was forbidden to adopt a new calling and he was restricted by law to a frugal way of living. Now farmers can be soldiers, merchants or officials and can live as they please. They begin to compare their standard of living with that of other callings.'[48]

Modernization was also making villagers less of a united community than idealists liked to think they were, or ought to be. The resident, reforming landlord of the Meiji era was still to be found, it is true, but in many cases his descendants were becoming absentees, living in cities, investing in business, taking part in politics. Even those who stayed on the land found themselves with a less important social function, since farming techniques were now learnt at schools, while the mediation of community disputes had become a task for local bureaucrats and voluntary associations. Another change was that tenants had become a more significant element in the village population. The area of land under tenancy reached a national average of 45 per cent of the whole at the end of the Meiji period and remained at that level until the Pacific War. Since tenant-farmers were the rural poor – a government survey in 1926–7 concluded that they had to spend 57 per cent of family income on food, compared with the owner-farmer's 49 per cent – this implies an important differentiation of living standards between one set of households and the rest.

After 1900 tenant associations became numerous and influential. Though often asserted to be for the study and improvement of farming methods, they soon came to represent collective tenant interests against landlords, notably with respect to rent and security of tenure. This prompted a rising level of tenancy disputes from 1917 onwards, sometimes involving violence and police intervention. The phenomenon has been variously interpreted. One school of thought argues that closer integration of agriculture into the commercial economy had increased the pressure on the less successful farmers to the point where resentment was expressed openly against landlord exploitation. Another, more recent one, holds that tenants were reflecting not so much an increase in hardship as an awareness of economic opportunity, that is, were seeking better terms of contract as a means of maximizing income. The fact that disputes occurred most often in areas where agriculture was technically most advanced – in the hinterland of Osaka and in silk-producing districts – is cited as evidence of this (though it must be said that these were also the regions where commerical crops were commonest and the pressures of the market most keenly felt).

Towns and cities, especially industrial ones, were as turbulent and problem-prone as the villages, though in different ways. In 1920 Japan had a work-force of approximately 27 million, of whom a little over one-sixth were engaged in manufacturing. About 1·6 million worked in factories (740,000 men; 870,000 women), another 400,000 in mining. Wages, though higher than the incomes to be derived from farming, were as far as possible held down by employers on the grounds that only in this way could Japan compete with the technologically-advanced and capital-intensive industries of the West. Even so, they increased more rapidly than the cost of living. Male factory workers in 1900 received an average 40 sen a day, the figure rising to just over 190 sen by 1920 (100 sen = 1 yen). Women received about half as much. This was ostensibly because they had no families to support, most of them being young, unmarried, and recruited from the countryside to work for textile companies under terms of engagement which made them little better than indentured labour. For both men and women conditions at work were harsh, often because of the extensive powers which employers entrusted to supervisors and foremen. Mining had an especially bad record for brutality and low safety standards, contributing to 600 deaths a year in the 1920s. Since its work-force was recruited in large part from the prisons in the Meiji years, then from underprivileged groups like outcastes and Koreans in the later ones, all of whom were treated as forced labourers, it is not surprising that protests, when they occurred, were violent. In February 1907, for example, workers at Furukawa's Ashio copper mine, having been refused an improvement in wages and conditions, staged a riot which was only put down when officials sent in the militia. A few months later there was a similar outbreak at Sumitomo's Besshi mine, once again requiring action by the army. Over a hundred miners were convicted on criminal charges after these two incidents.

Hours of work were long throughout industry, even women

and children working a norm of twelve-hour shifts in textile factories before 1900. Initiatives by bureaucrats to limit factory hours met with determined opposition from employers, but a wave of industrial unrest in 1907 gave stimulus to reform and led eventually to a Factory Act in 1911 (though it was not enforced until 1916). It introduced an eleven-hour working day for women and for children under fifteen years of age, the maximum being further reduced to ten hours in 1923. Night work for women and children was not prohibited until 1929.

Male workers lacked even this much protection, but from the late 1890s, beginning with skilled groups like printers and iron-workers, they began to organize themselves in unions. In 1897 Takano Fusataro and Katayama Sen founded the Society for the Formation of Labour Unions (Rodo Kumiai Kiseikai), which they modelled on the American Federation of Labor. The activities of its members, however, were little more than the provision of sickness and unemployment insurance, since the police – backed by the Public Order Law of 1900 – treated collective bargaining and strikes as illegal. As a result, the unions declined for the most part into intellectual study groups, though in 1912 Suzuki Bunji established the Yuaikai, a friendly society, avowedly to promote industrial harmony. The war years made it much more than this. High prices and an expanded work-force in heavy industry, followed by a postwar slump, created a state of affairs in which wage bargaining and labour solidarity won increasing numbers of adherents. The Yuaikai itself became involved in seventy disputes during 1917, while other more militant organizations also began to emerge. In 1919 Japan had 187 unions, which engaged in a total of nearly 500 disputes. Riots against high food prices in the cities were accompanied by major strikes among teachers, printers, postmen, and shipyard workers; the Yuaikai remodelled itself into the Federation of Labour (Sodomei), claiming 250,000 members by 1925; while attempted government repression, plus active strike-breaking by employers, turned the whole movement more and more to the left.

By this time unions faced a 'modern' cohort of entrepreneurs and managers. The men who had carried out the Meiji government's plans to establish Western-style enterprise in Japan had been drawn from varied backgrounds, including ex-samurai, old-style urban merchants, and 'rich peasants' (*gōnō*). Their origins gave them a commitment to the Confucian ethic as a guide to personal behaviour. Moreover, the experience of having lived through the turbulent years after the opening of the ports made them easily convinced that what they were doing was a patriotic duty. These were the twin pillars of their ideology. The next generation, however, drawn mostly from technical schools and universities, did not altogether share these attitudes. They were more the bureaucrats of big business, loyal as much to the firm as to the nation, measuring their achievements in terms of profit or market share; and they pursued their aspirations more through collective bodies, such as trade associations and chambers of commerce, than as individual tycoons. Many of these organizations were exceedingly influential. The Industrial Club, founded in 1917 to represent nearly two hundred *zaibatsu* and other large concerns, had a thousand members by 1928, while many comparable bodies for the smaller fry, some dating back to before 1890, were brought together under the aegis of the Japan Chamber of Commerce (Nissho) in 1922. They gave businessmen a voice in matters of national economic policy. They also constituted a political pressure group – hostile to socialism and the trade unions, opposed to large budgets, committed to private property and the rule of law – which governments ignored at their peril. In this respect, too, Japan acquired the familiar characteristics of an industrial society.

CONSERVATISM, LIBERALISM, SOCIALISM

The men who held power in late Meiji Japan as cabinet ministers and senior bureaucrats believed in tradition as an antidote to revolution. They had already made use of it in certain contexts by 1890: by incorporating parts of the Confucian ethic into the Education Rescript and into the teaching in schools; and by adopting the Shinto doctrine of imperial divine descent as a theme in the constitution. After 1905 they shifted their emphasis more specifically towards the preservation of social unity. It was to be secured, they maintained, through equality of all Japanese before the emperor and through the values of family and community, rather than through participation in the election of a representative government, as was customary in the West.

Ideas about the emperor were central to this kind of thinking.

His prestige was much enhanced by the credit he received as commander-in-chief for the victories over China and Russia. His presence was made more widely felt by the introduction of national holidays linked to the imperial house, such as Kigensetsu (11 February), celebrating the enthronement of the mythical first emperor, Jimmu. A great deal was written in school textbooks and the public press about his importance as a focus of family life and ancestor worship. In 1908 a rescript also associated him with the virtues of thrift, frugality, and hard work, which were the best guarantee of Japan's prosperity.

This appeal to an imperial ideology was reinforced by developments in policy and institutions. Among these was the so-called Local Improvement Movement, dating from the years after the Russo–Japanese War, which took as its point of departure a belief that Japan's farms and villages were not only the locus of traditional values, but also the segment of Japanese society which was most at risk from economic change. Their corruption by 'modern' thought and behaviour would entail, according to the *Tokyo Asahi* in 1914, 'first, the loss of the patriotic spirit, which forms the axis of our national character; second, the penetration of extreme individualism, which is the enemy of nationalism; third, the outbreak of socialism, which execrates those in power'.[49] Influenced by such arguments, political leaders moved in various ways to avert these dangers. One was to provide owner-cultivators with assistance in resisting the ill effects of commercialization: for example, by sponsoring rural co-operatives and savings associations; by supporting societies which were dedicated to promoting the virtues identified in the 1908 rescript; and by encouraging village residents and officials to work closely together in local economic planning. There were also efforts to attach loyalties in the countryside more directly to the central bureaucratic machine, especially by transferring sentiment from traditional hamlets (*buraku*) to the villages (*mura*) of the Meiji system, where officialdom had greater control. Not surprisingly, this provoked occasional resentment, the thrust of which ran counter to the government's objectives.

Other steps taken in these years had greater success in mobilizing mass support for Tokyo. One was the creation of a countrywide network of youth associations (Seinendan), which had originally been formed on local initiative, but were drawn into a national body under Home Ministry supervision in 1910. To the central authorities its purpose was to prolong into the early adult years the indoctrination provided by the ethics course in schools. Similar in this respect, though adding an ingredient of 'soldierly behaviour', was the Military Reserve Association (Zaigo Gunjinkai), established in 1910 by two politically-minded army officers, Terauchi Masatake and Tanaka Giichi (each was later to be Prime Minister). One of their aims was to provide Japan with the disciplined citizenry that modern warfare needed, while giving the army a firm base of popular approval for its role in national affairs. Another was to counter the 'immoral' influence of capitalism. To these ends the Gunjinkai advocated 'solidarity and co-operation' within a family-state organized in accordance with Confucian principles. Its members – there were three million of them by the 1930s – were expected to live by these ideals within their own communities, as well as to demonstrate the army's concern for the welfare of the people by undertaking voluntary social work.

Conservatism of this kind was an attempt to create defences against the less pleasing changes which economic development had caused, or was expected to cause, in Japanese society. By contrast, liberalism welcomed the changes and tried to push them further. One of its origins lay in the concept of *risshin-shusse*, 'making one's way in the world', which was derived, somewhat inaccurately, from Herbert Spencer and Samuel Smiles. Like the authors of the Education Code of 1872, liberals emphasized the importance of education as a stimulus to effort and a means to improve one's station in life. They also gave individualism a value much greater than it had had in any traditional system of ideas. Since Buddhism treated human ambitions as something to be negated, while Confucianism subordinated the individual to society and the state, liberalism thus laid itself open to the charge of being not only alien, but also subversive of Japan's own ethico-religious beliefs.

In a different context, liberals espoused the cause of groups which had gained or lost by the growth of commerce or industry: those who had acquired wealth, or at least a measure of prosperity, but were still shut out from political power; and those at the opposite extreme, whose poverty remained a problem to be solved. Japan, they argued, having achieved stability at home and reputation overseas, no longer needed to be preoccupied with 'strength', as she had been before 1894. Instead, she should turn to 'wealth', in order to build a better society: one that was less paternalistic, that could provide the common people with a higher standard of living, and would afford fuller scope for the extension of human rights.

Specific manifestations of this approach were to be found in the programmes of the 'bourgeois' parties, which will be discussed in the next section of this chapter. They focused on demands for universal suffrage, a more limited constitutional role for hereditary peers, election (rather than appointment) of prefectural governors, and restraints on the power of the police to suppress dissent. Socially and economically, as demonstrated, for example, in the writings of Ishibashi Tanzan, who became editor of the Oriental Economist (*Tōyō Keizai Shimpō*) in 1924, they ranged much wider: legalization of trade unions; effective factory laws; social insurance for workers; rent reform for tenants; industrialization in backward areas (to diversify employment); and every means available to free private enterprise from the dead hand of the government bureaucracy. To their long catalogue of contemporary ills, Ishibashi and his colleagues also added the contentious subject of the position of women in Japan, criticizing the wife-and-mother doctrine, so beloved of conservatives. Women, too, they maintained, should have the opportunity to make their way in the world.

Liberals of Ishibashi's kind, contributing to the many middlebrow journals that were founded in the early twentieth century, were gradualists, who did not wholly reject the Japan they had inherited, so much as wish to see it improved. Socialists, as one would expect, did not agree with them. Like the more radical members of the people's rights movement in the 1880s, they wanted something closer to a revolution, that is, the removal of authority from the existing establishment and its transfer to those who would use it directly on behalf of the poor and underprivileged. The point is well illustrated in the writings and career of Kotoku Shusui. There was a distinctly ethical tone in the judgements he made about his country just after the Sino-Japanese War: a government 'trampling down our constitutional system through the use of money'; politicians 'seeking influence and personal gain'. On the other hand, his conclusions were straightforwardly political: 'to prevent today's degeneration and corruption one must . . . fundamentally reform the organization of society'.[50] From this he found it a short step to a belief that change required extra-parliamentary action, in which he ought to take part. In 1907 he gave his support to rioting workers at the Ashio copper mines. When they were forcibly suppressed, he became involved in plans to assassinate the Meiji emperor, only to be arrested when the plot was discovered in 1910, and executed, along with ten others, in January of the following year.

Another strand in socialism was a moderate, Christian one, exemplified by the activities of Suzuki Bunji, a lawyer, Kagawa Tomohiko, an evangelist, and Abe Isoo, a professor at Waseda University, who took part in establishing the Socialist Study Association of 1898 and the Social Democratic Party of 1901. The party was promptly proscribed by government, because it listed among its goals the abolition of the class system, disarmament, and public ownership of land and capital, as was the quite separate Japan Socialist Party of 1906, which survived just over a year. In fact, it was not until the Russian Revolution and the defeat of Germany in 1917–18 had produced in Japan an atmosphere of intellectual turmoil and industrial unrest that socialism made any headway there. A Socialist League, reflecting the influence of European ideas, was founded in December 1920 for the purpose of bringing into existence a broad popular movement which would encompass all shades of left-wing thought, looking for support to industrial labour organizations and tenant unions, in the knowledge that they had at their disposal an array of manpower and resources far greater than the prewar radicals had been able to call upon.

Despite the existence of this body the left wing in Japan remained fragmented. There was a sharp division between those who favoured parliamentary methods and those who did not, such as had already been evidenced between Kotoku and the Christian socialists. It was exacerbated by the emergence of the Japan Communist Party in 1921, committed to a policy, dictated by the Comintern, which was based on the assumption that there would have to be a two-stage revolution in Japan, starting with a bourgeois-democratic one. Not all its members accepted the need for a popular front, which this implied. Nor, indeed, did the police have reason to believe in the legality of the communists' intentions, since they openly rejected the 'emperor system'. Police persecution, in turn, enhanced the party's extremist image, attracting some, but deterring others among those Japanese who might have joined it. The economist, Kawakami Hajime, for example, who was drawn to socialism because he believed it to be altruistic, and to Marxism as a path to economic modernization, shorn of poverty and selfishness, took more than twelve years after becoming a Marxist in 1919 to overcome his doubts about joining the Communist Party.

The presence of men like Abe and Kawakami in the socialist movement emphasizes another of its characteristics, which was an undue dependence on intellectuals. There was, to be sure, a substratum of organized labour, but very few socialist leaders emerged from the working class. Most were the disillusioned sons of landlords or ex-samurai. Nearly all were a great deal better at writing than doing, a circumstance that helped to make their socialism ineffectual when it came to the cut-and-thrust of politics. Kawai Eijiro, when on trial under the 'dangerous thoughts' legislation in 1939, exemplified a not uncommon attitude: 'Although I talk about socialism', he said, '. . . I do not address myself to the lowly plebs. I have never discussed socialism at a meeting of workers.'[51] Making all due allowance for the conditions under which this statement was made, it nevertheless tells us something about the failure of Japanese socialism to challenge the Meiji system effectively.

PARTY POLITICS

Although the Meiji constitution imposed serious disabilities on any group which offered opposition to the men in power, it did not guarantee that these would be decisive, or last for ever. Government leaders, after all, while they believed in cabinets that were 'transcendental', that is, above sectional interests and therefore above party, also required a measure of co-operation from the Diet in implementing their policies. Similarly, members of the parties, though engaged almost wholly before 1890 in the politics of protest, were not on that account immune to the temptations of office, even when office was divorced from power. It was not altogether beyond reason, therefore, to think that the constitution might be made to work.

The events of its first few years put that conclusion in doubt. Elections for the lower house were carried out in July 1890, while Yamagata Aritomo was Prime Minister. Only about half a million voters were qualified to vote out of a population of forty million, these being by definition men of substance, who seemed likely to opt for stability. Nevertheless, the judgements they made were not to Yamagata's satisfaction. Of the 300 seats, 160 were won by members of anti-government parties. It was a result which laid the foundation for clashes over the budget as soon as the session opened in November, only overcome by the extensive use of threats and bribery on the government's behalf. A similar trial of strength faced the cabinet of Matsukata Masayoshi in the following year, this time ending in a dissolution. Elections were held again in February 1892 – notorious for police interference which left 25 dead and nearly 400 injured – but the next session was no less stormy than that of 1891. Matsukata resigned, to be succeeded by Ito Hirobumi. In February 1893, facing a vote of impeachment, Ito secured an imperial message to the Diet on the cabinet's behalf, but even this device was not enough to quell the turbulence. There was another dissolution in December; fresh elections in March 1894; a session starting in May; and dissolution of the lower house again at the beginning of June.

The Sino-Japanese War brought a brief respite, while politicians of all persuasions joined in cheering Japanese victories. After it, parliamentary life began to move at last towards a compromise, born of a recognition by the cabinet and elder statesmen – it was at about this time that the term Genro began to be used to describe the dominant figures of the Meiji leadership, even though they were not necessarily in the cabinet of the day – that they could not make the constitutional machinery work if the Diet was permanently obstructive. There was also an acceptance by the parties that, short of revolution, the establishment's position was impregnable. As a result, when one side offered a modest number of cabinet posts and minor concessions on policy, the other agreed to take them as a sufficient basis for suspending hostilities.

In 1895 Ito gave the Home Ministry to Itagaki Taisuke, leader of the Liberal Party (Jiyuto). The following year, Matsukata made an alliance with Okuma Shigenobu's Progressives (Shimpoto) on much the same terms. Neither arrangement worked very well, so in 1898 Ito made the experiment of bringing in both men to lead what was nominally the first party government in Japanese history. It broke up in a matter of months, however, because of disagreements between their respective followers over taxation and political spoils, thereby letting in Yamagata.

At this stage Ito and Yamagata were emerging as settled rivals, diverging in their policies across a broad spectrum of domestic and foreign issues. Yamagata, who had always been determined to prevent any kind of party rule, had built up an influential following in the House of Peers and many segments of local government to reinforce his initial power-base in the army. Ito's close links with the Imperial Court were not enough to counter this fully. In September 1900, therefore, he decided to strengthen his hand by forming a party of his own. Called the Association of Political Friends (Seiyukai), it was for the most part a reworked version of Itagaki's Liberals, offered the prize of cabinet offices in return for acceptance of Ito's own constitutional belief that cabinets must remain independent of party. With its support Ito took over as Prime Minister, though his administration proved once again short-lived.

After it ended (June 1901), Ito and Yamagata ceased to take any personal part in cabinets, being represented by their respective protegés, Saionji Kinmochi and Katsura Taro. These two men alternated as Prime Minister for the next twelve years, a period known as the 'Katsura–Saionji truce', because there was a tacit understanding between the two main political groups. Saionji, having succeeded Ito as president of the Seiyukai in 1903, commanded a docile majority in the lower house and the backing of Ito's friends. Katsura could count on the Yamagata interests, including as a rule the House of Peers. Either could govern as long as he had the other's consent. Neither could do so without it.

It was the Seiyukai's Hara Kei, Saionji's deputy, an acute ex-samurai politician from outside the Satsuma-Choshu cliques, who shaped a new kind of party politics in this situation. The reforms introduced in the 1870s and 1880s had already made it possible for the country's more substantial citizens to play some part in public life: as recruits to the bureaucracy; as members of prefectural assemblies or chambers of commerce; as voters electing representatives to the Diet, or even as representatives themselves (the property qualification for suffrage in 1912 remained the payment of fifteen yen a year in national taxes, limiting the electorate to 3 per cent of the population). Hara sought to redirect the allegiance of such men towards the Seiyukai, that is, to change the balance of power within the existing framework by rallying to his party the well-to-do at intermediate and lower levels.

The lever he used was provided by the cabinet posts which the Seiyukai gained as the price of its support for Saionji after the Russo-Japanese War. Three times between 1905 and 1915 Hara himself served as Home Minister. From this vantage-point he was able to use his influence over promotions and dismissals to persuade many of the new university-trained bureaucrats in central and local government to join the Seiyukai. This gave him a following within officialdom comparable with that of Yamagata, though without the military element. He also wooed local interest groups by the manipulation of government spending, especially in railway-building and other development projects. By 1912, when the Meiji emperor died, these devices had made the Seiyukai a formidable political machine, controlling the lower house of the Diet and able to strike a hard bargain with those who wanted its help.

Nor were its opponents any longer as well disciplined as they once had been. Katsura Taro, taking over from Saionji again in December 1912, decided to make a bid for power on his own account, that is, to form a party, so escaping from dependence on the Seiyukai, and to manipulate the emperor's authority, as Ito had once done, in order to bring the Genro under some control. In the event he succeeded only in uniting almost everyone against his own 'dictatorship'. In February 1913 the Seiyukai launched violent attacks on him in the Diet. Outside the building thousands rioted, storming the offices of pro-government newspapers. Katsura resigned.

This failure to find an alternative formula for an essentially bureaucratic rule marked the end of an era in Japanese politics. The remaining Genro disappeared one by one from the scene – Ito had been assassinated in 1909, Inoue Kaoru died in 1915, Yamagata in 1922, Matsukata in 1924 – and only Saionji was left to perform their role. There was a change of generation among party leaders, too: Katsura survived only a few months after his resignation in 1913, Itagaki died in 1919, and Okuma Shigenobu three years later. Hara took over from Saionji as leader of the Seiyukai in 1913. He thought it wiser for a time to continue to support non-party cabinets, including that of General Terauchi Masatake, which came to power in 1916, but he exacted as his price for this the opening of some top posts in the bureaucracy to political appointment. He also reversed Yamagata's ruling, laid down in 1900, that the ministers of War and Navy must be serving officers, not reserves.

The strength which accrued to his party because of all this brought about a measure of polarization in the Diet, as smaller groups were forced into some kind of anti-Seiyukai coalition in order to have any hope of influence. In 1916 this took shape as the Kenseikai (Constitutional Association), under which name it continued until 1927 as the Seiyukai's principal parliamentary rival. Its outstanding figure was Kato Takaaki (Komei), son of a lower samurai from Nagoya, who had graduated in law from Tokyo University in 1881, joined the Mitsubishi company, marrying Iwasaki Yataro's eldest daughter in 1886, then taken up a career in diplomacy under the patronage of Mutsu Munemitsu and Okuma Shigenobu. He was Katsura's Foreign Minister in 1912, succeeding him in the following year as president of the Doshikai, one of the parties which was incorporated into the Kenseikai. In 1914 he served as Foreign Minister in Okuma Shigenobu's cabinet, but so offended the Genro by his handling of the Twenty-one Demands (see chapter 9) that he was left for some years thereafter in the political wilderness.

By comparison, the Seiyukai's Hara was altogether more acceptable to the bureaucratic leadership, having shown himself on numerous occasions to be willing to compromise with the realities of power. His reward was to be made Prime Minister in 1918, when rising prices brought popular discontent with Terauchi's cabinet to a dangerous level. Japan thus acquired a 'commoner' as premier, that is, a man who had never taken a title, though well enough born. Significantly, he chose as colleagues in government only members of his party, except for the 'specialists' who held the portfolios of war, navy and foreign affairs.

To those who hailed this as a victory for liberalism and democracy the next three years were disappointing. As a good party man, Hara tried with some success to get his followers into prefectural and colonial governorships, which had so far been reserved for bureaucrats, but he showed little enthusiasm for reform in the wider sense. His position still depended too much on the Genro and the House of Peers to permit constitutional adventures, ensuring that as long as he remained in office proposals for an extension of the franchise were steadfastly put aside. Socialist thought was ruthlessly suppressed, signs of corruption were ignored. Thus his assassination in November 1921 by a young fanatic, whose motives were never made clear, robbed the party movement of its ablest politician, but not of one likely to move Japan significantly in the direction of popular liberties.

Predictably, his successors, feeling uncertain of their ground, reverted to the practice of using the Seiyukai's majority to back non-party governments. The trend of the times was against them, however. Kato's insistent demands for responsible party cabinets on the British model, which he had learnt to admire while ambassador in London, received increasing support. He succeeded in forcing a dissolution on this issue early in 1924 and in winning the subsequent election. This left the way clear for Kato himself to form an administration, first on the basis of a coalition of non-Seiyukai groups, eventually (August 1925) from the Kenseikai alone.

Kato carried out several of the measures at which Hara had balked. Economies reduced the size of the bureaucracy by 20,000. Expenditure on the armed forces was cut to 30 per cent of the national budget, compared with 40 per cent a few years earlier, the army losing four divisions in the process. Reform of the House of Peers was still beyond reach, but in May 1925 the Universal Manhood Suffrage Act gave the vote to all males over 25, increasing the size of the electorate from three million to thirteen million. Against that, only a week later came a new Peace Preservation Law, providing penalties of up to ten years' imprisonment for taking part in the more extreme forms of left-wing activity.

Repressive legislation of this kind signalled another change that was taking place in Japanese politics. Both the existing parliamentary parties and those who voted for them came overwhelmingly from segments of the population to which socialism was anathema. They had been much alarmed by the growth of trade unions after 1918 and by the emergence of the Communist Party in 1921, not least because of the ambivalence towards parliamentary rule shown by the left as a whole. Moves to create a proletarian party in 1925, in order to take advantage of reform of the suffrage, did nothing to abate their hostility, since it heralded a challenge in the one area of Japanese political life where they had so far held an advantage. Support for the Peace Preservation Law was an almost inevitable response. And the law was quickly put to use. An extremist Farmer-Labour Party, formed in December 1925, was banned after only thirty minutes in existence. A moderate alternative, the Labour-Farmer Party, founded in 1926, escaped this fate, but broke up within a few months because of internal dissension. In the elections of 1928 those left-wing organizations which had managed to survive (one must exclude the Communists, who took no part) were able to poll less than half a million votes between them. The police at once took the opportunity to launch large-scale raids on left-wing activists and sympathizers of every kind.

Suppression of the left did not automatically enable the two 'liberal' parties – the Minseito (Democratic Party) replaced the Kenseikai in 1927 – to rally a mass following on their own account, because their own attitudes and behaviour met with a good deal of criticism. There were many reasons for this. Since policy differences were comparatively unimportant in parliamentary life, and success depended more on striking deals than on debate, decisions, even by party cabinets, tended to be bargains made behind closed doors, not always in accordance with election pledges. Party loyalty was a rare virtue, office being regularly put before principle. Rank-and-file Diet members showed no more scruple and a lot less decorum than their leaders: knowing that major issues did not depend on what happened in the chamber, they reduced debates to the level of the trivial, or simply howled their opponents down. Even the use of violence within the Diet building was not unknown. And as if this were not enough, the public was well aware that corruption remained a common feature of national politics. In 1914 the Yamamoto cabinet had had to resign after revelations of bribery over naval armaments contracts, involving the Siemens company. Under Hara in 1921 the South Manchuria Railway Company was accused of contributing illegally to the Seiyukai's funds. General Tanaka Giichi, who became the Seiyukai leader in 1925, was said to have taken bribes about the placing of army contracts, to have sold peerages, to have been improperly influenced in the making of a cabinet appointment.

Many such charges were exaggerated, and some were invented altogether, for this, too, was the way of Japanese politics, but there is no doubt that the nature of the relationship between the parties and business made some degree of corruption or political dishonesty all too likely. Money was always needed to lubricate the system. Nor was its influence exercised only over men in cabinet office. The *zaibatsu* families had a number of links by marriage with senior statesmen. In 1930 one in eight of the Diet's lower house, evenly distributed between the two main parties, and more than one in four of the Peers, either held posts in a *zaibatsu* concern, or had close relatives who did. Moreover, the fact that about a third of the members of both houses in that year described themselves as 'businessmen' suggests that lesser firms, lacking the *zaibatsu*'s powerful connections, could nevertheless expect the Diet to treat them sympathetically.

Business backing, though it strengthened the parties *vis-à-vis* the bureaucracy in the 1920s, was suspect not only because it contributed to their public ill-repute. Given the weakness of parliamentary institutions, businessmen did not need politicians to the same extent that politicians needed businessmen. That being so, in the contests for power that developed in the following decade the more important companies, at least, were not difficult to persuade that their better interests lay outside the Diet. And if capitalism had helped to give moderate politicians a greater voice in deciding the scheme of things, it had also nurtured socialism by way of rival, thereby giving impetus to a reaction from the right which proved a much more dangerous threat to democratic government.

9

INDEPENDENCE AND EMPIRE, 1873–1919

At the beginning of the Meiji period Japan still had to deal with the world from a position of weakness. The only realistic decision for the Meiji government to take in these circumstances, as it had been for the Bakufu before it, was to act with caution, despite the often vociferous or violent objections made by patriots. However, the successful implementation of plans for *fukoku-kyōhei*, 'enrich the country, strengthen the military', gradually removed the need for such restraint. By the 1890s Japan was militarily and economically strong enough to assert her independence, bringing the 'unequal treaties' to an end. What is more, the Japanese, like other peoples, found that a concern with defence led easily to arguments for expansion. Wars with China (1894–5) and Russia (1904–5) gave them the elements of an empire.

Victory brought problems of a different kind. Japan now became engaged in international rivalries at a level which threatened to exceed her resources. She also discovered that her territorial expansion aroused resentments among her neighbours that were a hindrance to her trade, becoming distasteful on that account to many Japanese whose livelihood depended on industry and commerce. As a result, the focus of debates on foreign policy changed. After 1905 the point at issue was not so much the choice between adventure and caution, as between different ways of extending Japanese influence overseas.

THE YEARS OF CAUTION, 1873–94

While the Iwakura mission was in America and Europe during 1872 and 1873, there was a crisis in Japan's relations with Korea. Trouble had started between the two countries in 1868, when the Korean government had taken offence at the language used by Japan to announce the Meiji Restoration (it implied that the Japanese ruler was superior in status to the Korean one). Korean rejection of the announcement was then held by the Japanese to be an affront to national dignity. Since further exchanges in the next year or two failed to pacify either side, there emerged in Japan a 'war party', seeking revenge for insult and an opportunity to demonstrate that Japanese power, inconsiderable though it was in face of the West, was still enough to deal with recalcitrant neighbours. The leader of this group was Saigo Takamori. In the summer of 1873 he persuaded the Executive Council to take the decision that he should go himself to Korea, either to seek a settlement or provoke a confrontation.

Kido, Okubo, and Iwakura, returning from their European travels at this point, armed with a much better knowledge of the world than their colleagues in government, believed that a clash with Korea might well be disastrous for their country. In their view the national finances were not stable enough to stand the cost of war. Energy and resources would in any case be better employed in carrying out reforms, which it was clear, in the light of the vast gap that existed between the West's strength and Japan's, would have to be a good deal more far-reaching than had originally been thought. Moreover, a Japanese-Korean struggle would make it all too easy for the powers to fish in troubled waters, undoubtedly to Japan's disadvantage. Saigo and his allies remained unmoved by these arguments. The 'reform party', as it was called, therefore had recourse to intrigue. Iwakura won over the emperor; Kido and Okubo canvassed samurai officials for support, threatening to quit office if they did not get their way; and all three put such pressure on Sanjo Sanetomi, the nominal head of government, as to bring him to the brink of mental collapse. Iwakura took over in his stead. Then, backed by Kido and Okubo, he successfully recommended that the emperor's final approval be withheld from the policy which had been agreed earlier in the year.

One result of the incident was to cause the first major split within the ruling coalition. Another was to commit those who had won the argument to a programme of Western-style reform at home, which would by implication be given priority over any attempt to assert the national interests overseas. It was not an easy position to maintain, given a background of rising self-confidence within the country, but for the next twenty years Japanese governments approached questions of foreign policy in a manner which was calculated to avoid serious conflict with the powers.

One continuing theme in the period was that of treaty revision. The Iwakura mission had first enquired about the possibility of amending the treaties, only to be rebuffed. Thereafter Japanese representatives took every opportunity to seek some alleviation of their principal grievances – extraterritoriality, which put foreign residents in Japan under the legal jurisdiction of their own consuls, and tariff control, which denied Japan the right unilaterally to change the customs duties on foreign trade – but they met with steadfast resistance from the treaty powers, led by Britain. In 1878–9 the United States was persuaded to agree to tariff autonomy, conditionally on others doing so, only for Britain to refuse. Again in 1882 Britain proved adamant over extraterritoriality. A compromise was then worked out, involving a plan for mixed courts under Japanese and foreign judges, but this had to be abandoned after an outburst of popular indignation in Japan in 1886.

Japan's leaders were themselves divided about arrangements of this kind. One strand of thought, represented by Inoue Kaoru, Ito Hirobumi's friend, was that the economic benefits arising from revision of the treaties would outweigh any temporary loss of national dignity over matters of law. Writing in 1887, Inoue argued that 'free contact with people from the West' would not only help Japan to establish a 'civilized state', but would also 'lead to the investment of foreign capital in Japan' and 'assist us to imitate foreign industries'. By contrast, the conservative, Tani Kanjo, insisted that Japan must 'act boldly in our dealings with foreign countries'. It was not right to revise Japanese laws because foreigners found them unacceptable, he wrote. To do so was to lose 'all sense of independence'.[52]

In view of the existence of such disagreements, it required

some courage for Okuma Shigemitsu, as Foreign Minister, to reopen talks in 1888, but he hoped to make headway by negotiating in the calmer atmosphere of the Western capitals, not in Tokyo. He was disappointed. Although he won general agreement to the abolition of extraterritoriality, subject to the use of mixed courts in cases of appeal, there was an immediate storm of public disapproval in Tokyo when the information was leaked in the London *Times*. In October 1889 Okuma was injured when a bomb was thrown at his carriage by a nationalist fanatic. The negotiations were allowed to drop.

After the opening of the Diet in the following year, opposition members, engaged in a bitter struggle with successive cabinets, made every use they could of popular feeling on foreign affairs. This was sometimes an embarrassment in the context of treaty revision, but at least it gave ministers a diplomatic argument they had not had before. When Mutsu Munemitsu, Foreign Minister in Ito Hirobumi's cabinet, decided to resume talks in London in the summer of 1893, he was able to claim that Japanese opinion would not be satisfied with anything less than the complete abolition of extraterritoriality. He was even able to hint that if the treaties were not revised they might have to be renounced; and since the veiled threat was accompanied by an offer of commercial advantages, it proved enough to get the discussions under way again. Details were settled in the next few months. They provided that extraterritoriality should end after Japan's new civil code came into force (ultimately this was in 1899); that foreign merchants should be given access to the whole of Japan outside the treaty ports; and that a fresh tariff agreement was to be substituted for the existing one. A treaty embodying these terms was signed in July 1894. Similar agreements with other treaty powers came soon after, for in these matters Britain's example was decisive.

The other main focus of foreign policy in these years was Japan's relationship with her neighbours. Russia, being too strong to be challenged, was the least problematical: in 1875 Japan took over the northern part of the Kuril chain in return for renouncing her claims to Sakhalin, but this was something to which Russia had readily agreed. Similarly, Britain and the United States made no objections to a Japanese claim to the Bonin Islands in 1873. As to China, in 1871 a treaty had opened trade between the two countries on equal terms – Japan had tried without success to get a status equivalent to that of the Western powers in China – but the next few years were punctuated by disagreement. After the abolition of the domains Japan had asserted that the Ryukyu Islands were part of her territory, citing as justification the authority which Satsuma had exercised there since the beginning of the seventeenth century. China protested. She did so again, equally unavailingly, when the islands became Okinawa prefecture in 1879. In 1873–4 there was a dispute over Taiwan, arising from a Japanese demand for compensation after Taiwan aborigines (under Chinese jurisdiction) attacked some Ryukyu sailors (taken to be Japanese subjects). Japan sent a punitive expedition in 1874 and there was talk in Tokyo of a possible occupation of the island, but when Okubo Toshimichi met Li Hung-chang in Peking later in the year, caution prevailed. It was agreed that Japan had had a right to intervene, but questions of sovereignty were carefully left aside.

Matters concerning Korea were even more contentious, as was to be expected after the furore in 1873. Both Chinese and Koreans saw themselves as sharing a special relationship which was many centuries old. By contrast, Japanese leaders of almost all shades of opinion wanted to draw Korea into the Japanese orbit, though they differed about how it should be done. Some, the spiritual descendants of Saigo's war party, were ready to use force. Others, more careful of the reactions of the West, preferred modes of penetration that could be held to conform with the treaty port system as already established in East Asia. Since each was able to exercise a dominant influence at different times, the result was to give Japanese actions in Korea a two-steps-forward-one-step-backward character in the period after 1873.

The first move was a naval expedition, not unlike that which Commodore Perry had brought to Uraga in 1853. It followed a clash between Japanese surveying vessels and Korean coastal batteries in September 1875 – which may have been stage-managed by Japan – and led to the negotiation of a treaty early in 1876, opening Korean ports to trade. Among its provisions was one which described Korea as an independent country, having 'the same sovereign rights as does Japan', which could be read as a denial that her place in China's traditional 'tribute system' made her a Chinese vassal state. China objected; and under the guidance of Li Hung-chang she used her good offices in the next few years to persuade Korea to conclude treaties with the Western powers as well, as a means of diluting Japanese influence. She also strengthened her links with Korea's royal family. Japan responded by seeking allies among Korean officials and inviting young Koreans to Japan to receive a modern education.

Almost inevitably, these manoeuvres brought turbulence in the Korean capital. It reached a crisis in December 1884, when a group of Japanese activists and Korean reformers, working closely with the Japanese legation, tried to carry out a coup d'état. However, conflict over such an incident was more than either Peking or Tokyo wanted – the one involved in a war with France, the other in a string of constitutional changes – so in the spring of 1885 Li Hung-chang and Ito Hirobumi met in Tientsin to conclude a hands-off agreement with respect to Korea. Its effect was to divert both parties towards less troublesome methods of pressing their policies, at least for a time, a task in which China was the more successful. During the next decade, represented in Seoul by Yuan Shih-k'ai, she strengthened her hold by enlarging Sino-Korean trade, largely at the expense of Japanese merchants.

The frustrations this caused, plus Japan's sense of growing strength, as economic and political modernization began to show results, ensured that the next crisis, when it came, was less easy to resolve. In June 1894 a number of local revolts broke out in Korea, organized by anti-Western, traditionalist groups called Tong-haks. The king, acknowledging his tribute status, called on China for help in suppressing them. This was quickly sent. Japan, however, held that the action was contrary to the Tientsin convention of 1885. She therefore sent forces to maintain her own position, shifting the focus from the Tong-hak outbreaks to the much more dangerous issue of Sino-Japanese rivalry.

There were several specific reasons why the Japanese government was not inclined on this occasion to act with restraint. Its army, led by Yamagata Aritomo, had come to view Korea as potentially an element in Japan's defences, not least because Russia had started to build a railway to her own possessions in the north. Political parties in the Diet, urged on by patriot-activists and a volatile public, claimed that national honour was at stake, making caution difficult. More soberly, the Prime Minister,

Ito Hirobumi, and the Foreign Minister, Mutsu Munemitsu, saw a prospect of political and economic gains, sufficient to make the international risks arising from war with China seem worthwhile. Hence Ito set out to force a confrontation. At the end of June 1894, far from withdrawing Japanese troops, as China demanded, he announced his intention of keeping them in the peninsula until the Korean government had carried out an extensive catalogue of reforms, the main thrust of which would be to substitute Japanese for Chinese influence. In July he warned China to send in no more men. Shortly afterwards his own took over the Korean royal palace. Since China's government, too, was under domestic pressures, there was from this point no hope of avoiding war. Its formal declaration came at the beginning of August.

POWER IN EAST ASIA, 1894–1905

By the end of September 1894 – to the surprise not only of China, but also of the world – the Japanese army controlled most of Korea, while the navy had command of the Yellow Sea. In October two divisions under Yamagata crossed into southern Manchuria. Three more under Oyama Iwao moved against the Liaotung peninsula, capturing Port Arthur the following month. Occupation of Weihaiwei in February 1895 then gave Japan outposts on both sides of the sea approaches to Peking, forcing China to come to terms. Li Hung-chang was sent to negotiate them with Ito Hirobumi at Shimonoseki.

Japanese ambitions had grown with the tale of victories until they exceeded by far the original aim of prising Korea loose from Chinese tutelage. As presented to Li Hung-chang early in 1895 they included demands for an indemnity; for the handing over to Japan of Taiwan (which she had not even occupied) and Liaotung; and for a commercial treaty, which would put Japanese privileges in China on a par with those of the Western powers. In addition, Weihaiwei was to be held by Japan until the indemnity was paid. Li Hung-chang had little choice but to accede, with the result that a peace treaty on these lines was signed in April.

To the Japanese people the fruits of victory seemed very sweet. Their government, however, knew them to be at risk, for they were subject to the concurrence of the powers. It was partly for this reason that the proposed commercial arrangements were to include several benefits, long sought by foreign merchants, which all the powers could share through the operation of the most-favoured-nation clause. However, no such benefit attached to the cession of Liaotung. Japan maintained that the peninsula was needed for the defence of Korea. Russia, on the other hand, saw it as a threat to her own route to China through Manchuria. Accordingly, on 23 April 1895 the Russian representative in Tokyo, supported by those of France and Germany, informed Mutsu Munemitsu that his government viewed with concern the prospect of Liaotung being transferred to Japan, since this would menace Peking and hence the peace of Asia. Japan was 'advised' to return the territory to China. Knowing that Russia, at least, seemed willing to back the demand with force, whereas there was little prospect of help from Britain or America, the Ito cabinet submitted (5 May). All Japan could get to salve her pride was an increase in the size of the indemnity.

Pride, there is no doubt, was at the heart of the matter, as seen from Tokyo. The loss of the clause concerning Liaotung did not by any means rob the treaty of its value, but the manner of the loss affected Japanese opinion as if it had. The war had brought a tremendous wave of enthusiasm at home, silencing even the government's critics in the Diet. Victory had been hailed with exultation. Then came a savage reminder that half a century's work had still not put Japan in a position to ignore or reject the 'advice' of one of the major powers. It is no wonder that the shock was great and that it engendered a mood of bitterness.

In the short term, however, the effect on responsible officials was to induce a return to caution after the euphoria of 1894. One evidence of it was rearmament, designed to ensure that on any future occasion indignity could be properly resented. In 1896 six new divisions were added to the regular army, almost doubling its first-line strength. In 1898 both cavalry and artillery were organized as independent entities. In addition, every effort was made to improve military equipment and the facilities for its manufacture in Japan. By 1904 this had been substantially achieved. The country was also made as far as possible self-sufficient in naval armaments, while the navy was greatly increased in size, a building programme being started in 1896–7 for the purpose of adding four battleships, sixteen cruisers and twenty-three destroyers to the fleet. The cost of all this was heavy. Army expenditure rose from just under 15 million yen in 1893 to 53 million in 1896, then remained at about that level. The naval budget, more variable, stood at 13 million yen in 1895, nearly four times that figure in 1898, then fell back to 28 million in 1903.

In the field of foreign affairs Korea continued to be a problem area, since the events of 1895 had substituted Russia for China as Japan's competitor there. Wartime efforts to bring the country more closely under Japanese influence, checked by the Triple Intervention in the spring of that year, had been sacrificed altogether by a bungled attempt to seize control of the palace in October. The groups involved were much as in 1884, as were their methods, but on this occasion the Korean queen was killed. A few months later the king fled from his Japanese protectors to seek refuge in the Russian legation, giving Russia an important political weapon. Soon there was a Russian loan to Korea, secured on the customs revenue; a Russian military mission in Seoul; and plans for a telegraph linking the city to the Russo–Korean border in the north. Japan was left with only economic opportunities, which she had to deal directly with Russia to confirm, though the Nishi-Rosen agreement of April 1898, by which both sides undertook to refrain from interference in Korean politics and to consult each other before sending military or financial advisers there, gave her some reassurance on that score.

Of more general importance for Japan were the changes which were taking place in China at this time. China's defeat in 1894–5 had led some of the powers to doubt the continued viability of the treaty port system and to consider other ways of insuring their interests. In the first place, those who had 'saved' China from Japan after Shimonoseki called in their debts by claiming spheres of influence in various parts of the country, that is, exclusive railway and mining rights in designated areas, each defended by a small leased territory and a naval base. France carved out such a sphere in the southern provinces, bordering Indo-China, and Germany in Shantung. Russia followed suit in Manchuria, where she took over Port Arthur in Liaotung – only recently denied at her instance to Japan – which was to be linked by rail to the Russian-owned Chinese Eastern Railway, already under construction between Baikal and Vladivostock.

These developments took place between 1896 and 1898. Britain and the United States viewed them with disapproval, but made no immediate attempt to stop what was going on. Japan, who also disapproved, was too weak to do anything on her own; and rejection of her approach to China, designed to pick up privileges in Fukien, opposite Taiwan, demonstrated that she lacked the means to compete in this kind of company. Her attention was in any case soon distracted by events in the north. In 1899 and 1900 a series of anti-foreign outbreaks, led by groups called Boxers, swept through China's northern provinces. The Peking legations of the powers came under siege, and in the next few months Japan won international reputation by providing the bulk of the troops for the expedition that relieved them. However, she found herself immediately afterwards faced by a more considerable challenge, especially to her position in Korea, when Russia seized most of Manchuria on the pretext that Boxers threatened the railway installations there.

Out of all this turbulence came a realignment of the powers. France and Germany continued to support Russia as they had done in 1895, though not wholeheartedly. Britain and America came together in what was called the policy of the Open Door, aimed at preserving equality of opportunity for foreign trade in China. This left Japan to make a choice between the rival groups, since she could not stand alone. She did not find it easy. On the one hand, free competition in the China trade was not altogether to her taste, because her industry had not yet reached a level at which it could challenge those of Britain and America on equal terms. On the other, co-operation with Russia was only likely to be possible at the cost of accepting Russian domination of the mainland north of the Great Wall. To put it differently, the choice was between extending trade with China's central and southern provinces under Britain's auspices, or securing a greater stake in Korea as the price of a deal with Russia. The dilemma was in one form or another to be central to Japanese policy decisions for the next thirty years.

The first occasion for debating it arose from proposals for an alliance with Britain in the summer of 1901. There had already been private overtures which suggested that such an arrangement might be feasible, on the grounds that both countries had an interest in opposing any further Russian advance. For Britain, the question still to be decided was whether Japanese help would make it worth abandoning 'splendid isolation'. For Japan, it was what Russia might be induced to concede by way of alternative. Ito Hirobumi preferred to wait until there had been an approach to St Petersburg to see what was on offer, but the Prime Minister, Katsura Taro, and his patron, Yamagata Aritomo, both believed that a show-down with Russia would be inevitable before very long, which made them reluctant to spend any effort to avoid it. Consequently, Ito was by-passed; the negotiations with Britain were pressed forward; and a treaty of alliance was signed on 30 January 1902, providing that each signatory would remain neutral if the other became involved in a Far East war, except that they would act together if either were attacked by two powers or more. This meant that Britain would hold the ring against any possible renewal of the Triple Intervention. In addition, Britain recognized that Japan possessed interests in Korea 'in a peculiar degree politically as well as commercially and industrially'.

In April 1902, apparently in response to this pressure, Russia agreed to withdraw her forces from Manchuria by six-month stages. However, the second stage of withdrawal, due in April 1903, was delayed without explanation. The Japanese government therefore decided to seek a more general settlement with Russia, now that it could be done from a position of greater strength, taking as its basis what her Foreign Minister, Komura Jutaro, called *Man-Kan kōkan*, 'exchanging Manchuria for Korea'. He envisaged, that is, an undertaking by both countries to respect the territorial integrity of China and Korea, coupled with recognition of Russian railway rights in Manchuria and of Japan's much broader interests in Korea. Russia's counter-claim (October 1903) sought more for Russia in Manchuria, less for Japan in Korea. These terms Komura, in the light of an increasingly aggressive public opinion at home, could not possible entertain. He restated his demands in the form of an ultimatum (January 1904), which was clearly a prelude to war.

War was declared on 10 February, but hostilities had already begun two days earlier. There was fighting at first in Korea and along the coast towards Liaotung. In April a naval victory outside Port Arthur gave Japan control of the seas across which she needed to move her reinforcements, thereby enabling her First Army to strike north across the Yalu River into Manchuria in May and her Second Army to land in the Liaotung peninsula a few days later. Within a month General Nogi Maresuke's Third Army had laid siege to Port Arthur itself. There followed nearly a year of campaigning: a battle round Liaoyang in August and early September 1904; the capture of Port Arthur at the beginning of January 1905; then an advance against Mukden in February and March, involving no less than sixteen Japanese divisions. As a final blow to Russian hopes, the Russian Baltic fleet, which had sailed halfway round the world to break the blockade of Vladivostock, was met by Admiral Togo Heihachiro's forces in the Tsushima Straits in May and decisively defeated.

Both sides had by then good reasons to end the struggle. Russia was facing revolution at home. Japan was unable any longer to sustain casualties and expenditure at existing levels. Accordingly, when America offered mediation, a truce was agreed, then a peace conference at Portsmouth, New Hampshire, held in August 1905. Japan's representative was Komura. His overriding objective had long been to secure for his country a position from which she could defend her mainland interests without outside help, should the rivalries of the powers bring China to collapse. Spelling this out, he had written in July 1904 that Korea 'must be brought effectively within the sphere of our sovereignty'; Manchuria 'must be made in some degree a sphere of interest'; and there should be an extension of Japan's economic privileges to the Russian territories in the north.[53] Despite Japan's weakness at the end of the war, much of this survived the peace negotiations. Japan gained Russian recognition of her freedom of action in Korea, and took over the Russian lease of Liaotung (Kwantung), plus that part of the railway which linked it with Harbin (renamed the South Manchuria Railway). She also secured the cession from Russia of the southern half of Sakhalin (Karafuto). There was no indemnity, but Komura had good cause to be pleased with the Treaty of Portsmouth, which he signed on 5 September 1905. It did not satisfy the extravagant expectations of the Japanese public, however. News of it caused riots in Tokyo, bringing martial law to the capital for a day or two.

FIRST AMONG EQUALS, 1905–19

The most vociferous calls for 'strong' action overseas at this time came from those Japanese who belonged to 'patriotic societies', the first of which, the Genyosha, had been formed in 1881 by men who wished to carry on the tradition of Saigo Takamori's policy towards Korea. At home its members constituted a pressure group, seeking to influence public and politicians. Abroad they engaged semi-officially in covert activities, which included taking part in the attempts to seize power at the Korean court in 1884 and 1895. In 1901 two of them, Toyama Mitsuru and Uchida Ryohei – ex-samurai with access to the highest circles in government – founded an even more famous body, the Kokuryukai, or Amur Society, which is better known to foreigners as the Black Dragon Society. Its avowed purpose was to extend 'the mission of imperial Japan' to Manchuria, Mongolia, and Siberia, as well as Korea, though in the fullness of time it also turned its attention to China farther south.

The ideas of such societies were popular among army officers, to whom Komura's formulation, sovereignty over Korea and a sphere of interest in Manchuria, became axiomatic after 1905. After all, Japanese blood had been shed to secure a foothold in those areas. They were sacred ground. What is more, there was the possibility of a Russian war of revenge, defence against which required something more than economic privileges in the region: at the very least, control over railways and communications, plus the means of maintaining law and order among the civilian population. Out of this ambition came the first confrontation between military and civilian leaders in the aftermath of the Russo-Japanese War.

Kodama Gentaro, the Army Chief of Staff, tried during the winter of 1905–6 to ensure that China be required to grant, as the price of Japan's postwar withdrawal from the south Manchurian provinces, a number of administrative rights which went some way beyond the usual definition of a sphere of interest. His civilian counterparts saw two dangers in this. One was that of offending Chinese sentiment, so imperilling Japanese trade in other parts of China. The other was that of provoking Britain and the United States, who had furnished wartime loans on the understanding that there was a firm Japanese commitment to the

Open Door. Men like Inoue Kaoru found this particularly alarming, since they believed that Japan would need further injections of foreign capital for the development of Manchuria's mines and railways (under the aegis of the South Manchuria Railway Company, formed in June 1906). They therefore called a meeting of senior statesmen and military leaders, at which Ito Hirobumi intervened decisively to secure the rejection of Kodama's views. Good relations with China and the powers, Ito argued, were more important than the ability to intervene in Manchuria. Nor was there any doubt about the legalities. 'Manchuria is in no respect Japanese territory', he said. 'The responsibility for administering Manchuria rests with the Chinese government.'[54]

Victory for Ito and his allies did not mean that the disagreement came to an end. In the years that followed, while the Foreign Ministry became spokesman for the Ito–Inoue line, looking to financial circles for support, the army – notably the Kwantung Army, which had been established in the leased territory of Liaotung – took every opportunity to assert its independence in this matter. One consequence was that Japan moved towards treating the Manchurian question as something apart, falling outside the policy of the Open Door. Another was a local rapprochement with Russia. In July 1910 the two countries concluded a secret agreement laying down a division of spheres in Manchuria, Russia in the north, Japan in the south, which implied a willingness to co-operate in the face of any attempts by other powers to enforce the Open Door there.

There were no such difficulties about framing policy towards Korea, on which the Japanese were broadly agreed among themselves and had no reason to fear intervention from outside. During the war years Japan had used her status as an 'ally' to secure a position of dominance in Korea. In November 1905, having had indications that neither Britain nor the United States would raise objections, she negotiated a treaty of protectorate, appointing Ito as Resident-General in Seoul. This made it possible to obtain privileges by way of railway, mining, and fishery rights, plus timber concessions and land for Japanese residents. However, it did not stifle Korean opposition. In June 1907 the Korean ruler sent envoys secretly to the Hague to seek an international declaration of Korea's independence. They failed.

Japan used the incident as a pretext to force the Korean emperor's abdication and to strengthen the hold of Japanese nominees on government. Most of the Korean army was thereupon disbanded.

After this, anti-Japanese dissidents in Korea turned to violence. Against a background of rising turbulence, the Japanese cabinet – Katsura was again Prime Minister – finally decided in the spring of 1909 that indirect control, such as was given by a protectorate, was not enough for its needs. It was resolved to move to outright annexation; the War Minister, Terauchi Masatake, was sent to Seoul as Resident-General (Ito had been assassinated by a Korean patriot in Harbin in October); and the Japanese garrison was strengthened. On 22 August 1910, once all preparations were complete, Terauchi signed a treaty of annexation which had been forced on the Korean court. He was then made Japan's first Governor-General of the colony.

During these years Japan had been building a considerable economic stake in China (see chapter 7), acting in concert with the other treaty powers. Like them, therefore, she had a good deal at risk when Chinese unrest at last became anti-Manchu revolution in the winter of 1911–12. The immediate outcome of the outbreak was confusion. It was some months before it was clear that there would be an end to Manchu rule, another year or more before Yuan Shih-k'ai, backed by much of the pre-revolutionary bureaucracy, overcame Sun Yat-sen in a contest for power. Japanese policy-makers found it difficult to decide how best to promote Japan's interests in this situation. The army sponsored two semi-official – and unsuccessful – attempts to organize an independent Manchuria under a Manchu figurehead. The Kokuryukai and its sympathizers gave their backing to Sun Yat-sen, providing arms for his followers with the help of Mitsui and other firms, which hoped to be given business advantages. Cabinets, by contrast, tended to follow the lead of the West in opting for Yuan Shih-k'ai, because he seemed more likely than any other Chinese to establish a state of order in which trade could flourish again; but they did not do so with enough conviction to persuade him that Japan could be counted as a friend. The result of these diverse interventions was that Yuan's victory over Sun in 1913 left Tokyo with little to show for nearly two years of meddling.

Despite this, all the Japanese groups which had been involved – government, army, businessmen, patriots – shared a conviction that Japan must seek a relationship with the new republican China that was closer and more clearly bilateral than that which the treaty port system had made possible so far. A fresh opportunity to develop it came with the outbreak of war in Europe in August 1914. The terms of the Anglo-Japanese alliance did not require Japan to join the hostilities against Gemany, but the Okuma cabinet decided that there was much to be gained by being a belligerent. It therefore demanded that Germany withdraw or disarm her warships in Far Eastern waters and surrender the leased territory which she held in Shantung. When the ultimatum was ignored, Japan declared war, landed troops in Shantung and seized the German bases there. In addition, naval operations, begun during October, brought the occupation of all German-held Pacific islands north of the equator.

Once these moves had been completed, the way was open to settle some of the outstanding issues in Japan's relations with China. As Foreign Minister, Kato Takaaki had inherited several items of unfinished business. In Manchuria Japan had for some time been trying to secure additional railway rights and to extend the duration of the leases taken over from Russia in 1905. Further south there was the question of the Hanyehping coal and iron company, which it was reported that Yuan Shih-k'ai was planning to nationalize. Since it was a major supplier to Japan's Yawata plant and heavily in debt to Japanese banks, significant economic interests were at stake. The disposal of German railway and mining rights in Shantung, which had now become an object of Japanese ambitions, was another matter to be decided. In a wider perspective, the army wanted to appoint military advisers to the Chinese government, for the sake of the influence this would give in matters of defence, and the Kokuryukai, in a document which Uchida Ryohei put forward in November, spoke of something more like a Japanese protectorate over China as a whole.

Late in 1914 these various pieces were put together by the Foreign Ministry to form what became known as the Twenty-one Demands. In addition to the specific items concerned with Manchuria, Shantung, and Hanyehping, they included a clause requiring Peking 'not to cede or lease to any other power any harbour or bay or any island along the coast of China', while a final section (Group V), which was to provoke the greatest controversy, called for railway concessions in the lower Yangtse valley, prior consultation with Japan about any proposed foreign loan for the development of transport in the province of Fukien, the employment of 'influential Japanese' as political, financial, and military advisers in China, and priority for Japanese firms in the provision of China's military equipment. Even allowing for the fact that the points cited in Group V were described as 'highly desirable', not 'absolutely essential' like the rest, it was impossible to conceive of such gains being conceded without straining the fabric of the treaty port system.[55]

The demands were presented privately to Yuan Shih-k'ai in January 1915, together with an offer of personal and political inducements for accepting them. Yuan appealed in vain for help to Britain and the United States. Once it was clear that this would not be forthcoming, Kato pressed his advantage home, dropping Group V, but making everything else the subject of an ultimatum. Treaties were signed on 25 May, accompanied by an exchange of supplementary notes, which together gave Japan everything her government, if not the Army and the patriots, sought.

This achievement was not received without criticism in Tokyo. Yamagata Aritomo, in particular, saw the manner by which it had been secured as holding dangers for the future. Kato, he said, had needlessly aroused the hostility of China and the treaty powers, which meant that Japan would not be able to count on Chinese goodwill when she faced, as inevitably she would, a renewal of rivalries with the West at the end of the war. His own preference by far would have been to effect a reconciliation with China's leaders, subject only to a recognition on their part of Japan's domination of Manchuria.

Something very much like this approach characterized the actions of his protegé, Terauchi Masatake, who became Prime Minister in October 1916. In February 1917 Terauchi sent Nishihara Kamezo, a businessman with experience in Korea, to be his personal representative in Peking. The Chinese government was at this time headed by Tuan Ch'i-jui – Yuan Shih-k'ai had died in June 1916 – and it was to be an object of Nishihara's mission, not only to ensure Tuan's friendship towards Japan, but also to help him against his domestic rivals. To this end a series of loans were negotiated during 1917 and 1918, by which Japan would ostensibly finance the development of China's economy, but would by so doing sustain Tuan's military and political power. The policy would also ensure that Japanese enterprise had pride of place in Chinese railways, telegraphs, and mining. It was hoped in this way, as Nishihara wrote to a colleague in Tokyo, 'to develop the limitless natural resources of China and the industry of Japan by co-ordinating the two, so as to make possible a plan for self-sufficiency under which Japan and China would become a single entity'.[56]

This first attempt to formulate an economic role for Japan in China which went beyond the normal trade and investment patterns of the treaty port system was a failure, partly because Tuan lacked a strong enough political base, partly because he was made to look uncommonly like a Japanese puppet at a time when the tide of Chinese nationalism was beginning to run strong. The 1915 treaties had inevitably aroused a great deal of popular hostility towards Japan in China. The most violent expression of nationalist sentiment, however, came at the end of the war with Germany, when Japan tried to entrench her gains in the peace settlement at Versailles.

Japan had worked hard to persuade the other treaty powers (who were in most cases her wartime allies) to accept the changes she had brought about in China. A secret treaty with Russia in July 1916 had included recognition of her expanded railway and mining interests in Manchuria. An agreement with Britain in February 1917 secured London's support for her claim to former German rights in Shantung and the Pacific islands. France and Italy made similar commitments shortly after. Towards the end of the year, the United States, upon becoming a belligerent, agreed to a vaguely-worded statement that 'territorial propinquity' gave Japan a special position on the Asian mainland, which she was entitled to protect.

Armed with these promises, Saionji Kinmochi set out for Versailles in the winter of 1918 as Japan's chief delegate. He met with mixed fortunes. His country's place in the world was indeed accorded respect – membership of the League of Nations Council after the conference, though not of the inner committee of the victors during it – but on the specific issues important to Japan he achieved less than had been hoped. His proposal for a racial equality clause in the League of Nations charter went down before American and Australian opposition. The German islands in the northern Pacific were put under Japanese control, but as a League mandate, not in outright ownership. On Shantung and other China questions the allies did in the end honour their undertakings; but the news brought such an outburst of popular indignation in China (the May Fourth demonstrations of 1919) that the Chinese delegation at Versailles refused to sign the treaty. Thus Japan was left in possession of her gains, but by no means unchallenged in her title to them.

10

SOLDIERS AND PATRIOTS, 1918–1933

As spokesmen for a 'transcendental' monarch, who was in theory absolute, but in practice a creature of his ministers, the Meiji leaders, notably the Genro, had ascribed to themselves the co-ordinating role in a system of government, the different elements of which were separately, not collectively, responsible to the Throne. It was their personal, extra-constitutional authority, exercised in the emperor's name, that held together the ministries, the armed forces, the Privy Council, and the Diet in a workable whole. By the 1920s that authority had vanished because of age and death. No successor – certainly not Saionji, the only surviving Genro – was able to inherit it intact. What is more, the cabinet, through which it had been chiefly exercised, proved too weak to impose priorities of its own, perhaps because the Genro had kept it so. As a result, a situation developed in which it was easier to keep order among the people than among those who ruled them. Various parts of the government machine – especially the army, but including also the lower house of the Diet, thanks to Hara – competed with each other for the control of decision-making, or, if they failed to secure it, claimed a right of veto over particular aspects of policy by virtue of their designated powers.

There are similarities between this state of affairs and that which had existed in the last years of the Tokugawa. In both periods too little of what happened did so at the behest of Japan's nominal rulers. In both, again, men were divided by fanatically-held beliefs which they were prepared to put above the law. Even the issues were broadly the same. In the 1930s, as in the 1860s, two things were held to be at stake: Japan's ability to maintain her 'proper' place in the world against external enemies; and the extent to which being 'Japanese' must be sacrificed to being 'modern'. Despite all the changes that had been made in society and the economy in the interval, it was not inappropriate that activists in the first part of the Showa era (the reign of Hirohito, 1926–89) spoke of another Restoration and used a vocabulary which echoed that of the Tokugawa 'men of spirit'. It is with these activists, their allies and their ideas that this chapter is principally concerned.

THE CHINA PROBLEM

China, as we have seen, loomed large in Japanese thinking about the outside world. To some Japanese the two countries, having shared the experience of being subjected to unequal treaties, had a duty to work together to resist Western dominance in East Asia. The anti-Manchu revolution had encouraged them to believe that China might be ready to take up that task. Others saw it as primarily Japan's duty, China being demonstrably too weak to do more than offer herself as a market and source of raw materials, by which Japan's capacity to carry it out could be ensured. A corollary of both arguments was that Japan needed to protect China from the Western powers, while maintaining her own advantages in that country and persuading the Chinese people to accept them.

Until 1917 such protection had been conceived as being directed towards limiting the growth of Western spheres of influence in China and preventing territorial partition. With the outbreak of the Russian Revolution, however, the situation changed. Not only were the Bolsheviks, if successful, likely to renounce the arrangements by which Japan and Russia had agreed to co-operate in defending their respective interests in Manchuria, but there was also a very real risk that communist ideas, penetrating China's own revolutionary movement, might imperil the stability of all East Asia. This in turn would put in danger those economic privileges within the treaty port system on which Japanese prosperity depended. Responses to the Russian Revolution were therefore a test of Japanese policy in the widest sense.

Opinions on the subject within Japan were divided very much as one would expect from the disagreements which had emerged in the previous ten or fifteen years. Senior statesmen and the Foreign Ministry, supported by political party leaders, put their emphasis on co-operation with Britain and the United States, pointing to the economic benefits it would bring. The army, especially the Kwantung Army, saw the prospect of intervention against the Bolsheviks in more narrowly continental terms, as something which held out the possibility of creating an anti-Bolshevik puppet state in Russia's eastern provinces, constituting a buffer for Manchuria's northern frontier. As had happened on previous occasions, the international emphasis proved the stronger of the two in Tokyo, but the armed forces found it easier to pursue their objectives in the field.

Failure to agree on which course to choose prevented action of any kind for several months, particularly as the United States, whose co-operation was widely thought to be essential, was suspicious of Japanese motives. Then in June and July 1918 Czech troops, fighting their way out of European Russia in an attempt to continue the war against Germany despite Russia's surrender, seized Vladivostock and the eastern sections of the Trans-Siberian railway. This provided the United States with a motive for proposing limited operations to cover the Czech withdrawal. The Terauchi government agreed, accepting on 2 August that each country should send one division to Siberia, supported by a smaller force in northern Manchuria, while other allies provided token contributions.

Notwithstanding this arrangement, it was the Japanese army's earlier plan, or something very much like it, that was actually carried out. By the end of 1918 four or five Japanese divisions were operating in the Amur basin and controlling the railway westward to Baikal. Even this brought no more than partial success. The cost was enormous; the allies bickered constantly among themselves; and no group of anti-Bolshevik Russians showed itself capable of setting up a stable government in the area. By November 1919 the Soviets were moving steadily eastward from Omsk. In January 1920 Washington announced the recall of its troops, on the grounds that the Czechs had been evacuated and nothing more that was useful could be done. The example was quickly followed by Britain, France, and Canada, leaving only the Japanese, who extended their operations to Sakhalin soon after, in retaliation for a massacre of Japanese citizens at Nikolaevsk. Even they were unwilling to carry the burden singlehanded for very long. In October 1922 they pulled back from the Amur and in 1925 evacuated Sakhalin.

Meanwhile there were a number of other issues concerning East Asia to be settled, closely involving Britain and America. Japan and the United States were engaged in disputes over immigration into California. Both the British and American governments were looking for ways to limit or reduce the wartime gains Japan had made in China and to provide a better framework for treaty port rights in the light of the growth of Chinese nationalism. They were also alarmed about the implications of the Anglo-Japanese alliance in the context of a possible Japanese–American conflict, as well as about naval armaments competition among the powers. Accordingly, the United States invited representatives of the countries with a stake in these matters, including China, to a conference in Washington, starting in November 1921.

During the next three months several important agreements were concluded. On naval armament it was decided to limit the size and firepower of capital ships, while fixing the tonnage held by America, Britain, and Japan at a ratio of 5:5:3. Japan, at the urging of a powerful section of her naval high command, had begun by demanding more, but she was persuaded to accept instead a promise halting the construction of naval fortifications at Guam, Hong Kong, and Singapore, which gave her naval predominance in the west Pacific. Against that she had to set the loss of the alliance with Britain. A Four Power Pact of December 1921 substituted for it a much looser arrangement, by which Britain, France, Japan, and the United States agreed to respect each other's rights in east Asia and to consult together if a crisis arose.

With respect to China, a Nine Power Treaty, signed by Belgium, Italy, the Netherlands, and Portugal, as well as China and the parties to the Four Power Pact, was concluded in

February 1922. It promised reconsideration of the tariff and extraterritoriality provisions of the treaty port system, while putting into due form the platitudes associated with the Open Door. The powers undertook to respect Chinese independence and integrity; to refrain from seeking special rights at each other's expense; and to avoid any interference with China's efforts 'to develop and maintain for herself an effective and stable government' (Article I). No machinery was created to enforce these promises, but at least the Chinese and Japanese delegates were able in this context to reach a separate agreement over Shantung. Japan promised to return the leased territory at Kiaochow and to withdraw her troops from the Tsingtao–Tsinan railway, China to buy back the railway itself and to transfer former German mining rights to a Sino-Japanese company.

This settlement provided an indication of the aims Japan was to set herself in China after the Washington Conference. Their architect was Shidehara Kijuro, a career diplomat, who was Foreign Minister in 1924–7 and 1929–31, and who, like Kato Takaaki, had married into the Iwasaki family, owners of Mitsubishi. This connection no doubt contributed to his belief in 'economic diplomacy', that is, the promotion of Japanese trade and investment overseas. So far as it applied to the Asian mainland, this implied, as he saw it, a refusal to undertake territorial adventures, such as were likely to damage trade (save only that Manchuria was a special case). In other words, Shidehara sought to preserve as far as possible the treaty port system, to work closely with Britain and America, and to come to terms with Chinese nationalism.

Unhappily, the various ingredients in this policy proved to be in conflict with each other. The Twenty-one Demands, the negotiations at Versailles, and Japan's continued presence in Manchuria, where the local warlord, Chang Tso-lin, depended heavily on Japanese help, had inevitably made Japan a target of Chinese resentment. Since nationalism in the 1920s was a major force in Chinese politics, no government in Peking could afford to ignore this fact in its diplomatic dealings. Moreover, Shidehara's interpretation of 'economic diplomacy' made it difficult for him to go along with any revision of the unequal treaties which would undermine his own country's advantages, notwithstanding the promises that had been made at Washington. In this he found himself at odds with Britain and the United States. Thus when discussions of tariff reform began in 1925–6, he stood out for measures that would protect Japan's textile markets and offer some hope of repayment of the Nishihara loans. Similarly, in the talks about extraterritoriality during 1929 and 1930 he tried to reserve Japan's position in Kwantung and south Manchuria. None of these questions had been satisfactorily settled by the time the Manchurian Incident changed the whole pattern of the Sino-Japanese relationship in 1931.

Shidehara thus gained very little from his willingness to work within an order of things in China which seemed to many Japanese to have been designed mostly for the benefit of America and Britain. He put at risk specific Japanese rights, which by his own definition were vital to the Japanese economy. He went some way towards sacrificing symbols of international status, like extraterritoriality, which had been painfully acquired in the years since Japan's own unequal treaties had come to an end. And with it all he had apparently done nothing to reduce China's hostility, since anti-Japanese strikes and boycotts remained regular occurrences. If this was what was meant by international co-operation, his critics said, Japan could do without it. She would do better to opt for 'autonomy'.

THE NATIONALIST REACTION

Shidehara's policies were defended by liberals in Japan in terms which were offensive to conservatives and nationalists. Ishibashi Tanzan, for example, had opposed intervention in Siberia on the grounds that Japan should avoid 'making enemies of our neighbours', who were also customers, by the 'reckless' use of troops.[57] He later developed the argument into an attack on Japanese imperialism in a much more general sense. As he saw it, the profits to be made from colonies were less than those which would derive from trade; the military action that had to be undertaken to acquire colonies put trade at risk; and by necessitating a high level of defence expenditure, the very possession of an empire was a hindrance to the growth of Japan's domestic economy. Hence 'strength', in the form of political authority and exclusive rights outside Japan, was much less desirable than 'wealth', defined as foreign trade and investment.

This was liberalism of a more far-reaching kind than Shidehara's, but both varieties flouted the prejudices of those traditionalists to whom wealth in its modern guise was a cause of undesirable extravagance. What is more, its unequal distribution, such traditionalists believed, prompted 'dangerous thoughts' like socialism and communism, the existence of which implied that something was seriously wrong with the body politic. Thus dance-halls, luxury, corruption, big business, trade unions, strikes, and agrarian unrest, as well as Shidehara's foreign policy, could all in the last resort be lumped together as results of an over-indulgence in foreign ways. They threatened not only Japan's position on the Asian continent, but even such fundamentals of the national life as the emperor system, the Confucian ethic, and samurai values.

Before about 1930 these opinions were most conspicuously voiced by an influential minority of Japanese, members of the so-called 'patriotic societies', who had always acknowledged a close connection between the nature of Japanese society and the country's relations with the outside world. The Kokuryukai, for instance, had at the outset stated its purpose to be to 'renovate the present system, foster a foreign policy aiming at expansion overseas, revolutionize domestic policies to increase the happiness of the people, and establish a social policy that will settle problems between labour and capital'.[58] Some of the later organizations, like the Dai Nihon Kokusuikai (Japan National Essence Society), dating from 1919, and the Kokuhonsha (National Foundation Society) of 1924, were openly designed to save Japan from the perils of socialism. Of the two, the Kokuhonsha was particularly respectable and influential. Its members included three future prime ministers (Saito Makoto, Hiranuma Kiichiro, Koiso Kuniaki) and several famous generals (Ugaki Kazushige, Araki Sadao, Mazaki Jinzaburo), in addition to party politicians, senior bureaucrats and representatives of *zaibatsu* companies.

In sharp contrast were a number of smaller, extremist groups which existed on the fringes of politics, dependent for funds on the contributions of non-members – obtained by methods ranging from cajolery to moral blackmail – and for cohesion on the leadership of individual 'bosses'. Often they were little more than strong-arm squads, capitalizing on the fashion for patriotism instead of crime. Sometimes, however, they were the personal following of politically much more dangerous men, fanatics whose views were as violent as the means by which they tried to spread them. Such a one was Kita Ikki, author and revolutionary, who was executed in 1937 for his part in an attempted coup d'état. With Okawa Shumei he founded the Yuzonsha (Society for the Preservation of the National Essence) in 1919 and became the inspiration of several others like it.

Kita's chief contribution was to the ideology of the movement. In 1923 at the age of forty he published a much-acclaimed book entitled *Nihon kaizō hōan taikō* (An Outline Plan for the Reconstruction of Japan), which advocated radical changes in order to fit Japan for leadership in the revolutionary Asia which Kita thought bound to come. The first step would be a military coup, making possible a clean sweep of the country's existing élites and the substitution of a regime based on a direct relationship between emperor and people. Next would come the confiscation of personal fortunes greater than one million yen, the nationalization of major industries, the seizure and redistribution of private landholdings above 100,000 yen in value, and the renunciation by the emperor of his family estates. Thus purified, Japan would be ready to act more vigorously in foreign affairs than recent governments had ever done. After all, Kita argued, as a member of the proletariat of nations Japan had a duty to secure justice from the wealthy (Britain, the millionaire; Russia, the great landowner) by launching an expansionist policy on the Asian mainland and supporting the interests of Asians everywhere against the West.

Logically this was a hodgepodge, but it was popular. Equally so were the views of Gondo Seikyo, apostle of an agrarian-centred nationalism that looked to the village instead of the town as the nucleus of political and economic life. Like Kita, he emphasized the role of the emperor in the national polity and accepted the doctrine of Japan's racial mission overseas. Unlike him, however, he wished not to socialize industry, but to bring it low, because it signified a capitalist exploitation of the countryside. Centralization, bureaucracy, and almost all things Western, too, were in his view to be condemned. In other words, he rejected the Meiji achievement of creating a modern state, because it contradicted – and had done much to destroy – the true

Japaneseness of family and lineage, as they were to be found in the farming community.

Gondo's ideas, first published in 1920, were propagated through an institute which he established for that purpose. In much the same way, another agrarian nationalist, Tachibana Kosaburo, founded a communal village near Mito and opened a school at which he taught a blend of farming and patriotism to a handful of devoted students. Unlike Gondo, Tachibana had no hesitation in endorsing the use of force. From about 1929 he formed a connection with Inoue Nissho's Ketsumeidan, a blood brotherhood, committed to bringing about the agrarian millennium by assassinating selected financiers and industrialists.

The attitudes and interests represented in such societies were too varied to make it likely that they could devise a concrete programme or co-operate in promoting it. Moreover, small numbers and lack of regular funds were bound to make them ineffective if they tried to act alone. Hence their importance was catalytical, like the 'men of spirit' of the 1860s, on whom they often chose to model themselves. In addition, they communicated their anti-capitalist, anti-Western prejudices to many young officers of the armed services, whose ability to influence policy proved greater than their own. Many of these, as a result of reforms carried out by the Kato cabinet in 1924–5, were drawn from families of shopkeepers, small landowners, and minor officials, who had not the same loyalty to the established social order as their ex-samurai predecessors, but were nevertheless unwilling to espouse the cause of socialism or the urban poor. Such men inclined towards the radical right, as they did in other industrial states. They also had specific grievances as members of the military. As they saw things, civilian control, exercised by political parties, had contributed to a decline in the services' prestige; good neighbourliness abroad and retrenchment at home had combined to threaten their careers; and the way of life enjoyed by the well-to-do, especially in the cities, contrasted strangely with the low pay and spartan habits which they themselves were expected to accept.

As a result, a number of officers began to form connections with the nationalist movement at a level quite distinct from that of the recognized channels between the high command, senior bureaucrats, and politicians. Some came to terms with Kita Ikki,

Okawa Shumei and their like, founding joint military–civilian groups to discuss the prospects of achieving 'reform' by force. Others established new societies having a membership drawn entirely from the army and navy. The most famous of these was Lieutenant-Colonel Hashimoto Kingoro's Sakurakai (Cherry Society), originating in September 1930, which at its peak had a hundred members, all of the rank of lieutenant colonel and below. They were mostly drawn from the War Ministry and General Staff, together with the military training establishments and units stationed in the Tokyo area.

Two phrases constantly recurred in the speeches and writings of these patriots, both military and civilian. One was *Kōdō*, 'the Imperial Way', the other *Shōwa Ishin*, 'the Showa Restoration'. Both implied that the emperor had a special place in the country's political structure, though neither was precise about what he should actually do. For the rest, the Imperial Way had connotations of high moral purpose and of action to restore the traditional values of Japan, while the Showa Restoration sought to invoke the atmosphere of the mid-nineteenth century, when Japan had been beset by enemies without and by disunity within, as it seemed to be again in the 1920s and 1930s. What was needed, the nationalists maintained, was action as radical and decisive as that which had saved the country in 1868. It was to be directed on this occasion, however, against those who typified the new corruption: big business, especially the *zaibatsu*; party politicians; and the bureaucrats who worked with them. And the men who carried it out were to be modern 'men of spirit', patriots willing to use force against individuals or governments at the risk of their lives.

This aspect of nationalist thought concerned what should be done within Japan itself, but there was another which focused on the country's place in the world at large. As expressed, for example, by Ishiwara Kanji, one of the army's ablest young strategists, who taught military history at the Staff College in and after 1926, this characterized the Japanese army as the guardian of Japan's mystic *kokutai*, or national polity, and as such destined to save the world from Marxism and other Western ideologies by means of a righteous war. Japan was to appear as Asia's champion. The struggle in which she engaged would be directed ultimately against the arch-representative of capitalist corruption, the United States; but before that Armageddon came, it would be necessary first to dispose of the other powers which had long exploited Asia, namely, Britain and Russia. Indeed, such preliminary campaigns were essential to final victory: 'war', as Ishiwara saw it, 'can maintain war',[59] each successful phase contributing strength and resources for the next. It was for this reason that action ought to begin with Manchuria, he believed. Manchuria was not only the key to defence against Russia and expansion into China, but also the source of food, coal, and iron of which Japan had urgent need.

Ishiwara was not just a militarist visionary, like so many of his contemporaries, for he recognized that the task to be undertaken would require a careful marshalling of Japan's resources. The whole of the population and the economy would have to be deployed and put under strict control. For the sake of armaments, there must be central management of finance and industry; for the sake of unity, a suppression of dangerous thoughts and corruption in politics. In other words, the modern state was not to be dismantled, as Gondo Seikyo recommended, but disciplined and purified, so as to become a fit instrument to carry out Japan's 'Asian' mission. It was a formulation that attracted widespread sympathy and support.

THE MANCHURIAN INCIDENT

Towards the end of the 1920s the struggle for power between different factions and warlords in China began to impinge on Manchuria. In 1926 Chiang Kai-shek, who had taken over the leadership of the Kuomintang (Nationalist Party) two years earlier, began a series of campaigns designed to win control of the Yangtse valley and the north. By the spring of 1927 he had established his capital in Nanking, while further victories in that and the following year extended his authority towards Peking. As a result, he came into conflict with Chang Tso-lin, whom Japan had been supporting in Manchuria since 1921. A confrontation between the two appeared inevitable, threatening not only to involve Manchuria in China's civil war, but also to draw Chiang Kai-shek, if he were successful, into challenging Japan's whole position north of the Great Wall. This the Tokyo government had every desire to avoid.

The cabinet in 1927 was that of General Tanaka Giichi, who served also as Foreign Minister. In June, at a meeting of senior diplomatic and military officials which Tanaka held in Tokyo, it was agreed, as it had been several times before, that keeping Manchuria as a sphere of influence, detached from China's political instability, must remain a prime object of Japanese policy. A Kwantung Army proposal, which envisaged some form of self-government for the region under Chang Tso-lin, was set aside, but when Chiang Kai-shek visited Tokyo in November Tanaka tried to persuade him to halt any future advance at the Manchurian border. He sent troops into Shantung early in 1928, threatening Nationalist communications, to reinforce the warning. Clashes then occurred with the Chinese in Tsinan, followed by Japanese occupation – once again – of the Kiaochow–Tsinan railway.

As it became clear that the Nationalists were soon going to take Peking, Tanaka put pressure on Chang Tso-lin to withdraw from northern China into Manchuria, where the Japanese forces could give him protection. Chang reluctantly agreed. Some members of the Kwantung Army staff, however, remained dissatisfied with the move, believing that Japan needed a more direct hold on Manchuria than a puppet warlord provided. One of them, Colonel Komoto Daisaku, decided to manufacture a pretext for getting something better, and ordered men under his command to detonate a bomb under Chang Tso-lin's train on the morning of 4 June 1928 as it was approaching Mukden. Chang died from his injuries within a few hours.

The incident did not in fact trigger Japanese intervention in the Manchurian provinces, as Komoto intended, because neither Komoto's superiors nor the Tokyo cabinet were willing to authorize such a move. Komoto, indeed, barely escaped a court martial. Hence for a time the situation on the mainland returned to normal: Chang Tso-lin's son, Hsueh-liang, took over in Mukden, coming to terms with Chiang Kai-shek; and Japanese troops were recalled from Shantung. Nevertheless, Komoto's colleagues in the Kwantung Army did not abandon their ambitions. Two new staff officers took over the planning, Lieutenant-Colonel Itagaki Seishiro and the new chief of the operations section, Lieutenant-Colonel Ishiwara Kanji.

While Shidehara, back as Foreign Minister in a Minseito

cabinet – Tanaka resigned in July 1929 – resumed the discussion of Chinese tariffs and extraterritoriality, Ishiwara and Itagaki drew up contingency plans for an occupation of Manchuria, should a suitable opportunity arise. Changes that were taking place in the political climate at home because of economic crisis gave their actions urgency. The collapse in the American stock market in 1929, followed by a slump in world trade, had had a devastating effect on Japanese businessmen and farmers, especially as an ill-timed return to the gold standard in June 1929 had made the value of the yen uncomfortably high. Total exports fell from 2,513 million yen in 1929 to 1,426 million in 1931. For many small firms in the textile trade this spelt catastrophe. Farmers fared even worse. The index of raw silk prices (1914 = 100) fell from 151 to 67 in 1929–31, while rice prices, suffering from colonial competition and the effect of several years' good harvests, dropped over 50 per cent in the second half of 1930 alone. The result was to add widespread poverty in rural areas to the bankruptcies and unemployment already evident in cities. To the Minseito's opponents the lesson was clear: the government's leaders and their policies were no longer tolerable. The outcry was led by officers of the armed forces and members of the patriotic societies, to whom, after all, Japan's farmers and their villages embodied the 'national essence'.

Controversy focused first on the negotiations covering naval armament. Initial proposals for the London Naval Treaty of 1930, designed to extend to smaller warships the limitations already agreed for battleships and aircraft carriers at Washington in 1922, were opposed by Japan's Naval General Staff on the grounds that they would make more difficult – some said impossible – the task of defending the western Pacific against the United States. These objections were overruled by the Minseito cabinet, both for reasons of economy and from a wish to preserve good relations with the powers. The treaty was therefore signed and ratified. To many serving officers, not only in the navy, this decision was outrageous. That is, they held it to be unconstitutional, as well as strategically unwise. The service ministers, who were members of the cabinet, and the chiefs of staff, who were not, had separate functions, which could be broadly distinguished as administration, on the one hand, and planning on the other. It could therefore be argued that it was not within the competence of the minister – nor of his civilian colleagues in government – to overrule the chief of staff on operational matters, in which he was responsible to the emperor as commander-in-chief. The level of naval armament for defence, it was maintained, was a case in point.

The same reasoning was employed on several occasions in the next ten years to justify overseas commanders in evading or ignoring Tokyo's orders, but in 1930 the immediate repercussions were domestic. In November the Prime Minister, Hamaguchi Yuko, was shot by a youth connected with one of the lesser patriotic societies, dying of his wounds in 1931. When this did not produce any change in policy – he was succeeded by Wakatsuki Reijiro, a man of similar background and ideas – the patriots went further: Hashimoto's Sakurakai, together with some civilian extremists, planned a coup d'état, which was intended to bring about martial law and the installation of a military government. The scheme had to be abandoned in March 1931, because senior officers refused to participate, but in the autumn it was revived on an even larger scale. This time, the cabinet was to be eliminated by air attack during one of its meetings; a Guards division was to be called out in the resulting confusion; and the War Ministry was to be isolated until martial law had been declared. Although the plan was betrayed and its authors arrested in October, the patriotism of their motives duly won them lenient treatment in the courts.

It is against this background that one has to set what Itagaki Seishiro and Ishiwara Kanji were doing in Manchuria. They were convinced that Japan's position on the mainland was being seriously undermined, not only by signs that Chang Hsueh-liang might transfer his loyalty to the Kuomintang, but also by the slump in world trade, which had greatly reduced the South Manchuria Railway Company's profits. A collapse of the company, if it came to that extreme, was likely to put in peril Japan's supplies of food and important raw materials, just at the moment when the need for them was increasing because of the growth of protectionism in the world at large. What is more, Manchuria under the Kuomintang would be a threat to the Korean frontier. From a military point of view, these considerations made action imperative – and soon.

The action needed, as the Kwantung Army's staff conceived it, was the occupation of key points in Manchuria, a step which might be justified by some manufactured incident on the South Manchuria railway. During the summer of 1931 they completed plans for carrying this out, securing the co-operation of like-minded colleagues in the War Ministry and General Staff in Tokyo, as well as in army headquarters in Korea. Not surprisingly, in view of the number of men involved, rumours of what they proposed to do came to the ears of officials of the Imperial Court and members of the cabinet. Caution was urged on the high command. Early in September it was decided to send a messenger to Mukden to order the conspirators to desist, or at least delay until wider consultations could be held. Unhappily, the messenger chosen, Tatekawa Yoshitsugu, an officer on the General Staff, was himself a party to the plot; and sending word to Itagaki and Ishiwara why he was coming, he travelled slowly enough to give them time to set up their plans before his message was delivered. This they did. On the night of 18 September 1931 a bomb exploded on the railway outside Mukden. Troops were immediately moved to seize the city, and by next morning the occupation of southern Manchuria had begun. Within a matter of days reinforcements arrived from Korea, making it possible to extend operations to the whole of the three Manchurian provinces.

All this had been done, not only against the known wishes of the cabinet, but also without the authority of the army high command and possibly without that of the Kwantung Army's own commander (it is not certain how much he knew about what was ordered in his name). Yet once taken, action proved impossible to halt. The General Staff and the War Ministry, now at the most senior levels, insisted that troops already in the field must be fully supported, thus ensuring that instructions from the government to check the advance would be ignored. Indeed, the end of January 1932 saw hostilities spread to China further south, when a clash between Chinese and Japanese troops at Shanghai was followed by a naval bombardment of Nanking.

In only one respect were the civil authorities able to impose a measure of restraint. The Itagaki–Ishiwara group in the Kwantung Army had anticipated that when all was done, Manchuria would be under Japanese military rule. At this Tokyo balked, partly because it would be an affront to vested bureaucratic interests (in the Foreign Ministry, for example), partly because it would throw down the gauntlet to all the other treaty powers in China. The Kwantung Army accordingly turned instead – with cabinet acquiescence – to the kind of arrangement it had attempted several times before, namely, a puppet regime, headed nominally by a Manchu. Pu Yi, the Manchu emperor deposed in 1912, was brought out of retirement in Tientsin, to be installed as Head of State (March 1932) in what was renamed Manchukuo. Japan recognized the regime six months later. The commander-in-chief of the Kwantung Army was appointed as Japanese ambassador, responsible for the country's defence and for maintaining law and order. Japanese advisers were nominated to all key posts in the Manchukuo administration.

Meanwhile, diplomacy was doing what it could to limit the damage to Japan's international reputation. On 21 September 1931 China had appealed to the League of Nations, calling forth from Japan a denial that she had any territorial ambitions on the mainland and a promise to withdraw her troops. This, it transpired, Tokyo lacked the power to do, in view of the Army's intransigence. In due course the League appointed a commission of enquiry, chaired by Lord Lytton, whose members arrived in Yokohama early in 1932, to be met almost at once by the announcement creating Manchukuo. Nothing they saw or heard on their subsequent travels lent credence to the Japanese case that this was a spontaneous choice on the part of the region's population. Hence the report they wrote, while cautious and moderate in its tone, left little prospect that the League would find against China. When the matter came finally to debate in Geneva in February 1933, Japan chose to withdraw from the League rather than listen to condemnation.

Uchida Yasuya, her Foreign Minister, explaining this decision, argued that the fault lay in China's turbulence, not Japanese ambitions. The world, he wrote, must recognize 'that China is not an organized state; that its internal conditions and external relations are characterized by extreme confusion and complexity and by many abnormal and exceptional features; and that, accordingly, the general principles and usages of international law which govern the ordinary relations between nations are found to be considerably modified in their operation so far as China is concerned'.[60] That being so, he concluded, Japan intended to follow her own path towards order in East Asia and 'a durable peace'.

11

THE NEW ORDER IN JAPAN, 1931–1945

After the seizure of Manchuria in 1931 there was a level of turbulence in Japanese life unmatched since the decade following the treaties of 1858. Abroad there was almost constant war. Intermittent fighting went on in northern China until the summer of 1937. It then escalated into full-scale campaigns, extending to the whole of the country. Though at first expected to be brief – and not dignified by the Japanese government with the designation 'war' – hostilities in fact continued until 1945, merging during the last four years into a wider conflict, the Pacific War. This began in December 1941, when Japan attacked the United States and the colonial territories of the powers in South East Asia.

In the most general sense, the aim of Japanese policy-makers in mounting these operations was to create a Japan-dominated international order in East Asia to replace that which, as they saw it, the West had devised in the nineteenth century for its own advantage. This aspect of the period will be considered in the next chapter. Here our concern will be domestic events, which were also violent, including as they did a number of assassinations and attempted coups d'état. Most of them were carried out by patriots who sought to regenerate Japanese society, in such a way as to cleanse it of those elements of Western-style 'corruption' which had accrued since the Meiji Restoration in the search for 'wealth and strength'.

One way of looking at these political activities is to compare them with those taking place in Germany and Italy at the time, because they, too, involved a rejection of parliamentary democracy, plus the imposition of tight controls on finance and industry for the sake of building a war economy. In such a context developments in Japan have often been labelled 'fascist'. True, Japan had no charismatic dictator or genuinely one-party state, replacing the old order through an appeal to popular discontents. Nor was there any wholesale destruction of established institutions. Nevertheless, there is a broad similarity in other respects between the three regimes, sufficient to have led Maruyama Masao to describe what happened in Japan as 'fascism from above' (emphasizing the leadership's reliance on sections of the military and the bureaucracy).[61]

An alternative approach to the 1930s is the particularistic one, looking at the role of nationalism (or better, ultra-nationalism, since it was raised to a pitch at which no other values competed with it). The vocabulary of Japanese politics in these years was traditionalist: men sought authority in the emperor's divinity and a unique national polity (*kokutai*), while justifying expansion as a racial and cultural 'mission'. It is therefore tempting to characterize the confrontation in which they were engaged as being between a Japanese 'way' and one that was alien, not between political ideologies in the European sense. This is certainly how most Japanese patriots saw it at the time. It is also the view that has had the widest appeal to revisionists since the end of the war.

THE MILITARY IN POLITICS

One proposition that has been almost universally accepted by historians is that after 1930 the influence of the military in Japanese politics increased to the point of dominance. To carry the analysis further than that, however, by asking who took which decisions, and why, is to enter a quagmire. The complexities of army–navy rivalry, of competing factions within both services, of shifting allegiances over time, and of the confused relationships which existed between officers, bureaucrats, and politicians, make any summary statement hard to formulate.

In trying to clarify the situation, it is useful to begin by making a distinction between senior officers (chiefly those holding top posts in the War and Navy Ministries, the two General Staffs, and the Kwantung Army) and the so-called Young Officers, having rank as lieutenant-colonel and below at the beginning of the period, most of whom were stationed in and around Tokyo on the relevant occasions. All these men shared a belief that the armed forces had a duty to defend Japan which might in certain circumstances override that which they owed to a civilian government. A majority were convinced that the task should involve political reform as well as military efficiency. Beyond that, however, they were divided. At the highest levels – more so in the navy than the army – political activity was envisaged as being directed towards controlling the existing institutions of power, rather than destroying or radically changing them. At lower ones, whether from impatience or from revolutionary commitment, the model was more often that of the 'men of spirit' of the Meiji Restoration, that is, fanatics who were willing to use violence to make complacent seniors do their bidding.

Within the army there were in the end two factions. One, the Control faction (Tōsei-ha), had its origins in the movement for military reform instituted under Ugaki Kazushige and Minami Jiro, who successively held office as War Minister between 1929 and 1931. Its prime objective was to speed up the modernization of military structure and equipment, especially aircraft and tanks, in such a manner as to ensure greater striking power without an increase in troop numbers. Another was to prepare for the kind of national, economic, and political mobilization which modern warfare required. At the heart of the group was a staff officer, Nagata Tetsuzan. Associated with him were several of the most famous soldiers and soldier-politicians of the period after 1937: Matsui Iwane, Tojo Hideki, and Koiso Kuniaki.

Their principal rivals were the members of the Imperial Way faction (Kōdō-ha), centring on Generals Araki Sadao and Mazaki Jinzaburo, who put their trust much more in the traditional martial virtues of morale and *esprit de corps*. Politically their concern was with a comparable phenomenon, national unity, which they conceived as finding its spiritual focus in the emperor, rather than deriving from bureaucratic or parliamentary rule. It is not altogether clear how far they were prepared to countenance rebellion as a means to achieve their ends, but many patriots, both military and civilian (see chapter 10), who believed that Japan must be given a new purity and sense of purpose by another Restoration, undoubtedly looked to them as the leaders who would come forward, when a crisis gave them the opportunity, to declare martial law and reform the Japanese polity.

In the event the patriots were to be disappointed. The first of a succession of plots came in March 1931, when Hashimoto Kingoro's Sakura-kai, working with Okawa Shumei and other civilians, planned political assassinations to bring Ugaki Kazushige to power. Abandoned because of lack of support from senior officers, the plan was then revived in October as a domestic extension of the Kwantung Army's actions in Manchuria. This time Araki Sadao was the chosen figurehead, expected to emerge as leader of a military regime after removal of the existing cabinet, but premature disclosure enabled the high command to put a stop to the affair. The participants in it were only lightly punished. Indeed, one consequence was that Araki, who seems to have had no knowledge of what was being arranged on his behalf, became War Minister in December, it being widely held in government circles that some such step was needed in order to keep the hotheads within bounds.

Early in 1932 civilian extremists gave the violence a new dimension, when Inoue Nissho's blood brotherhood carried out attacks on those whom they blamed for agrarian distress. Inoue Junnosuke, a former Finance Minister, was killed in February; Dan Takuma, executive head of Mitsui, in March. Two months later (15 May) a group of young naval officers, together with a few army cadets and a handful of agrarian extremists, led by Tachibana Kosaburo, carried out extensive attacks on ministers and public offices in Tokyo, in which the Prime Minister, Inukai Tsuyoshi, was one of the victims.

The disorder which had suddenly entered Japanese political life was made very plain by the trials which followed these incidents: separate civil trials for Inoue Nissho and Tachibana Kosaburo, each with his followers; two court martials, one army and one navy, for the servicemen involved. All were public, long drawn out and wordy, the defendants being allowed to engage in fierce diatribes, sometimes lasting two or three days, against everything and everybody they thought they had reason to hate.

This was their defence, an assertion of patriotic motive. What is more, they were encouraged in it by judge and prosecuting counsel. And the sentences they received, when one considers the nature of the crimes, were minimal, ranging from four years' imprisonment for the army cadets to life for Tachibana. Such leniency did not escape the notice of others who had reason to fear attack.

The next phase of the struggle took the form, not of patriots *versus* cabinet, but of faction *versus* faction. From late 1931, with Araki as War Minister and Mazaki as Vice Chief of Staff, the Imperial Way faction was in a strong position within the army. In January 1934, however, Araki resigned because of ill health, and his successor, Hayashi Senjuro, began to fall under the influence of Nagata Tetsuzan. In July 1935 Mazaki, who had become Director General of Military Education – only the minister and the Chief of Staff were of greater consequence – was dismissed, while in the following month Nagata was murdered by Lieutenant-Colonel Aizawa Saburo, one of Mazaki's supporters. The leaders of the Control faction promptly brought Aizawa to trial.

This deterioration in the Imperial Way faction's access to senior office triggered another attempt by the Young Officers to change the course of political history. Early on the morning of 26 February 1936 a thousand men of the First Division, led by company commanders of Kōdō sympathies, took over the centre of the capital. Some attacked the official residence of the Prime Minister, Okada Keisuke, killing his brother-in-law, whom they mistook for Okada. Others murdered the Finance Minister, the Lord Privy Seal and the new Inspector General of Military Education (Mazaki's successor). Pamphlets were distributed calling for the establishment of a reformed regime, which it was hoped would be led by Mazaki. However, neither Mazaki nor Araki made any move, while the high command – at the emperor's urging – called out units of the navy and the Imperial Guards, surrounded the rebels, and invited them to surrender. They did so on the afternoon of the 29th.

This time surrender did not bring publicity or nominal sentences. Thirteen of the rebels were tried and executed in secrecy and haste, as was Aizawa; four of their civilian contacts, including Kita Ikki, met a similar fate in the following year; Araki and Mazaki were placed on the reserve (and were prevented from re-entering politics by the revival of the old rule, requiring the War Minister to be an officer on the active list, which had been abandoned in 1913). Radical Young Officers who had not been directly involved in the *putsch* were posted to the provinces or abroad.

Taken as a whole, the outbreaks of violence between 1932 and 1936 not only led to victory for the Control faction within the army – at least in Tokyo, for the situation sometimes differed overseas – but also changed the balance of power in Japanese politics. One result was to relegate the Diet parties to a position of impotence. The formation of the Minseito in June 1927, bringing together those elements in the lower house which opposed the Seiyukai, had given Japan for a time the semblance of a two-party system. The reward for electoral success, it was assumed, would henceforth be the formation of party cabinets. In July 1929 Tanaka Giichi's Seiyukai administration was replaced by a Minseito one under Hamaguchi Yuko; Hamaguchi's murder in 1930 brought a transfer of office to the same party's Wakatsuki Reijiro; and at the end of 1931, when Wakatsuki's position had been undermined by his failure to control events in Manchuria, he gave way to the Seiyukai's Inukai Tsuyoshi. That ended the sequence, however. From that time on, party leadership, weakened by assassinations and threats, showed itself unable to command the loyalty of other segments of the ruling élite – the armed forces, the bureaucracy – in what was undeniably a period of national crisis. Instead of party cabinets, there were cabinets having a proportion of party representatives, whose numbers decreased over the years. Nor did the emergence of a stronger left-wing group in the Diet materially alter things. The Shakai Taishuto (Social Mass Party), formed in 1932 to pursue an anti-communist, anti-capitalist line, polled half a million votes and won eighteen Diet seats in the 1936 election, then twice as much in 1937, but it did not win a voice in policy.

In fact, after 1932 there was a reversion to the kind of 'transcendental' cabinets that had existed earlier in the century. Their Prime Ministers were drawn for the most part from the services: Admiral Saito Makoto, 1932–4, killed as Lord Privy Seal in February 1936; Admiral Okada Keisuke, 1934–6, who escaped the same fate by chance; General Hayashi Senjuro, foisted briefly on the country by the army in 1937, in order to keep out General

Ugaki Kazushige; General Abe Nobuyuki, 1939–40; Admiral Yonai Mitsumasa in the first half of 1940; General Tojo Hideki, Japan's principal war leader, 1941–4; General Koiso Kuniaki, 1944–5; and Admiral Suzuki Kantaro for the last few months before surrender in the summer of 1945. That left room for just three others. Two were ex-bureaucrats: Hirota Koki, 1936–7, a former diplomat; and Hiranuma Kiichiro, in office during 1939, who had come into politics via the Justice Ministry. The third was a Court noble, Konoe Fumimaro, who headed cabinets in 1937–9 and again in 1940–1.

Not all the military members of this group were spokesmen for their fellow-officers. Some generals were chosen by the Genro and the Court in the hope that they might maintain the army's fragile discipline. Admirals were occasionally a compromise choice, when army and civilians were at loggerheads. Nevertheless, the rule requiring the War and Navy Ministers to be on the active list gave senior officers of the two services a collective voice in the composition of the cabinet, which they did not hesitate to use; and it was about military influence in this sense that those who still sought to preserve the Meiji settlement were most concerned.

Notable among these defenders of the established order was Saionji Kinmochi, the last survivor of the elder statesmen (Genro), whose job it had been to advise the emperor on his choice of Prime Minister from time to time. As Ito's protegé, Saionji had been twice Prime Minister early in the century. Diplomatic experience, including service as head of the Japanese delegation at Versailles, had given him close links with the Foreign Ministry, while as a member of a distinguished Court family he was on terms of intimacy with the emperor. He used these connections to ensure that the men who held posts close to the throne shared his political sympathies – Makino Nobuaki, Okubo Toshimichi's second son, who was Lord Privy Seal from 1925 to 1935, is an outstanding example – and occasionally to persuade the emperor in person to give the cabinet or military leadership a nudge. Until his death in 1940 Saionji continued by such means to do what he could to preserve both his country's membership of an Anglo-American international order and the continuation of a constitutional monarchy on the Meiji model.

Yet 'what he could' was proving to be not enough by the

middle of the 1930s. Men who were willing to use troops against the government seemed more likely to seize the emperor's person than obey those close to him. Moreover, in 1935 their civilian allies began for the first time openly to criticize Saionji and his friends, claiming that the way they used their influence was contrary to the national polity (*kokutai*). Makino resigned as Lord Privy Seal. Saionji changed course, drawing more apart from Tokyo politics and exerting himself chiefly to preserve the imperial institution against the day when 'the trend of the times' would enable it once more to perform its 'proper' role. In his judgement, this meant that the emperor, too, must be separated as far as possible from political events. He must 'absolutely not . . . participate in decision-making'. Nor must his personal opinions 'be advanced as if they were Imperial decisions'.[62]

In these circumstances, Saionji turned to another Court noble, Konoe Fumimaro, who was thought to be acceptable to the army because of his views on foreign affairs, as the man to put together a compromise that might save the monarchy. What was required was somehow – without fundamental change in political institutions – to reconcile the Control faction's plans for a 'national defence state' (*kokubō-kokka*), Imperial Way notions of the emperor's 'transcendentalism', and the desire of civil bureaucrats and politicians to keep some at least of their existing prerogatives. It was a formidable task. As it turned out, Konoe lacked the character and resolution to carry it through successfully. On the one hand, he declared himself willing 'to fight poison with poison', by which he meant giving some extremists responsibility in the hope of controlling the rest. On the other, he set out to bring bureaucrats, businessmen, and politicians into a single organization, broader than the parties, but looser in its structure than the all-embracing, one-party system that Japan's totalitarians favoured (on the German model). This was the Imperial Rule Assistance Association (Taisei Yokusankai), founded in October 1940.

Neither device gave Japan the political coherence and stability Konoe wanted. The first promoted men who in the end were willing to disregard his wishes, like his War Minister, Tojo Hideki, who was also his successor. The second proved totally unavailing as a means of imposing restraint upon the military, at least outside Japan. At home, it is true, it helped to ensure the survival in some degree of sections of the Meiji establishment: within the Imperial Rule Assistance Association, for example, party politicians still ran Diet business and retained the prestige that came from conferring legality on wartime regulations; local government officials actually increased their powers, exercising the new ones (for rationing, war savings, civil defence) largely through neighbourhood associations (*tonari-gumi*), set up in September 1940; and Tokyo bureaucrats held on to most of their time-honoured procedures and practices, sometimes using them to frustrate the aspirations of the military in the allocation of economic resources. In other words, while Japan after 1937 was subject to an uncomfortable range of controls and prohibitions, it was still too pluralistic to be fully totalitarian. Nor was it quite as militarist as the military would have liked.

DANGEROUS THOUGHTS

All countries at war engage in censorship and attempt to suppress ideas that are believed to threaten political stability, but the use of police against socialists and communists in Japan did not begin only with the outbreak of hostilities in Manchuria in 1931. Quite apart from the regulations invoked against the popular rights movement in the 1880s and trade unions in the early twentieth century – though these are relevant precedents – the Peace Preservation Law of 1925 had given the thought police (*tokkō*, under the Home Ministry) and gendarmerie (*kempei*, under the War Ministry) ample powers against any organization which advocated the overthrow of the Japanese form of government or the abolition of private property. These powers were employed in March 1928, when the police rounded up about a thousand communists and communist sympathizers. A year later a further series of raids brought in many non-communist radicals as well; and thereafter men and women of known left-wing proclivities were always liable to arrest, imprisonment, and often torture without warning or apparent cause. By 1945 over 75,000 people had been arrested under this law, though only about 5,000 were actually brought to trial. Approximately half the latter were still in custody when hostilities came to an end in 1945.

Nor was the removal of political subversives by any means the whole of what was envisaged. Araki Sadao, when War Minister early in 1934, recommended the cabinet to impose tight controls on the publication of books and newspapers for the purpose of banning 'views which would impair fundamental national policies', while encouraging those which would 'contribute to state prosperity, social order, the smooth functioning of national life, and to wholesome public entertainment'. Restraints were to be imposed on groups which 'disseminate anti-war and anti-imperialist ideas'.[63] In addition, popular hostility towards dangerous thoughts of all kinds was to be mobilized through the Military Reservists Association, the Youth Association, the Boy Scouts, the Red Cross, and various women's organizations, as well as through religious and welfare bodies.

Censorship of publishing and the press, operated by the police, grew increasingly severe in the years that followed, though with respect to books it seems to have been directed chiefly at authors well enough known to have an influence with the general public. Even so, the effect was more pervasive than such a qualification might make it seem. Self-censorship, reflecting fear of imprisonment or threats from employers, undoubtedly existed, although it is not always easy to identify. Nor was overtly political material the only thing to come under scrutiny. Tsuda Sokichi's writings on ancient history, because they dealt with the origins of the imperial line, and novels like Tanizaki Junichiro's *Sasameyuki* (translated as *The Makioka Sisters*), which implied a doubt about conventional values, were also suspect. And in the fullness of time Araki's reference to 'wholesome public entertainment' came to justify official disapprobation of jazz, of love scenes in Western drama and films, and of the American expressions which were used in baseball.

The impact of all this is difficult to judge. There is no doubt that the Japanese public was kept in ignorance of many events at home and abroad such as might show Japan in a bad light. In addition, persons who were nonconformists, or spokesmen for unpopular ideas, came under very considerable pressure. Of those arrested in this period, for example, about 1,800 were Christians, chiefly of the less orthodox and less amenable kind, like Jehovah's Witnesses. Action was also taken against some Shinto and Buddhist sects, whose beliefs were critical of the state, or war, or approved social norms, or whose practices were unduly heterodox. State Shinto, by contrast, received more government support than ever, not only on account of its relevance to the emperor's divinity, but also because it was held to be a truly Japanese type of thought, which could be used to bolster empire overseas. Holtom quotes a Japanese official in Korea, who in 1936 sought to justify an instruction that Koreans take part in Shinto ritual by the argument that this was not a religious act, but one of 'patriotism and loyalty', reflecting 'the basic moral virtues of our nation'.[64] In 1938 the Home Ministry laid it down that shrines established overseas should be dedicated to Amaterasu, the progenitor of the imperial line, not to lesser deities; they should be Japanese in architectural style, subject to variations 'suitable to climate and locality'; and should have Japanese as priests.

Where the context was directly political, the requirement for conformity was almost absolute. The Minobe affair amply illustrates this. Minobe Tatsukichi, professor of constitutional law at Tokyo's Imperial University and an appointed member of the House of Peers, was hysterically criticized in the press and Diet during 1934–5, because some of his writings had described the emperor as an 'organ' of the state, which traditionalists held to be lèse-majesté. In one sense the campaign was directed against those, including Saionji Kimmochi, who had used Minobe's theories as a defence of constitutional monarchy. More personally, it spelt tragedy for the man himself. Minobe was forced to resign from the Peers and relinquish all his honours. His books were banned. Early in 1936 he narrowly escaped assassination.

Such incidents, plus the known harshness of prison conditions and the expectation of torture at the hands of the police, help to explain the response of many other intellectuals. Often they made public declarations of *tenkō*, renouncing their former beliefs, a phenomenon described by Tsurumi Shunsuke as 'a conversion which occurs under the pressure of state power'.[65] They did not do this solely as a result of fear and hardship, though these played their part, since the statements were commonly made on leaving jail. There was also the fact that the authorities were able to bring home to a person under arrest and interrogation the extent to which he or she was out of step with almost all their fellow-Japanese, that is, to appeal to a sense of racial and national 'belonging'. A famous case was that of two communists, Sano Manabu and Nabeyama Sadachika, who in 1933 were brought to disavow the anti-imperialist elements of their creed, in so far as these might be applied to Japan. Since Japan, they explained, was leading Asia against Western capitalism, it was right that she should expand in 'backward' China and bring Manchuria, as well as Taiwan and Korea, under her sway. In such an undertaking notions of 'independence for colonies and national self-determination are outdated bourgeois ideas'.[66]

Not all Japanese radicals succumbed to pressures of this kind, though few were able to resist them when they were made particular targets. Some withdrew into intellectual seclusion, some into the more esoteric byways of scholarship, while a few continued to write critically of events in privately-produced magazines; but neither they nor the country's surviving political dissidents engaged in active protest, or created a resistance movement in Japan. One important reason for this was the weight of public and private propaganda directed towards showing that individualism and antipathy to consensus – hence liberalism, voting, confrontational politics –was unJapanese. The process began in schools, where the ethics course was more than ever concerned with showing that these things were undesirable imports from the West. Along with a heavy dose of admiration for Japan's military achievements, past and present, which was instilled through the study of history and literature, pupils were taught in the principal ethics text, *Kokutai no Hongi* (Principles of the National Polity, issued in 1937), to put nation always before self. Individuals, they were told, 'are essentially not beings isolated from the state, but each has his allotted share as forming parts of the state'. To believe otherwise, as certain Western political thinkers did, was to promote 'the setting up of an individual against an individual and classes against classes'. Indeed, the 'ideological and social evils of present-day Japan' could be attributed to the fact 'that since the days of Meiji so many aspects of European and American culture, systems, and learning have been imported, and that, too rapidly'. What was needed in their stead was something Japanese, a harmony achieved because there was 'under the emperor a body of people of one blood and one mind'.[67]

There was nevertheless a difficulty about this particular route to national unity. What Araki Sadao called 'spiritual mobilization' had its limitations. If Japan's war effort were to be effective, the rejection of Western thought could not be extended to Western science, as was evidenced by the fact that the proportion of students graduating from science and engineering departments in Japanese universities rose from 15 per cent of the whole in 1931–5 to 23 per cent in 1941–5. Nor could purely 'nativist' principles be applied to the organization of a wartime economy.

A CONTROLLED ECONOMY

The policies which did most to bring Japan out of the economic crisis caused by the slump in world trade were the work of Takahashi Korekiyo, who was Finance Minister from the end of 1931 to the beginning of 1936. His first step (December 1931) was to abandon the gold standard, in order to reduce the value of the yen and stimulate exports. During 1932 he substantially increased government spending, much of it going into agricultural relief. Coupled with a reduction in interest rates, this brought over the next few years a gradual revival in demand and hence in private investment. Agricultural production, the index for which (1925–9 = 100) was still only 103 in 1935, having fallen from 110 in 1930, began to edge upwards again. In manufacturing, the index by volume (1910–14 = 100) almost doubled between 1925–9 and 1935–9, while some sectors out-performed the average by quite large margins. In particular, the metals and machinery index moved from 255 to 920, chemicals and ceramics from 453 to 1,255. In ship-building, annual gross tonnage launched recovered from 106,000 tons in 1929–33 to 259,000 tons in 1934–7, that is, to approximately the same level as during the 1914–18 war.

Several important changes in emphasis accompanied this recovery, mostly connected with Japan's position in the world economy. The drop in the value of the yen, which made imports more expensive and exports less profitable, encouraged the country's traders to look for sources of supply where currency ratios were in their favour, and for markets where there were fewest barriers to Japanese sales. On both counts this produced a growth of trade with East and South East Asia, especially with Japanese dependencies, rather than Europe and America. By

1934–6 (the years which are usually taken as the prewar norm, since the figures for later ones are distorted by military factors) nearly 60 per cent of Japan's exports went to China, Korea, Taiwan, and the countries of South East Asia, while 50 per cent of imports came from those areas.

Another change was the more rapid growth of heavy industry within Japan, reflecting both an increase in military spending and a pattern of import substitution, designed to avoid high-priced sources of supply. There was significant development in the electrical and machinery industries, plus the growth of new enterprises in fields like aircraft and automobiles. This had the effect of bringing into existence a sector of manufacturing dominated by what were called the 'new' *zaibatsu*. The older conglomerates to which the term applied had concentrated their attention on finance and commerce, including foreign trade. They chose to defend their position when times were hard by an increasing use of cartels and similar business agreements, not by extending their activities in manufacturing. In the latter, the initiative therefore passed to newcomers, some of whom had formerly been *zaibatsu* associates – Japan Nitrogen (Nihon Chisso) had links with Mitsubishi, Toyota with Mitsui – while others, like Nissan, had emerged independently. All these were to benefit from the expansion of military industry after 1936. Nissan's automobile plant in Yokohama, for example, was completely eclipsed in importance by its stake in Manchukuo.

The victory of the Control faction in the army, committed to a programme of military modernization, together with the outbreak of full-scale hostilities in China in 1937, resulted in further economic problems and opportunities for Japan. Military spending rose from just over 9 per cent of gross national expenditure in 1933–7 to 38 per cent in 1938–42, that is, to 11,900 million yen out of a total of 31,000 million. Baba Eiichi, who took over as Finance Minister when Takahashi was killed in the attempted coup of February 1936, was quite unable to hold back the trend, which led inexorably to a balance of payments crisis. It is true that territorial expansion on the Asian mainland gave Japan access to much-needed coal and iron at feasible prices, but much of what was required – machine tools, oil, some of the rarer metals used in steel alloys – came from countries where it proved hard to increase, or even maintain, her purchasing power. That left only one recourse: to balance supply and demand by a system of planning and controls.

During 1936 and 1937 the army General Staff made the first coherent attempt to solve this problem. Ishiwara Kanji, working in conjunction with Miyazaki Masayoshi, formerly of the South Manchuria Railway Company, drafted a Five Year Plan, covering the years 1937 to 1941, which set production and investment targets for iron and steel, oil, coal, electric power, chemicals, machinery, and other industries vital to military strength. Though not finally approved by the cabinet until early 1939, its contents were widely known among officials and prompted a steady diversion of capital and resources from civilian to military use well before that date. New institutions were established to supervise the process. In the Ministry of Commerce and Industry there already existed an instrument of government intervention in the economy, used to assist recovery from slump and to strengthen Japanese firms against foreign competitors (mostly by encouraging cartels). To this was added the Cabinet Planning Board in October 1937, initially to co-ordinate the work of the various ministries concerned with the war effort in China. Its staff included military officers on secondment, as well as central government bureaucrats with appropriate economic expertise; and in 1943, as wartime difficulties grew, it was merged with the Ministry of Commerce and Industry to form the Ministry of Munitions. Members of all these bodies were expected to co-operate with Imperial Headquarters (Daihonei), which had been activated in November 1937 to concert the strategic aims – and hence the economic needs – of the army and navy.

Late in 1937 controls were instituted over capital and foreign trade for the purpose of giving priority to military requirements. The National Mobilization Law of April 1938 then put these into a wider framework of emergency powers, providing for the direction of labour and materials, the regulation of wages and prices, government operation of key industries, if required, and even a compulsory savings scheme. Some of its provisions were to remain for a time inactive, but in theory, at least, they gave the government the weapons with which to tackle all the key questions with respect to war production, resource allocation, and balance of payments.

Despite the existence of the Cabinet Planning Board, the

Japanese government machine in the 1930s lacked any central body which was capable of both identifying and enforcing economic priorities. The insistence of the army and navy, jointly and separately, that their own needs took first place; the presence at Court and in the Foreign Ministry of powerful men who disagreed with both, in that they put foreign trade before territorial expansion; the reluctance of the old *zaibatsu* and some other large firms to sacrifice their profits to what they were told was the national interest, or to bow to state interference in their businesses; all these things made life exceptionally difficult for those who tried to plan. Nor, given that all these groups had extensive political influence, which made them difficult to overbear, is it surprising that several constitutional innovations of the period were devoted to a search for unity in the making and enforcing of decisions. The Liaison Conference (Renraku Kaigi) provided a forum at which cabinet ministers could debate high-level policy with the representatives of the army and navy. The Imperial Conference (Gozen Kaigi), meeting in the emperor's presence, had a similar function, though usually with reference to critical issues. Yet much of the time the best that could be achieved, even by such distinguished gatherings, was verbal compromise, which fell apart as soon as it was put to the test of implementation.

The fact is that the situation was not capable of compromise, only of resolution, requiring a degree of authority that in the last resort was lacking. The armed forces, fighting a war in China much greater in scale than they had ever predicted, needed more and more matériel, most of which used steel. To provide it was possible only at the expense of the capital, manpower, and manufacturing capacity which might otherwise have gone to consumer industries. This in turn put two things in jeopardy. One was exports – of textiles, for example – which were Japan's only means of paying for imports of strategic raw materials (these included oil, as well as iron and coal). The other was civilian morale, which depended in part on standards of living. What is more, a conflict between short-term needs (for munitions for the China battlefield) and long-term aims (the expansion of resources for a confrontation with America and Russia) prompted disputes among the strategists themselves. In April 1941 these cross-currents reached a point where the army insisted on the arrest of some civilian members of the Cabinet Planning Board, on the grounds that by speaking up for industrialists they had revealed themselves as sympathizers of the political left.

The implications of this state of affairs for Japan's external policies will be considered in the next chapter. Here we should add by way of conclusion that wartime experiences in this context did much to determine the manner of postwar industrial development. For example, by an ordinance of August 1939 domestic manufacturers were made subject to compulsory cartels, headed by prominent businessmen under the guidance of the relevant ministry, a decision which greatly strengthened the power of bureaucrats and the conglomerates over smaller firms. Again, the need to implement controls over wages and the movement of labour brought into existence a government-sponsored programme of 'industrial service to the nation' (*sangyō-hōkoku*, abbreviated as *sampō*), under which works councils became a substitute for unions. This gave stimulus to the process by which the company, rather than the industry, was becoming the key unit for industrial relations. It also hastened the trend towards seniority wages and life employment by making them an approved alternative to strikes.

On a shorter time base, the conversion of consumer industry to war production had a sharp impact on standards of living, as it did in contemporary Europe. The resulting hardship also had significance for the postwar scene. People learnt to work harder than ever, but for less material reward. Consumer goods, like clothes and household equipment, became unobtainable in pre-1937 variety and quality. Food became scarce, because of price controls and a shortage of chemical fertilizer for the farms; queues became a normal feature of urban life; eating in restaurants and buying in black markets became a means by which the well-to-do evaded the regulations. There is at least one witness who claims that conditions were worse in Japan than in wartime Britain. John Morris, who was not repatriated until the summer of 1942, records that on his return to London 'one of the things that struck me most was the abundance of food'.[68]

12

AN EMPIRE WON AND LOST, 1937–1945

This chapter will be concerned with Japan's foreign relations in the period between 1937 and 1945, that is to say, chiefly with the New Order in East Asia and the Greater East Asia Co-prosperity Sphere, together with the wars which brought them about. To call this a phase of empire-building, though usual among historians, has not always been acceptable to Japanese opinion, either at the time or since. Some Japanese have preferred to describe it as a search for 'autonomy', because their country sought a freedom of action in East Asia which had previously been denied her, because of 'dependence' on an international order dominated by America and Britain. Others put it in the context of a cultural, as well as political, conflict between Asia and the West, in which Japan had a duty to take Asia's side.

This second approach has always posed problems of definition. Most Japanese agreed in the 1930s that equality and independence for Asian peoples should be an ingredient in whatever eventually replaced Western imperialism: hence their emphasis on 'coexistence and co-prosperity' (*kyōson-kyōei*). On the other hand, China and the other countries of East and South East Asia had, they believed, been so reduced to weakness and disunity by the events of the past hundred years that they could not in reality be treated as equal partners with Japan. Indeed, if the struggle to free them involved large-scale war, as seemed inevitable, then Japan would have to provide both the leadership for it and most of the effective force. It followed that she would need to have at her disposal for this purpose the greater part of the region's resources, whether willingly offered or not. This in turn implied that the route to Asia's independence lay through something very much akin to Japanese empire.

THE NEW ORDER IN EAST ASIA

After 1932 the staff of the Kwantung Army planned further moves into the Chinese provinces immediately south of Manchukuo. One reason was that Japan's gains in the region would never seem quite secure while the Chinese Nationalists under Chiang Kai-shek held the territory just across the border. Another was that a relatively small advance into north China and Inner Mongolia would bring a substantial increase in the reserves of coal and iron available to Japan, thereby taking her one step closer to economic self-sufficiency. On both counts the army's leaders could expect some backing from Tokyo. Certainly in the political atmosphere prevailing in the capital in the next few years (see chapter 11) it was hard to see who was likely to prevent a repetition of 1931, this time on new ground.

In the first few weeks of 1933 a pretext was found for adding Jehol to Manchukuo. In May of that year a truce at Tangku, negotiated without reference to the Foreign Ministry, created a demilitarized zone, insulating the Japanese-held areas in the north from those under Nationalist control. This move then became the basis for demanding in June 1935 that Chinese troops be withdrawn from the provinces of Hopei and Chahar in the interest of 'preserving peace'. It was a familiar form of frontier imperialism, reinforced by giving recognition to such Chinese political movements in that vicinity as might be willing to accept 'autonomy' under Japanese patronage. The most conspicuous outcome was the creation of the Hopei–Chahar Political Council in December 1935.

In Tokyo, governments tried to frame some kind of overall policy within which to set these actions. In April 1934 it was announced by a Foreign Ministry spokesman that the relationship between China and Japan was not considered to be the business of the League of Nations or of any other power. Late in

1935 there came an indication of the terms that would be acceptable for a China setlement: Chinese recognition of Manchukuo; suppression of anti-Japanese activities in China; and an anti-communist Sino-Japanese alliance. Finally, in August 1936 Tokyo approved a statement known as the Fundamentals of National Policy, from which the essential features of both the New Order and the Co-prosperity Sphere were eventually to be developed. Central to them was the elimination of 'the tyrannical policies of the powers in East Asia' and the substitution of 'cordial relations' with the peoples of the area, 'founded on the principles of coexistence and co-prosperity'. To achieve it there was to be 'a strong coalition between Japan, Manchukuo, and China', in which north China was to be a 'special region', because of its economic significance. Farther afield, Japan would extend her interests into South East Asia, though only in 'gradual and peaceful' ways.[69]

Implicit in these aims, as Japan's military leaders understood them – and they had, after all, played an important role in drafting the document – was a willingness to detach north China from the rest of that country in much the same way as Manchuria had been in 1931. However, the growing determination of the Nationalists to prevent China's fragmentation, especially after Chiang Kai-shek reached agreement with the communists at the end of 1936 on making common cause against Japan, virtually ruled out the attainment of Japanese ends without a general conflagration. It came in 1937, when an incident at Marco Polo Bridge outside Peking provoked another local clash. The Chinese refused to bow to the demands of the Japanese commander; both sides committed more troops; and since the Japanese General Staff was able to persuade both itself and its government that a rapid and total victory was possible, what had been an incident became a campaign. By the end of the year Japan had 200,000 men in the field and a new command, the North China Army, to handle them.

Once the fighting had properly begun, Tokyo, as in 1931, was in no position to prevent its escalation. By early August Tientsin and Peking had both been occupied. Hostilities then spread south, beginning at Shanghai, where there was heavy fighting, and moving up the Yangtse to Nanking. This city, Chiang Kai-shek's capital, was captured in mid-December amid the largest-scale atrocities of the war. The Chinese government thereupon withdrew to the interior, eventually to Chungking, while Japan extended a naval blockade to the whole of China's coastline. Many Chinese cities were heavily bombed, and Japanese control was established over all major political and economic centres in the lower Yangtse valley and the north, together with the transport and communication routes connecting them. During 1938 the North China Army linked up with the forces along the Yangtse; Hankow was taken; and a separate attack on south China captured Canton.

The refusal of the Kuomintang to surrender despite these reverses brought a change in Japanese tactics. Beginning in February 1939 with the occupation of Hainan, followed in June by a blockade of French and British concessions in Tientsin, a combination of political and military pressures was used in an attempt to isolate Chiang Kai-shek from any foreign help. Meanwhile, operations in China continued in a lower key. The outbreak of war in Europe in September made this plan easier to carry out, since it left the European powers in no position to disregard Japanese threats. France granted Japan access to China's southern frontiers through Indo-China; Britain temporarily closed the supply route from Burma to Yunnan. Yet Chinese resistance was still not brought to an end. In the southwest, Chiang Kai-shek kept a substantial army in the field. In the north, communist guerrillas took over much of the area outside the towns, sapping Japanese strength and pinning down sizeable forces.

The fact that fighting went on in one part of China or another until the end of the Pacific War in 1945 had a considerable impact on Japan's approach to control and integration of the region. There never was a time when she enjoyed to the south of the Great Wall the degree of stability and co-operation that existed to the north of it. Politically, she tried, as she had in Manchukuo, to establish indirect rule. However, the cabinet and the army were unable to agree on exactly what they wanted in China, or to find a figure of sufficient standing to work with them in securing it. Wang Ching-wei, formerly a senior member of the Kuomintang, came closest to it. In 1940 he was made head of a puppet regime in the Yangtse valley, but in practice was never given the kind of authority that might have enabled him to win Chinese popular support: Tokyo still toyed with the idea of a deal with Chiang Kai-shek, while Japanese field commanders were reluctant to sacrifice their local puppets for the sake of giving Wang prestige. Accordingly, China remained as fragmented under Japanese rule as it had been under the Chinese warlords.

In December 1938 Konoe Fumimaro, speaking as Prime Minister, made a public declaration about the New Order in East Asia. Japan, he said, should come to terms with 'those far-sighted Chinese who share our ideals and aspirations', as she had already been trying to do for several years. Although it was true that in bringing together Japan, China, and Manchukuo in an anti-communist league Japan must insist on certain military rights – in Inner Mongolia, for example – she did not wish to 'exercise an economic monopoly'. There must be freedom of residence and trade for Japanese subjects, but what she chiefly required was that China 'should extend to Japan facilities for the development of China's natural resources'.[70]

In the event, Japanese economic planning envisaged something a good deal more exploitative than this might seem to imply. As expressed by Ishiwara Kanji and Miyazaki Masayoshi in formulating their Five Year Plan, the intention was to create in Manchuria and north China an industrial complex, integrated with that of Japan, which would make a major contribution to the Japanese war machine. They had set separate targets for Manchukuo for the years 1937–41 in items like steel, which were to be locally produced. They had also looked to the manufacture there of arms, aircraft, automobiles, and railway rolling-stock. From north China and Inner Mongolia both Japan and Manchukuo were to secure principally coal and iron, though making it available to them would entail in addition some investment in power and transport.

The implementation of plans of this kind had begun in Manchukuo as soon after 1931 as the Japanese hold on the area was secure. A range of 'special' and 'semi-special' companies, each dominating one field of industrial activity, was entrusted with expanding the appropriate sectors of production under the overall supervision of the South Manchuria Railway Company, in which the Japanese government held half the stock. Chinese railways were taken over and the Chinese Eastern Railway was bought from Russia in 1935, in order to ensure fuller control of the movement of supplies, but in other respects development was at first disappointing. Army men tended to blame this on the fact that the railway company remained more concerned with profits than the national interest. Consequently, when hostilities with China gave added urgency to the need for munitions in 1937, matters were taken out of the company's hands. In December the Manchuria Industrial Development Company (Mangyō) was formed to assume the task of co-ordination, headed by Nissan's Ayukawa Yoshisuke, whose own concern transferred its headquarters to Manchukuo. A year later, just before Konoe's announcement of the New Order, similar companies were established in north and central China.

The result of these changes was a very substantial rise in Japanese investment on the mainland – alongside a great deal of carpet-bagging and expropriation of Chinese firms – which brought sharp increases in production, especially of coal and iron. North and central China, together with Inner Mongolia, produced nearly 23 million tons of coal and 5 million tons of iron ore in 1941–2. Manchukuo alone was eventually responsible for 20 per cent of Japan's total output of pig iron and 8 per cent of its steel. Nevertheless, these figures were lower than had originally been hoped, as were those for other kinds of industrial activity. One reason was shortages of capital and skilled manpower, which hampered every part of Japan's war effort. Another was the change in priorities after the end of 1937, when growing military commitments in China – and recognition that they might last some time – brought a greater emphasis on immediate needs, such as munitions, and less on long-term development. This meant in practice that industrial concerns within Japan got the lion's share of available finance, skills, and technology, leaving those overseas more and more to revert to their traditional task of providing raw or semi-processed materials for the metropolitan economy.

Yet, this said, the achievements were not inconsiderable. By the end of the war the southern part of Manchukuo was quite heavily industrialized, as were some areas in north China, Korea, and Taiwan. In this respect the New Order left a significant postwar heritage.

THE ROAD TO PEARL HARBOR

Ishiwara Kanji had argued that Japan's action in Manchuria was only the first stage of a struggle which would ultimately have to be waged against Russia, Britain, and the United States. His assumption was that Japan could choose her moment for each of its stages, meeting her enemies one by one. However, the invasion of China, of which he disapproved, together with world events over which Japan had no control, were to invalidate this assumption. Britain and the United States were alienated at an early date, not only by specific incidents in China, in which their ships and citizens were attacked, but still more by the fact that each had much to lose economically, if the treaty port system were destroyed. Meanwhile, Russia, uninvolved, was left free to build up her military force in Siberia and the Maritime Provinces. In these circumstances Japanese decision-makers came to believe that they had to choose between two courses, one described as 'defend to the north, advance to the south', the other, its opposite. Whichever they settled upon, the ramifications would obviously not be confined to East Asia, as the term was usually understood.

Wariness about Russia's strength and intentions was enhanced by two clashes on the long Russo-Japanese frontier on the mainland, the first of which came in July 1938 at Changkufeng (near the Manchukuo–Korea border in the north), the second in the following summer at Nomonhan (between Manchukuo and Outer Mongolia). Large forces were employed in both, including armour, and the Kwantung Army suffered on each occasion a serious reverse. This fact, plus an awareness of British and American hostility, led some groups in the army to urge a much closer relationship with Germany, in the expectation that it would serve to keep Russia in check until the China problem had been 'solved'. Japan had already moved some way in that direction by signing the Anti-Comintern Pact in November 1936, committing her publicly to co-operation with Germany against international communism. What was now envisaged was something much more positive, leading to a co-ordination of plans and a division of spoils.

The reasoning in favour of it was strengthened by events in Europe: the Russo-German non-aggression pact (August 1939);

the outbreak of war (September 1939); and the string of German victories in the spring and early summer of 1940. When Konoe's second cabinet took office in July 1940, its Foreign Minister, Matsuoka Yosuke, enthusiastically endorsed the army's ideas. He was sure of German success in Europe. From this he drew the conclusion that Japan must lose no time in negotiating about what might follow it, since the defeat of Britain, France, and Holland would leave their colonies in Asia without defence. The prospect was sufficiently enticing to overcome the qualms of other members of the cabinet, with the result that a Tripartite Pact with Germany and Italy was signed on 27 September of that year. A neutrality agreement with Russia was then concluded in April 1941, helping to remove any remaining uncertainty about the northern frontiers.

Matsuoka's calculations proved to be in several respects erroneous. Britain did not succumb to the German assault, while Hitler, having given no warning to Japan, launched an invasion of Russia in June 1941. One by-product was Matsuoka's fall. Another was a full-scale review of Japanese strategy. Some members of the inner councils now argued strongly that this was more than ever the time to strike south, since Japan's rear would demonstrably be safe. Others, including Matsuoka, maintained that Germany had created an unparalleled opportunity to secure Japan's position in the north, that is, to attack Russia's eastern provinces. On 2 July an Imperial Conference of senior ministers and service leaders, held in the emperor's presence, refused, almost predictably, to opt for one or the other. Japan would act in the north, it resolved, if the European situation still favoured such a step when the army had completed the necessary preparations, which would not be before September; but the alternative would be kept open in the interval by occupying positions in the southern half of Indo-China. This action, which began at the end of the month, in fact set in train the moves which were to lead to war in the Pacific before the end of the year.

Behind the government's uncertainty there lay a fundamentally economic dilemma. Although control of north China and Manchukuo had done much to ensure supplies of coal and iron, there were other raw materials, vital to modern war, which the regions adjacent to Japan did not produce. Oil was the most notable of these, but the list also included rubber, tin, tungsten, chrome, and nickel. What is more, war in Europe had increased the world demand for all of them, raising prices and making them more difficult to obtain, especially for a country like Japan, which was short of bullion and foreign currency. Of the possible sources of supply, one was the United States, to which Japan turned chiefly for scrap metal and petroleum. Another was South East Asia. Since the South East Asian territories in question were mostly colonies, their resources were in the first place at the disposal of their respective metropolitan states. This implied that any determined attempt to divert their output to Japan carried a risk of international confrontation on a major scale. And if an advance into South East Asia also brought Japan into open conflict with America, there was the further danger that the warfare would reach a level at which even domination of South East Asia would not be enough to sustain it.

In October 1939 the Cabinet Planning Board carried out a study which concluded that the country's growing demands for strategic materials made it necessary 'to bring within our economic sphere areas on the East Asian mainland and in the southern region'.[71] Preferably, as the Fundamentals of National Policy had indicated three years earlier, this was to be achieved by diplomatic pressure, accompanied by financial support for Japanese firms engaged in the enterprise, but in the months that followed, as it became more and more certain that the European powers were in no position to resist, attitudes hardened. In August 1940, when negotiation of the Tripartite Pact was already under way, Matsuoka Yosuke spoke publicly for the first time of creating a Greater East Asia Co-prosperity Sphere, which would be 'the same as the New Order in East Asia', except that it was to include 'areas such as the Netherlands Indies and French Indo-China'.[72] Koiso Kuniaki, who was Colonial Minister, warned that Japan's role in such a sphere must be more than economic, since it would involve 'guidance' of the internal affairs of the relevant countries and military protection of their lands. This was presumably to be on the lines of what was being done in China and Manchukuo. On the other hand, another Planning Board document, dated only a few days after Matsuoka's statement, still identified the aims of Japanese policy, if not its methods, as being economic: unrestricted export to Japan of the materials she required; special Japanese rights in trade, transport, and communications; and a number of mining concessions. In other words, there was not at this stage an agreed plan, identifying precisely what should be done.

It proved none too difficult to browbeat the French in Indo-China into granting facilities for Japanese troops and aircraft there, notionally for use against China. This came in September 1940. In May 1941 the French conceded economic privileges as well. The Dutch in Indonesia, however, were much more stubborn. Throughout the autumn and winter of 1940–1, backed by America and Britain, they rejected Japanese demands for larger quotas of oil, making it evident to Tokyo that nothing short of force would move them. Against this background the Konoe government decided in July 1941 to send substantial forces into southern Indo-China, which was an indispensable springboard for action farther south.

The result was sharply to worsen Japan's relations with the United States. These had been deteriorating ever since the beginning of 1940, partly because of Japanese expansion in Asia, partly because of Washington's hostility to the Axis, which spilled over to Germany's partner, Japan. Licences were introduced for exports of some types of oil and scrap iron to Japan in July 1940, that is, as soon as the situation in Europe became desperate for Britain; there was an embargo on all scrap metal from September; and this was extended to iron and steel exports after the presidential elections in November. There was then a lull of several months until the occupation of southern Indo-China, but this at once brought a freeze on Japanese assets in the United States (26 July 1941) and a complete embargo on oil exports (1 August). Since the Dutch soon followed suit with a ban on exports of oil and bauxite, Japan's planners now faced crisis. To seize what oil there was in Indonesia seemed likely on existing evidence to precipitate American intervention, while not to do so would quickly reduce stocks to the point where an 'advance to the south' became impossible. For Japan, in fact, time was running out. A decision for war, both services agreed, had to be made within weeks, if it were ever to be made at all.

Japan and the United States had for some months been engaged in direct negotiations, though the exchanges in April, May, and June 1941 had done no more than clarify their differences. Washington sought an undertaking that Japan would respect the territorial integrity of her neighbours, including China and the Philippines; that she would pursue her policies by peaceful means; and that she would guarantee equality of economic opportunity (the Open Door) in the areas under her control. Japan wanted a settlement with China on the terms she had stated previously – which she believed America had encouraged the Chinese Nationalists to refuse – plus access to the raw materials she needed, especially oil. Neither side gave any sign of giving way. In August Konoe tried unsuccessfully to break the deadlock by proposing a personal meeting between himself and President Roosevelt. When this was rejected as a futile gesture, he sent a special envoy, Kurusu Saburo, to give greater weight to the efforts of his Washington ambassador.

In Tokyo, meanwhile, staff officers were considering the alternatives to diplomacy. The state of stockpiles and the climatic conditions to be expected in South East Asia led them to believe that a drive to the south should start no later than December. Preparations for it would have to begin some two months earlier than that (and were irreversible, in the sense that Japan already had too little oil to make the necessary dispositions twice). October, therefore, was the moment of decision. When that month came, however, the country's leadership was still divided. The services saw no alternative but to go ahead in South East Asia. The civilians, or some of them, were adamantly against a war with the United States. Konoe resigned, naming as his successor the War Minister, General Tojo Hideki, whom he believed had the standing to resolve the disagreements.

On 5 November the Tojo cabinet gave its negotiators one last chance to secure acceptance of Japanese demands by Washington. When this failed, the die was cast. A formal statement breaking off relations was prepared for transmission to the American government – it was intended to arrive just before the first hostilities, but a combination of excessive security consciousness and secretarial inefficiency delayed its delivery until after they began – while the final preparations were made for an initial series of attacks. These were directed first against the bases from which American or British forces might be able to interdict an assault on South East Asia: an air strike against the American Pacific fleet's Hawaiian base, Pearl Harbor, carried out by planes from a naval carrier force on the morning of Sunday 7

December 1941, which left eight battleships sunk or damaged and large numbers of aircraft destroyed on the ground; and simultaneous raids, equally successful, on targets in Wake, Guam, Midway, the Philippines, and Hong Kong. A few days later a British battleship and battlecruiser, operating from Singapore, were sunk by aircraft off the coast of Malaya.

These operations, carefully planned and brilliantly executed, signalled the start of land campaigns in South East Asia. Hong Kong was forced to surrender on Christmas Day. Landings in Luzon brought the capture of Manila on 2 January 1942, followed quickly by the occupation of the whole of the Philippines (except for Bataan, where an American force held out until the beginning of May). Other Japanese troops landed on the east coast of Malaya, crossed the Kra isthmus, then advanced down both sides of the peninsula, taking Kuala Lumpur on 11 January and Singapore – supposedly impregnable – on 15 February. This freed men for an invasion of the Netherlands Indies, where the Dutch surrendered on 9 March, and on Burma, most of which was overrun by the end of April. At this point, Japan dominated an area from Rangoon to the mid-Pacific, from Timor to the Mongolian steppe. She had also taken many thousands of American and European prisoners of war. All were to be harshly treated in the next three years, as were their Asian counterparts, while a considerable number suffered torture and execution.

THE CO-PROSPERITY SPHERE

Public statements about the nature of the Co-prosperity Sphere, made before the outbreak of war, tended to be more idealistic than practical. Even Tojo Hideki, speaking as Prime Minister to the House of Peers in January 1942, used language that was vague about the long-term future. The object of the war, he said, was to establish 'an order of coexistence and co-prosperity based on ethical principles with Japan serving as its nucleus'. Burma and the Philippines might ultimately be given their independence, but areas which were 'absolutely essential for the defence of Greater East Asia' – Hong Kong and Malaya both came in that category – would remain under Japanese rule, while the Netherlands Indies would be treated 'with full understanding for their welfare and progress'.[73] What was meant by this might be judged from a Liaison Conference decision of 20 November 1941, that Japan should avoid 'premature encouragement of native independence movements'.[74]

Initially the territories conquered by Japan were under the supervision of military government sections attached to the various army and navy headquarters in the occupied areas, reinforced in the spring of 1942 by the addition of a number of civilians as political and economic advisers. In the districts for which they were responsible military government officers were instructed to make as much use as possible of existing administrative organizations – mostly colonial ones, stripped of their Western officials – and to try to win popular support without conceding any real authority. They proved to be generally suspicious of the Chinese communities in South East Asia. By contrast, they showed favour to anti-British nationalists in Burma, to Malay sultans, and to Muslims in both Malaya and Indonesia. In some countries they were able to find puppet leaders, as they had in China: Ba Maw, who became head of a Japanese-sponsored regime in Burma; Jorge Vargas in the Philippines. Thailand retained its existing political regime and a nominal independence, though it signed a treaty of alliance with Japan. Indo-China was still recognized as French, despite the presence of a Japanese occupation force.

In November 1942 this varied structure was put under the aegis of a new central body, the Greater East Asia Ministry, though army and navy officers, who were responsible to Imperial Headquarters, continued to have an important part in running it until the end of the war. This step, which brought together the Colonial Ministry and various special agencies dealing with occupied China, Manchukuo, and other areas to form a single body, was opposed by the Foreign Ministry, partly out of bureaucratic pique, but also because the diplomats foresaw, more clearly than the generals and admirals, the difficulties that would arise in persuading the peoples of the Sphere that they were not part of an 'empire', if their affairs were handled alongside those of colonies and other dependencies.

The Foreign Ministry proved right about this, the more so when the fighting turned to Japan's disadvantage. By the middle of 1943 it was evident that she was on the defensive. Hence there was perceived to be military value in any measure that might reduce unrest – of which there was a great deal, especially in Malaya and the Philippines – and gain positive support from non-Japanese peoples. Accordingly, Burma and the Philippines were made 'independent' in August and October 1943, respectively – subject to the authority of a Japanese ambassador, much as in Manchukuo – at the price of declarations of war against Britain and the United States. In Malaya and Indonesia modest political rights were granted to the local population (which was not told that a decision had been taken to keep both territories indefinitely Japanese). Wang Ching-wei's regime in China, which had declared war on Japan's enemies in January 1943, was rewarded by abolition of some Japanese privileges in the old treaty ports. Finally, a conference of heads of state and political leaders from countries within the Sphere was held in Tokyo in November of that year. Tojo's speech of welcome made much of the 'spiritual essence' of Greater East Asia, which he contrasted with the 'materialistic civilization' of the West. The members of the conference responded by pledging solidarity in pursuing the Great East Asia War.

Despite this, there was a good deal of reluctance among the peoples of the Sphere to accept what they saw as Japanese domination. In the north it had proved possible for Japan to appeal to a shared Chinese tradition, notably the Confucian element in it, as a basis on which conservatives, at least, could co-operate with her against those, like the Kuomintang and the communists, who rejected much or all of what that tradition stood for. The Concordia Association (Kyōwakai) in Manchukuo and the New People's Society (Hsin-min Hui) in China were both formed to exploit such sentiment, which was reinforced by privileges (jobs, rations, housing) made available to their members. In South East Asia there was no equivalent lever. Confucianism existed among the overseas Chinese, but they were politically suspect as long-time supporters of Chiang Kai-shek. Showing favour towards Buddhist and Muslim groups was useful as a weapon against Western influence, but did not obviously consolidate opinion behind Japan. Introducing Shinto, together with a knowledge of the Japanese language, as was widely attempted, simply added an extra ingredient to the cultural mix, more likely to provoke resentment than induce conformity.

Nevertheless, economic discontents created more political disturbance than cultural ones. Japan's broad intention, as set out by the Cabinet Planning Board at the end of 1939, had been to establish in south China and South East Asia a Japanese special interest zone within which it would be possible to secure not only strategic raw materials, but also export markets, earning foreign currency. The fact of war distorted this plan in a number of ways. For one thing, it gave Japan's war needs absolute priority, no matter what the cost to the region's economic structure and standards of living. As a government document of November 1941 had stated, the hardship 'imposed upon native livelihood as a result of the acquisition of resources vital to the national defence . . . must be endured'.[75] In accordance with this policy, military government sections diverted to Japan all available supplies of oil and other strategic materials; channelled investment towards increasing production of them; ensured that local consumption of such items was reduced by banning their use as far as possible in South East Asian industries; and gave priority in shipping and other transport for their shipment to Japan.

A further economic distortion was caused by the fact that those types of product which had been developed in Malaya, Indonesia, and the Philippines for export to Western markets, such as tea, coffee, sugar, even tin, were now cut off from their previous customers. They found Japan's 'industrial heartland' to the north no sufficient substitute. Nor was a Japanese war economy, in which the consumer industries were being starved of capital and raw materials, in any position to meet the return demand for goods in southern areas, previously met by the West. One response to this problem was an attempt to divert production in South East Asia away from 'plantation' exports towards food and other necessities, that is, to increase the region's self-sufficiency. Even that, however, required a level of fresh investment which was often not forthcoming.

Several factors arising from this situation contributed to a drop in standards of living for South East Asian peoples. Despite an increase in the operations of those Japanese firms, such as Mitsui and Mitsubishi, which had long had a stake in mining and foreign trade – there was no attempt to set up new 'national policy' industries for the region, as there had been in north China and Manchukuo – there was a decline in the level of general economic activity which was reflected in shortages of food and consumer goods. This, plus widespread use of military scrip, led to inflation. Prices rose, while wages were controlled. Unemployment spread. War damage, originally caused in the process of conquest (including a 'scorched earth' type of defence in certain areas), was extended by enemy air and submarine attacks, disrupting communications. The results were a destabilization of the economy and a considerable degree of popular discontent, manifested in nationalist movements, or even in guerilla warfare in places where Japanese attempts to suppress it were exceptionally harsh. This made the reimposition of Western colonial control at the end of the war wellnigh impossible, though not in the way Tokyo had intended. It also made the Co-prosperity Sphere of only limited value to the Japanese war effort.

DEFEAT

There had always been reasons to doubt the durability of Japan's military success. Her merchant fleet was only just large enough to sustain a maritime empire on the scale envisaged in 1941, even if all went well. As it was, the unexpected severity and effectiveness of American attacks on Japanese commercial shipping – three-quarters had been sunk by 1945 – coupled with the inability of Japanese shipbuilders to replace the losses, largely because of shortage of steel, put the whole enterprise at risk. Japan also lacked the military manpower for the task she had undertaken. The conquest of South East Asia had been accomplished by remarkably few troops, but the need to guard against a Russian incursion into Manchukuo tied down many more, as did garrison duties everywhere. There were costly campaigns in China against both Nationalists and Communists, while fighting in Burma along the frontier with British India was another significant call on available reserves. By the later stages of the war the armed forces had drained the country of men, even of youths, and still demanded more. It has been estimated that some 2·3 million Japanese servicemen and civilians died from war-related causes between 1937 and 1945.

It was in the Pacific, however, where the land fighting was by comparison on a minor scale, that the decisive engagements were fought. In the ocean areas naval air power quickly became a crucial factor. Thanks largely to the American aircraft carriers, which had escaped at Pearl Harbor, Japanese thrusts towards Australasia and Hawaii were foiled in the naval battles of the Coral Sea in May 1942 and of Midway a month later. Thereafter American forces under the command of Admiral Chester Nimitz evolved a new pattern of warfare by which to push the Japanese westward. Called 'island-hopping', it involved bringing together land, sea, and air forces in overwhelming strength to isolate and seize small island targets, which could then be used as bases to cover the next similar advance. Japanese garrisons outside the chosen targets were left in possession of their 'real estate'. In November 1943 the technique was applied in the Marshall Islands, the key point, Kwajalein, being captured in February 1944. Saipan in the Mariana Islands followed (mid-June to early July 1944), a full fleet action, the battle of the Philippine Sea, being fought to cover the landing force. Guam fell in August, the Palau group in September, thus completing an 'advance' of over two thousand miles in less than a year.

In the southwest Pacific, where General Douglas MacArthur had the command, warfare was more orthodox. Japan's first serious repulse, following the successful defence of southern New Guinea by Australian forces during 1942, came with the American capture of Guadalcanal in February 1943 after six months' bitter fighting. Subsequently there was steady progress through the islands and along the north coast of New Guinea, culminating in September 1944 with landings on Morotai, half-way to Mindanao. A month later came an assault on Leyte, which was occupied by the end of December, then an invastion of Luzon in January 1945. Manila was taken at the beginning of February. Coupled with the capture of Saipan six months earlier, this made it possible for the two prongs under Nimitz and MacArthur to join for a drive against the Japanese home islands. Meanwhile, in Burma the land forces of Lord Louis Mountbatten's command had also taken the offensive, reopening communications with China via the Burma Road in January 1945 and taking Mandalay in March.

Defeats on this scale had important results within Japan, where Tojo Hideki became more and more isolated politically. He resigned under pressure in July 1944. His replacement, General Koiso Kuniaki, was a man equally determined to pursue the struggle, but he faced a military situation that was deteriorating rapidly. What was left of Japan's fleet was almost destroyed in the battle of the Leyte Gulf in October 1944. She already had too few aircraft to defend the homeland properly, and attacks on industry by land-based bombers from Saipan severely hampered her attempts to build more. The American capture of Iwojima in March 1945 made the work of the bombers easier still. Rangoon fell in May to Mountbatten. A few weeks later Okinawa fell to the Americans. Koiso had by this time resigned, making way for an aged and much respected admiral, Suzuki Kantaro, who was known privately to favour a negotiated peace.

He was by no means alone in this. Former diplomats like Shigemitsu Mamoru and Yoshida Shigeru had begun to think in terms of a possible settlement as early as 1943. As the war situation grew worse during 1944 they won over a number of persons close to the emperor to their views, including Konoe Fumimaro, and were influential in getting rid of Tojo in July. Their next step was to make secret overtures to Russia – still technically neutral in the Pacific War – in the hope of persuading Stalin to mediate with the United States and Britain; but before they could make any headway in the face of Russian delays, the allied leaders, meeting at Potsdam, issued a declaration (26 July 1945) calling for Japan's unconditional surrender. It was to be followed, the statement said, by demilitarization, military occupation, and loss of territory.

So discouraging a prospect did not immediately bring a weakening of will in Japan, so much as an apparent closing of the ranks behind those who called for resistance *à l'outrance*. This was a policy of despair, however, for the country had little left with which to fight. Since the end of 1944 the only possibility of counter-attack by air against the American fleet had come to depend on the special attack corps, known as *kamikaze*: suicide bombers who set out to crash their antiquated planes on American ships. They caused a good deal of damage during the Okinawa campaign, but not to the extent of affecting the outcome. Nevertheless, it was planned in Tokyo that they should be a major element in defence against invasion, together with other suicide units, which would use midget submarines, human torpedoes, and high-speed boats. Facilities for preparing such weapons were given priority, the factories entrusted with the task being as far as possible moved underground to escape the bombing. Supplementing the defence was to be a volunteer fighting corps organized among civilians – all men from 15 to 60 and women from 17 to 40 were required to join – to engage in guerilla action against any enemy who landed on Japanese soil.

The American air assault on Japan contrasted greatly with these desperate and makeshift measures. Heavy bombers, which had attacked munitions and aircraft factories in the last months of 1944, extended their targets from the spring of 1945 to other industrial and transport centres. In addition, there were huge fire-bomb raids on cities, designed to break civilian morale. The most devastating of these was made on Tokyo on 9 March 1945, leaving 120,000 of its inhabitants killed or injured, but nearly all Japan's large cities, except Kyoto, suffered heavily. Still more so did Hiroshima, where a single atomic bomb, dropped on 6 August, caused perhaps 50 per cent more casualities than the incendiaries on Tokyo. Since this failed to produce immediate Japanese surrender, another similar bomb destroyed a large part of Nagasaki three days later.

On 8 August Russia declared war on Japan, an act designed to influence Japan's leaders to accept the Potsdam terms, as well as to open the way for Russian gains on the mainland. Despite this blow, the War Minister and the two service Chiefs of Staff continued to resist the calls for peace. By so doing they produced a deadlock at the Imperial Conference, which only the emperor was able to resolve. He first ruled in favour of those who urged surrender, subject to a reservation of the imperial prerogatives; but when this condition was ignored by the allies, he intervened again to make surrender unconditional. These discussions took up several days. It was therefore 15 August before the decision was made public in Tokyo.

Throughout the period since 1931 the army had shown more respect for the emperor's status than for his opinions. August 1945 was to prove no exception. On the night before the surrender announcement, officers from the War Ministry and army General Staff broke into the palace in an unsuccessful attempt to find and destroy the recording in which the emperor was to give the news to the nation. Others set fire to the homes of the Prime Minister and President of the Privy Council. When all this failed to reverse the decision, many, including War Minister

Anami Korechika, committed suicide. It was in this turbulent atmosphere that orders were given for a cease-fire on 16 August and a new government, headed by an imperial prince to give it greater moment, took office to see that they were carried out. On 2 September members of it signed the instrument of surrender aboard the American flagship in Tokyo Bay.

13

MILITARY OCCUPATION, 1945–1952

The language in which the Japanese emperor told his people of the decision to surrender was elliptical in the extreme. 'Despite the best that has been done by everyone,' he said, '. . . the war situation has developed not necessarily to Japan's advantage'. In order to avoid further bloodshed, perhaps even 'the total extinction of human civilization', Japan would have to 'endure the unendurable and suffer what is insufferable'.[76]

What this meant in practice was very soon made clear. The appearance of American airborne forces in Tokyo and of an allied fleet at anchor off Yokosuka, the orders given to Japanese troops overseas to lay down their arms, and to those in Japan to disperse quietly to their towns and villages, brought home vividly the reality of defeat. Japan was for the first time under foreign military occupation. In the Tokyo–Yokohama area the population stayed as much as possible indoors, fearing atrocities and reprisals. Everywhere they found their country's administration, like its economy, in chaos: production at a standstill; few trains; less road transport; hardly any food, at least in the cities. To a nation that had for weeks been exhorted to prepare itself for a last-ditch stand, the change was bewildering, notwithstanding the bombing and the other signs of disaster which had multiplied on every side for the previous year. The war's ending brought a sense of relief, therefore, but also a shock of disillusion. In its train came a dull apathy, evident in the way people walked, in the silence of the streets, in the conscientious provision of entertainment for the conqueror.

So sharp was the break with what had gone before that one is tempted to treat September 1945 as the end, not of a chapter, but of a story, making all that followed part of a fresh beginning. Indeed, in many ways it was. Defeat acted as a catharsis, exhausting the emotions which the Japanese had hitherto focused on their relations with the outside world. It also opened the way for radical changes in social and political institutions, imposed by the victors. Yet this change of direction can be overstated. Once the shock wore off, and the Japanese again began to take the initiative in directing their own affairs, they gave to the new something of the attitudes and the personalities of the old: less of America of the 1940s, more of Japan of the 1920s and 1930s. The result is that in many contexts one can trace today a far greater continuity with the recent past than would at one time have seemed possible.

THE POSTWAR POLITICAL SETTLEMENT

The policies to be followed in occupied Japan were worked out by the American government after a minimum of consultation with its allies. Their basic purpose, as stated in a directive sent to the allied commander in Japan at the beginning of November 1945, was to ensure 'that Japan will not again become a menace to the peace and security of the world', and could eventually be readmitted 'as a responsible and peaceful member of the family of nations'. The steps to be taken to this end were to include 'the abolition of militarism and ultra-nationalism in all their forms; the disarmament and demilitarization of Japan, with continuing control over Japan's capacity to make war; the strengthening of democratic tendencies and processes in governmental, economic, and social institutions; and the encouragement and support of liberal political tendencies.'[77]

The implementation of this policy was in all vital respects an American undertaking, though a small British Commonwealth force, mostly Australian, shared the military tasks. There was an elaborate façade of international control under a Far Eastern Commission in Washington, on which were represented all the countries that had fought against Japan, but authority in Tokyo rested firmly in the hands of General Douglas MacArthur, the Supreme Commander for the Allied Powers (SCAP). As American commander-in-chief in the area he took orders only from the United States government, through which the decisions of the Far Eastern Commission were transmitted to him; and a natural tendency for the distinction between his 'allied' and 'American' functions to be blurred left him a good deal of discretion in carrying those decisions out. This was especially so because the various international committees supposed to be advising him were often deadlocked.

To assist him, the Supreme Commander had a considerable staff, both military and civil, forming a bureaucracy nearly as complex, if not so large, as that of Japan itself. Few of its members had much knowledge or experience of the country they had to govern. This led them at times to transplant American institutions to Japan, not because they were appropriate, but because they were familiar. Moreover, they lacked the means by which to ensure that SCAP directives were put fully into effect. It was a basic assumption of post-surrender policy that the occupation authorities would work through a Japanese government, not try to rule direct; but the difficulty of checking on that government's operations, because of a shortage of trained allied personnel – to say nothing of genuine misunderstandings, which arose from differences of political culture – made for many divergencies between intention and result.

The most immediate task was that of dismantling the Japanese war machine. Military supplies and installations were destroyed and over two million men were demobilized at home. Another three million, plus as many civilians, were repatriated from overseas as a consequence of the allied decision to deprive Japan of all the territorial gains she had made since 1868. This included both the Ryukyu and the Kuril islands. In addition, those Japanese who were identified as war criminals were put on trial. Twenty-eight political leaders, accused of planning and initiating an unjust war, were brought before an international tribunal in Tokyo between May 1946 and November 1948. Seven, including Tojo Hideki, were condemned to hang, and eighteen to prison sentences; two died during the trial; another suffered mental collapse. Twenty senior officers of the armed forces, who had commanded in areas where atrocities occurred, were also arraigned, though only two were found guilty and executed, while thousands of their juniors were charged with individual acts of cruelty and murder, both at home and abroad. In Yokohama alone 700 were sentenced to death and another 3,000 to various terms in prison.

As to politics, the peerage, being undemocratic in American eyes, was abolished. That apart, all those whose close connection with the old order was thought likely to make them enemies of the new were removed from public life, that is, from key posts in government, education, press and radio, even certain businesses. A few of them were selected personally on the basis of their records. Most were identified simply by the jobs they had held, a method which was easy to operate, but not always just. This 'purge', as it was called, starting in January 1946, affected over 200,000 persons, making heavy inroads into the Japanese leadership. By way of corollary, an amnesty was announced in October 1945, by which all those who had tried unsuccessfully to oppose the prewar and wartime governments in Japan – communists, socialists, and liberals of every shade – were freed from gaol or other personal restraints.

Since it was widely held that the great financial and industrial conglomerates, the *zaibatsu*, had not only played an important part in bringing about the war, by which they had profited, but were also a barrier to domestic competition, hence to 'economic democracy', they, too, became targets of action by SCAP. Starting in November 1945, orders were given to dissolve the family holding companies which bound together their various components, so releasing the latter to engage in business on their own account. Shares of the holding companies were then sold to the public, providing compensation (at levels quickly eroded by inflation) to their former owners. An anti-monopoly law was passed in April 1947 to prevent the emergence of any comparable successors. However, an attempt at the end of that year to impose further legal restrictions on excessive business concentrations aroused such fierce opposition in Japan (and to some extent in America) that it was never put properly into effect.

The position of the emperor posed a special problem. Many people outside Japan – and some at home, notably Marxists – called for him to be tried as a war criminal, or forced to abdicate, on the grounds that he had been party to the decisions taken in the 1930s. To this there were two objections. One, advanced by conservatives in Japan and a handful of foreigners who knew the country well, was that by constitutional convention the emperor was required to confirm any decision that was presented to him as having the support of his principal advisers. Only when the senior members of his government were irretrievably divided, as had happened over surrender, could he make a personal choice between the courses they proposed. This was in substance true, though the case was often overstated. The other argument, which was that of expediency, appealed more strongly to the occupation authorities and the American government. Sentiment attaching to the emperor was clearly very strong in 1945. To offend it by seeming to make him a martyr – most Japanese saw the fate of the 'political' war criminals as a necessary sacrifice for their country's sake – might arouse such resentments as would make Japan impossible to govern. Hence Washington ordered SCAP to work through existing political institutions, 'including the emperor', in order to ensure 'a minimum commitment' of American forces. General MacArthur in turn opposed any attempt to bring the emperor to trial, because to do so might cause 'a tremendous convulsion among the Japanese people', which would negate all prospects of indirect rule.[78]

It did not follow from this that the United States would accept any Japanese postwar government at all, regardless of its membership, as being satisfactory for its purposes. The first (August to October 1945) was not of significance in this context, since it was no more than a caretaker cabinet, having an imperial prince as Prime Minister. The next, lasting until May 1946, was led by Shidehara Kijuro, an anti-militarist liberal who had twice been Foreign Minister before 1931. His record made him respectable, but he lacked a parliamentary following, so there were doubts about whether he qualified under the terms of the instructions to MacArthur, which had required him to establish a government 'in accordance with the freely expressed will of the Japanese people'. For this among other reasons, efforts were made during the winter of 1945–6 to promote the formation of new political parties, from which an elected leadership might emerge. The two most influential were the Liberals (Jiyuto) and Progressives (Shimpoto), largely composed of experienced men from the prewar Seiyukai and Minseito. Both were conservative in varying degrees. However, they were soon hard hit by the purge, especially the Progressives, who lost 243 of their 270 Diet representatives because of it. Slightly to the left of these two groups was an uneasy combination of socialist and non-socialist moderates, the Social Democratic Party. Farther to the left again were the Communists, given greater cohesion by the return to Japan in January 1946 of Nosaka Sanzo, who had worked with the Comintern in Russia, then in China with Mao Tse-tung. There were also all sorts of small, local parties, their numbers estimated at over three hundred by the spring of 1946, representing everything from the lunatic fringe to ambitious but unaffiliated individuals.

In an election held in April 1946 the Liberals won a plurality of seats in the lower house (140 to the Progressives' 94), but their leader, Hatoyama Ichiro, was promptly purged by SCAP. The party's presidency then passed to Yoshida Shigeru, an ex-diplomat, serving as Foreign Minister in Shidehara's cabinet. Yoshida was a conservative much alarmed by the threat from communism in a country almost destroyed by war, and willing for that reason to accept a degree of reform under American tutelage as a defence against it. He became Prime Minister in May, holding office for a year, during which the Progressives were dissolved and the moderate right was reorganized as the Democratic Party (Minshuto), led by Ashida Hitoshi. The outcome was a split in the conservative vote in the 1947 elections. It dislodged Yoshida, enabling Ashida to take the Democrats into an alliance with the Socialists under Katayama Tetsu, who formed a coalition government; but this in turn disintegrated in October 1948, making way once more for the Liberals, who confirmed their position in the election of January 1949 by winning a clear majority – the first since the war – with 264 lower house seats. The Democrats, reduced to 69 representatives, now showed signs of dividing into a parliamentary right and a Marxist left; the Communists, profiting from Nosaka's insistence on 'peaceful revolution', made important gains (35 seats); and Japanese politics began to take on its characteristic postwar pattern, that is, a conservative majority, facing a fragmented left-wing opposition. Yoshida was able to exploit the situation to stay in power until December 1954.

DEMOCRACY BY DECREE

In his memoirs Yoshida was dismissive about his achievements in 1946–7. 'I do not recall the Cabinet doing anything tangible enough to merit recording here in detail', he wrote.[79] This is a remarkable statement, when one considers that these were the months which saw the working out of almost all the major reforms introduced by the occupation. No doubt it reflects Yoshida's distaste for much of what was done, as well as his estimate of the part played by Japanese in doing it. Certainly it serves to point the difference between those reforming members of American GHQ, who saw Japanese society as being by nature militarist and 'feudalistic', needing fundamental change, and those senior Japanese politicians and officials, to whom the years since 1930 had been an aberrant interlude, calling for nothing more than the restoration of things as they were before it. In 1946–7 the former had their way. After 1951 Yoshida set out to push the pendulum back a little.

Central to the introduction of democracy, as required by Washington, was a new constitution to replace that of 1889, which would strengthen the position of the elected Diet and eliminate the power of the military and the Imperial Court. In the winter of 1945–6 the Japanese authorities responded slowly and half-heartedly to indications that they should produce a draft along these lines. Accordingly, SCAP officials took it upon themselves to do so in their stead. Their version, foisted on a reluctant Japanese cabinet, was made public in March 1946; considered and in a few respects amended by the Diet and the Privy Council during the summer; promulgated in the emperor's name on 3 November; and brought into force from 3 May 1947. It provided that the Diet was still to be bicameral, but both houses were to be elected by universal adult suffrage: a House of Councillors of 250 members, half standing for election every three years (three-fifths were to represent prefectures, the rest a single national constituency); and a House of Representatives of 467 members (later enlarged in step with population growth), drawn from 118 multi-member electoral districts. The lower house, like the British House of Commons, could be dissolved before the end of its four-year term, a step which would bring about a general election. The upper house, like the American

Senate, could not. The right of decision on all key issues rested in the last resort with the lower house. In the event of a deadlock between the two, a finance bill would become law thirty days after the Representatives passed it, while any other bill rejected by the Councillors would become law if the lower house passed it again by a two-thirds majority. The lower house was also to elect the Prime Minister, who had to be a civilian and a member of the Diet. Moreover, it was to the Diet that his cabinet was responsible, not the emperor, as in the past. Indeed, the only important limitation on the theoretical power of the Representatives was that revision of the constitution required a two-thirds vote of each house, ratified by a simple majority in a national referendum.

One significant feature of the constitution was its restatement of the emperor's position. At SCAP's instigation he had already issued a New Year rescript in 1946 renouncing his supposed divinity. He was now described (Article I) as 'the symbol of the state and of the unity of the people, deriving his position from the will of the people in whom resides sovereign power'.[80] Although this aroused profound misgivings among conservatives – and has continued to do so – it provided a starting-point for remodelling the monarchy in a different image, emphasizing respect, rather than awe.

At least equally controversial was the so-called 'peace clause' (Article IX), introduced, it is said, on General MacArthur's own initiative. It stated that 'the Japanese people forever renounce war as a sovereign right of the nation', undertaking on that account not to maintain 'land, sea, and air forces, as well as other war potential'. Looking back from 1946 to the Pacific War, this seemed unexceptionable, if of doubtful effect. For the future, however, it was to be a source of embarrassment. Once the occupation had ended and Japan became independent again, it occasioned regular disputes about the legality of her defence forces and of the security treaties which she concluded with the United States.

The constitution also stated the principles on which local government was to be based. The changes arising as a result, which were introduced piecemeal, before being consolidated in the Local Autonomy Law of April 1947, brought about the transfer of many functions formerly performed by central government to prefectural and city administrations, headed by elected governors and mayors. Local assemblies were given more extensive powers. The Home Ministry, which was held by SCAP to be obstructing these reforms, was abolished in December 1947. Police forces were decentralized, also in December 1947, and Public Safety Commissions in the American manner were created to supervise them, both locally and nationally. However, giving substance to some of these policies ran into difficulties over finance. Local governments lacked adequate tax resources and borrowing rights, which left them still substantially dependent on Tokyo; and although Dr Carl Shoup of Columbia University, brought in to advise on these and related matters in 1949, recommended a revision of local tax arrangements and central government subsidies, with a view to giving local authorities greater self-reliance, his proposals in this particular respect aroused so much opposition in the Diet and from the bureaucracy that very little was done to put them into effect.

American example was also followed in separating the judiciary from the executive. Administrative supervision of the legal system was transferred from the Ministry of Justice to a newly-established Supreme Court, to which was deputed the task of appointing judges (except its own members, who were to be cabinet nominees) and of pronouncing on the constitutionality of laws. This made it the guardian of a wide range of human rights provisions which had been written into the constitution, not least those giving women legal and political equality with men. The Civil Code had to be revised to take account of these, especially to remove or alter some provisions concerning the family (for example, the powers of the family head, and rights of succession). This was highly controversial and led to fierce public debate, not unlike the exchanges about civil law in the 1890s, but the necessary legislation was finally accepted by the Diet in November 1947, becoming law in January 1948.

Equally important was the revision of the labour laws. A Trade Union Act in 1945 and a Labour Relations Act in 1946 gave Japanese workers the right to organize and strike, while a Labour Standards Act in 1947 gave them a guarantee of better conditions of work, including a health insurance scheme and accident compensation. They were quick to seize the opportunities this offered. By the end of 1948 some 34,000 unions had been formed, having nearly seven million members (over 40 per cent of the industrial labour force).

Education was also held to need reform, because of its role in shaping public attitudes. The first step was a ban on 'militaristic and ultra-nationalistic ideology' in October 1945, soon followed by the suspension of courses in ethics. As an alternative, the Fundamental Law of Education (March 1947) set out the aim of developing personality so as to produce citizens 'sound in body and mind, who shall love truth and justice'.[81] Compulsory education under this law was to be free; to be based on the principles of equal opportunity and religious toleration; and to provide for, but not enforce, coeducation. In so far as it included a training in citizenship, this was to be neither 'for nor against any specific political party'.

Early in 1946 SCAP had the benefit of advice from an educational mission sent from the United States. Among its recommendations, that which urged a change in teaching methods, so as to inculcate 'independent thinking' in place of 'memorization, conformity, and a vertical system of duties and loyalties',[82] proved much the most difficult to put into practice. The issue was still a live one forty years later, as we shall see (chapter 16). By comparison, revising the educational structure proved relatively straightforward. The School Education Act of 1947 provided for nine years of compulsory education (six years primary, three years secondary), followed by an optional three years of high school and four years of university. Control of the school system was to be decentralized, that is, put under the direction of elected boards of education in prefectures and cities. Universities were to be increased in number – to the extent of at least one in each prefecture – and given both academic and economic freedom under the Education Ministry. They were also to be encouraged to broaden their curricula.

Another major contribution to social change was land reform, undertaken in the belief that agrarian unrest had contributed to extreme forms of nationalism, hence to Japanese aggression. The first proposals concerning it, prepared by Japanese officials, were submitted to the Shidehara cabinet in November 1945, but were emasculated by landlord interests in the Diet. The Diet's revisions were then vetoed by MacArthur, who substituted a scheme put forward by the Australian representative in Japan,

W. MacMahon Ball, which was sent to the Japanese government in June 1946 and forced through a reluctant lower house, becoming law in October. It provided for the compulsory purchase of all land held by absentee landlords. Owner-farmers and resident landlords were to be allowed to retain an area ranging from 12 *chō* (about 12 hectares) in Hokkaido to 3 *chō* elsewhere, not more than a third of which was to be let to tenants. Everything above those limits was to be sold to the government – at rates fixed in relation to the controlled prices for agricultural products ruling in 1945, which were artificially low and had long since been overtaken by inflation – in order to be offered to existing tenants on easy terms. The terms were made all the easier in the event by a continuing fall in the value of money and the farmer's ability to charge black market prices for food.

Some idea of the scope of what was done can be gathered from the fact that more than a million *chō* of rice-paddy and a little less than 800,000 *chō* of upland was bought from 2·3 million landlords by August 1950 and sold to 4·7 million tenants. Land under tenancy agreements, amounting to over 40 per cent of the whole before 1946, dropped to a mere 10 per cent. There were still inequalities, of course. Since small landowners, who were the great majority, had to get rid of only a small proportion of their land, their tenants had less chance of acquiring it than did those of former absentees. There was also much room for manoeuvre in the choice of plots to be sold, a topic which greatly exercised the land committees, each consisting of five tenants, three landlords, and two owner-farmers, which were set up in every village to oversee the operation. All the same, the reform made Japan substantially a country of peasant proprietors. Their natural conservatism was to be a key factor in sustaining a succession of right-wing governments, while their improved economic status helped to create a wider domestic market, which was crucial to industrial growth.

THE PEACE TREATY AND DEFENCE AGREEMENT

American policy-makers had never been unanimous on the subject of Japan. Within MacArthur's headquarters in Tokyo some sections were primarily concerned with reform, others with promoting the economic and strategic interests of the United

States. Similar differences of emphasis existed in Washington. In both places, however, the influence of the reformers weakened with the passage of time, partly because their plans made unwelcome calls on American tax resources, partly because they began to seem less relevant as the international context changed. In particular, once the Cold War imposed its grip on Russo-American relations, Japan's value as a base began to outweigh her interest as an object of social experiment. Such attitudes became more pronounced when Mao Tse-tung's victory in the Chinese civil war in 1949 deprived the United States of her chosen ally in East Asia. They were accentuated by the hostilities which broke out in Korea in June 1950 between a communist north and an anti-communist south, the effect of which was to make Japan look more and more like an alternative choice as partner. At this point, in other words, her international future became of more concern to America than her democracy.

Since General MacArthur's reports had been consistently optimistic about the success of 'democratization', implying that his mission in Japan had been completed, talk about the possibility of a peace treaty began as early as 1947. Even so, it was not until 1951 – against the background of events in Korea – that negotiations were begun. The resulting treaty, restoring Japanese sovereignty, confirming her loss of all territory she had seized since 1895, and leaving the way open for a future settlement about war reparations, was signed at San Francisco in September of that year by most of the countries which had fought in the Pacific War; and although Russia refused to accept it, as did India and mainland China, these three were not in a position to prevent the occupation from coming to an end when the treaty was ratified in April 1952.

There were still a number of associated problems to be settled. One was that of the 'two Chinas', Japan being under American pressure to recognize Chiang Kai-shek as a legitimate ruler in Taiwan, whence he had withdrawn after his defeat on the mainland. China's intervention in the Korean war (December 1950), constituting an apparent threat to Japan and America's foothold there, made it inconceivable that Yoshida could follow his own preference for recognizing Mao Tse-tung, as Britain had done. He therefore came to terms with Taiwan in January 1952, putting Japan's relations with Peking into a state of limbo which lasted for another twenty years.

Russia had to be treated with greater circumspection, because she was in a better position than China to drive a hard bargain. Having occupied the Kuril islands and southern Sakhalin (Karafuto) under the Potsdam agreements, she dominated the area to the north and controlled all routes of access to Japan's former fishing grounds in the Sea of Okhotsk. This meant that in any negotiations she had a choice of menaces or bribes: she could threaten to close or restrict Japanese fisheries, or hold out the hope that Japan might, if amenable, recover the islands of Habomai and Shikotan, nearest to Hokkaido, which Tokyo had consistently argued were part of Japan's national territory, not former conquests, subject to seizure by the victorious powers. When the two countries opened peace talks through their ambassadors in London in June 1955, they ended in deadlock over this territorial question. Nor did the Japanese Foreign Minister, Shigemitsu Mamoru, make any progress on a visit to Moscow in August of the following year, when he faced additional Russian pressure in the form of a veto on Japan's entry to the United Nations. Accordingly, in October 1956 Prime Minister Hatoyama Ichiro (who had succeeded Yoshida) went himself to Moscow. There he signed an agreement which ended hostilities and restored diplomatic relations. A fisheries pact was agreed and a commercial treaty promised, but the territorial question was set aside until a peace treaty proper could be concluded. This has not yet (early 1989) been done, though talks have taken place on a number of occasions.

The ending of the occupation of Japan, for which the San Francisco treaty had made way, was something by which the United States had always expected to benefit, in the sense of reducing its military commitment in that country. The implication was that there would have to be some sort of Japanese force to ensure domestic security, while an American one remained to provide external defence; but neither proposition was very acceptable to Japanese opinion, which had made Yoshida wary of any suggestion of rearmament. The outbreak of the Korean war in 1950, making fresh demands on American manpower in the region, caused him to relax his opposition to the extent of creating a paramilitary National Police Reserve with a strength of 75,000 men. The negotiation of a peace treaty then pushed him one step farther: in September 1951 he signed a defence agreement, by which Japan promised to continue providing bases for American troops, aircraft, and ships. When it came into force in 1952, the National Police Reserve became the National Safety Force. Renamed again in July 1954, it was known thereafter as the Self-Defence Force (Jiei-tai), administered by a Defence Agency (Boei-cho) under a director holding cabinet rank.

Part of Japan's reward for these concessions was economic. Japanese leaders, in particular Yoshida, once they had been persuaded to provide the resources for a measure of rearmament, continued to argue that economic recovery at home was a prerequisite for effective participation in defence. Washington, which looked to the Japanese economy to contribute to its wider plans for Asia – that is, setting up barriers against communism by promoting economic growth – was inclined to accept this view. It therefore played a part in expanding Japan's overseas trade, especially in South East Asia. What is more, the Korean war afforded an occasion for a different kind of economic assistance to Japan, taking the form of American purchases of war material and related goods, which gave an important stimulus to Japanese industry (see chapter 15). Even after a Korean truce had been concluded in 1953 the same kind of arrangement was continued, this time through a Mutual Security Agreement, signed in March 1954, under which America undertook to provide Japan with military equipment to the value of $150 million, while contributing another $100 million in offshore purchases and agricultural supplies.

Underlying these agreements and decisions was a recognition by the two governments concerned that Japan's independence, as confirmed at San Francisco, was conditional on a military and economic alliance with the United States, though this had also to be subject in its turn to the constraints imposed by the Japanese constitution and the state of the Japanese economy. This was to prove the most emotive issue in Japanese politics for the next ten years or more. One reason was the tacit affront to a slowly-recovering Japanese national pride. Another was the link, as perceived by the Japanese, between the defence agreement and the power of conservatives in Japan.

14

CONSERVATIVE DEMOCRACY AND THE AMERICAN ALLIANCE, 1951–1972

In one respect the institutional reforms carried out under military occupation appear to have brought about a lasting transformation of Japanese politics. Power thereafter remained publicly in the hands of an elected Diet, exercised on the Diet's behalf by a Prime Minister and cabinet responsible to the lower house. Winning and retaining it involved the familiar trappings of parliamentary rule: parties, composed of local 'machines' and professional representatives of the people; business associations and trade unions, each promoting their sectional interests; all the panoply of electioneering. Yet there were important changes after 1951 in the way in which power was shared and used, not least because industrial growth (see chapter 15) brought about a shift in the relative standing of different groups, as well as in popular aspirations. One feature of these post-treaty years was the 'reverse course', an attempt on the part of conservative leaders to undo some of the occupation reforms. Another was that decision-making came more and more to depend on a close relationship between the civil bureaucracy, Japanese business, especially 'big' business, and one dominant political party, the Liberal Democrats.

Critics overseas gave the political society which resulted the pejorative label, 'Japan Inc.', implying both that there was an uncommonly disciplined approach to relations with the outside world, and that business considerations had an undue influence over national policy. There were objections, too, to some of the consequences of the American alliance, which, it was said, enabled Japan to divert financial resources from defence, greatly to the advantage of domestic industry. Opponents of the Liberal Democrats within Japan also found aspects of the alliance not to their taste. In their view, it committed their country to a type of international alignment of which they did not approve – in extreme cases they spoke of a form of surrogate imperialism, carried out under American auspices – while giving such support to right-wing cabinets at home as to put democracy in peril. The American connection was to remain in this sense a central issue in Japanese politics for the best part of a generation.

THE POLITICAL SYSTEM AFTER 1951

The nature and objectives of the 'reverse course' can be judged from a passage in Yoshida Shigeru's memoirs, written in 1960, setting out what he believed had been badly or wrongly done before 1951. The record showed, he wrote, 'how a purge was enforced which deprived our nation of a trained body of men at a crucial moment; how the financial concerns were disintegrated through the complete break-up of *zaibatsu* and by the institution of severe anti-monopoly measures, gravely retarding our economic recovery; how notorious Communist leaders were released from prison and praised for their fanatical agitation, causing untold injury to our body politic; how organized labour was encouraged in radical actions, thus endangering law and order; how education was reformed, sapping the moral fibre of our bewildered youth'.[83]

American concern about the danger from international communism gave Yoshida an opportunity to start putting some of these things right even before the occupation came to an end. In 1949 the purge regulations were amended, so as to make them apply to communists and other left-wing radicals. At the same time the Yoshida government was authorized by SCAP to review the application of the purge of militarists carried out in 1946 and 1947. It did so with enthusiasm, especially after the outbreak of the Korean war in the following summer; and although not many of those whose political rights were restored were able to regain positions of command – their successors were by this time too well entrenched to want to make room for an older generation at the top – their reappearance in the Diet, occasionally in the cabinet, or in company boardrooms, helped to augment the growing conservatism of Japanese public life. Meanwhile, the Red Purge, as it was called, removed some 22,000 left-wing workers from their jobs, drawn about equally from the public and private sectors. Not surprisingly, the position of trade unions was a good deal weakened. The right to strike had always been subject to veto by American GHQ, as had been demonstrated in February 1947, when a proposed general stoppage of work was banned because of its serious implications for a shaky economy. In July 1948 the constraint was codified as a prohibition of strikes by civil servants, later extended to all workers in public enterprise. Employees of local government were brought within its scope in December 1950.

Given this foundation, Yoshida turned his attention to attacking 'excessive' decentralization, a task in which politicians could always count on support from the capital's bureaucracy. In 1951 the law was amended to permit towns and villages, which were having difficulty in funding separate police forces of their own, to put themselves under the jurisdiction of the National Rural Police. About 90 per cent did so. Two years later a bill to impose central control on all police forces was put to the Diet, but was thrown out amidst public indignation. Brought forward again in revised form in 1954, it passed after some disorder. This made it possible to bring together the whole of the country's police under the National Police Agency, whose director was to be appointed by the National Public Safety Commission, acting with the consent of the Prime Minister. In addition, some of the functions of the former Home Ministry (Naimusho), which had been dispersed among other departments after its abolition in December 1947, were brought back together under the Autonomy Agency in 1952. In 1960 this was given status as a ministry (Jichisho), a title sometimes translated as Ministry of Home Affairs.

Yoshida had hoped also to undo some of the reforms in education – he tried, for example, to reintroduce the teaching of ethics in 1951, only to be frustrated by a public outcry when his plans leaked to the press – but in the event this had to be left to his sucessor, Hatoyama Ichiro. Hatoyama pushed through a Local Education Law in 1956. It weakened the powers of education boards, which were no longer to be chosen by direct election, putting them instead under the supervision of prefectural assemblies, dominated for the most part by conservative politicians; and it gave the Education Ministry (Mombusho) the right to provide guidance on matters concerning curricula and textbooks. This provision was strengthened in 1958 by an order establishing a uniform curriculum for primary and secondary schools. There followed a revival of the teaching of ethics in 1959.

As Prime Minister, Yoshida had laid down a formulation of national policy which had considerable public support: implementation of a conservative brand of parliamentary democracy; adherence to the American alliance; a concentration of effort on economic recovery and growth. On the other hand, partly because he was disliked for his stubbornness and intolerance, partly because he was a better administrator than parliamentarian, he failed to create a stable party structure which would help both his colleagues and his policies to endure. In fact, the Liberals, when he stepped down at the end of 1954, faced rivals who were to put them severely to the test. There were other right-wing politicians, like Hatoyama Ichiro, released from the purge in the summer of 1951, capable of offering an alternative leadership. Hatoyama took over as head of the Democratic Party – Ashida had been arrested in a bribery scandal – and became premier in December 1954. There were also substantial numbers of socialists in the Diet, bitterly opposed to the 'reverse course' and the alignment with America. In a lower house election in February 1955 the new party of government, the Democrats, held only 185 seats. Ominously, the two main socialist groups, Right and Left, between them won 156, polling 29 per cent of the popular vote; and when they came together in October, forming a single Socialist Party, the whole of Japan's conservative establishment began to fear for its future. Under considerable pressure from business interests, the Liberals and Democrats agreed to merge in the following month, forming the Liberal Democrat Party (LDP), which has remained in office ever since.

The LDP was less united than its durability might lead one to suppose. It had ample access to funds, mostly provided by business, as we shall see. These enabled it to mount expensive election campaigns, the cost of which exceeded by many times the limits on expenditure imposed by the electoral law. It had solid backing from the farm vote as a result of land reform, which it took care to reinforce by a policy of agricultural price support. In addition, its Diet representatives individually cultivated a network of 'men of influence' within their constituencies, whose ability to deliver votes made it relatively unimportant for the party to have a genuine popular base (it has claimed anything from one million to three million members at various times, but a high proportion of these have been nominal, often enrolled by their employers). Co-ordinating the party's activities was a well-articulated central machine, concerned above all with election tactics. What was conspicuously lacking, both in 1955 and for thirty years thereafter, was unity of leadership. The groups which had existed among conservatives at the time of the party's formation were incorporated into the Liberal Democrats as factions, which retained their own identity and funding. Because the differences between them were concerned less with policy than with political ambition, they have always been identified with the names of senior politicians, not with issues; but the regularity of their place in Japanese politics is demonstrated by the fact that one can trace a quasi-geneaological lineage for the principal ones over the whole period since 1955. Their rivalries focus on the election of a party president, who is destined at once to become Prime Minister, provided the LDP retains a majority in the Diet's lower house. This translation puts him in a position to dispense patronage, that is, government posts to reward his followers and cabinet office to some from other factions, in such proportion as he sees fit.

A major source of strength for the Liberal Democrats has been their close relationship with the bureaucracy. In one respect this is a reflection of their many years in power. In another, it results from the continuation of the prewar practice of appointing ex-bureaucrats to political office (except that the military are no longer eligible). Sometimes there was a continuity of personnel between the prewar and postwar periods. For example, Yoshida was a high-ranking diplomat before 1941. Kishi Nobusuke, who became Prime Minister in 1957, had been vice-minister in the departments of Commerce and Industry and of Munitions under Konoe and Tojo; had been arrested, but not indicted, as a war criminal in the 'political' category; and had first become a party politician (as a member of the Liberal Party) after being depurged in 1952. His numerous links with officialdom and business, arising from this experience, enabled him to play a key part in bringing the Liberal Democrats into existence in 1955. He was in this typical of many senior ex-bureaucrats in postwar politics. Their background was frequently in those sectors of the civil service which had the greatest relevance to economic growth, while their 'connections' with former colleagues in the central ministries greatly facilitated the drafting and planning of legislation. Their numbers were substantial. It has been estimated that on average about one-fifth of cabinet ministers after 1955 were former bureaucrats, who joined the Liberal Democrats on retirement. What is more, between 1955 and 1980 ex-bureaucrats held office as Prime Minister for a total of twenty years, compared with only five years for those who had risen through the party's ranks.

The third leg of the tripod of power was Japanese business, represented after the war by several widely-based organizations, rather than by a few outstanding companies, as in the past. One such organization was the Japan Chamber of Commerce and Industry, dating from 1922. Another was Nikkeiren (Japan Federation of Employers Associations), founded in 1948 to help management deal with militant trade unions. Both came to exercise a good deal of influence, but neither matched the high public profile of Keidanren (Federation of Economic Organizations), which had (and has) in its membership several hundred of the country's largest firms. Although it was established in 1946, Keidanren suffered at first from SCAP's hostility towards potential monopolies and cartels, with the result that it did not come into prominence until 1952. Thereafter, however, it played a dual role on the national stage. First, it sought to mediate the interests of different business groups and sectors, where these came into conflict with each other. Second, it served as spokesman for big business in dealing with major economic issues, both inside and outside Japan. In the latter capacity, it has acted as a pressure group, setting out, usually in general terms, the policies which businessmen expected their governments to adopt.

Keidanren derived its ability to insist on these, not so much from businessmen entering politics – though quite a large number did – as from money, which it provided through a variety of intermediaries. There was in fact at all times after 1952 a heavy flow of funds, contributed by business associations, as well as by single firms, to the Liberal Democrat Party, to its various factions, and to many of its representatives in the Diet. Altogether this amounted to over 90 per cent of the contributions received by conservative political groups in the 1960s. Much the largest share came from Keidanren, especially when vast sums were needed at short notice for elections to the lower house. Usually the price exacted was simply a recognition that the cabinet had a responsibility to induce a climate politically and financially favourable to the business economy. Sometimes it went farther, however. Business leaders not only argued in favour of a coalition between Liberals and Democrats in 1955, they also underwrote its costs. When Kishi resigned in 1960, they made it clear that they would be more willing to finance Ikeda Hayato than any of his rivals for the post of Prime Minister. Their reward was Ikeda's 'income-doubling' plan, designed to give Japan an annual compound growth rate of over 7 per cent for the next ten years.

One logical consequence of business backing was to give the Liberal Democrats an immense advantage over their rivals. Of these, the Japan Socialist Party (JSP) remained the most important, despite the scornful comment that it achieved for Japan nothing better than a one-and-a-half party system. It had from the beginning been split between a Marxist left and a social democratic right, whose differences had been by no means healed, any more than were those of the Liberal Democrats, by the creation of a single party in 1955. In the election of May 1958 socialists won a total of 166 lower house seats, evenly divided between urban and rural constituencies. From that time on, however, there was a gradual decline. A right-wing group broke away to form the Democratic Socialist Party (DSP) in 1960, while the disunity of those who remained was enhanced by some very public disagreements about the defence relationship with America, to which the party's left was totally opposed, while the right was ambivalent. Moreover, rapid industrial growth encouraged the trade unions, on which the socialists depended heavily for candidates and funds, to pay more attention to standards of living than to party politics, and this in turn pushed the politicians into greater reliance on radicals who had little popular appeal. In the election of December 1969 the JSP won only 90 lower house seats. There was a modest recovery in the next few years, as socialists profited from the unease that followed various setbacks to the economy (see chapter 15), but after the middle of the 1970s the decline resumed.

The Japan Communist Party (JCP), which was the other main element of opposition in the early part of this period, was for some years bedevilled by leadership struggles reflecting partisan attitudes towards the Sino-Soviet dispute. The disagreements were not resolved until 1965 when the party adopted a more detached approach under Miyamoto Kanji. This accomplished, it began once again to furbish its parliamentary image, pursuing specifically Japanese issues and building up mass membership. And the policy gradually showed results. The party organ, *Akahata* (Red Flag), was transformed into a family newspaper, earning substantial profits for the party coffers. A youth organization, holding aloof from the more extreme forms of student violence – to the extent that student rebels began to talk of the Communist Party as being 'on the right' – broadened the popular base. As a consequence, there was a steady rise in communist successes at the polls: 3 lower house seats in 1960, 5 in 1967, 14 in 1969, 38 in 1972. This level was then approximately maintained until 1980.

The fact that neither socialists nor communists seemed able to make very much political headway in a period of economic growth was highlighted by the emergence of a new opposition party in 1964. It was sponsored by a Buddhist organization, Sokagakkai, an offshoot of the Nichiren sect, which had achieved rapid development in the postwar years, especially among urban groups who had failed to win a share in industrial success; and although the new party took the name Komeito (Clean Government Party) to emphasize that its purposes were ethical as well as political, in practice its programme reflected its social composition more than any Buddhist ideas. That is, it appealed for a form of Asian neutralism (to include recognition of communist China), but also for a better deal for small and medium businesses, and more welfare provision for the under-privileged. Electorally Komeito benefited from Sokagakkai's very large membership, even though the two formally severed their ties in 1970. When the party first took part in lower house elections in 1967 it fielded 32 candidates, elected 25 of them, and polled nearly 2·5 million votes. In 1969 it raised its total of Diet seats to 47. The number fell back to 29 in 1972, but the reverse was temporary: in both 1976 and 1979 Komeito won over 50 seats, becoming the third largest party.

As a result of this fragmentation of the opposition, whose members showed little sign of co-operating with each other, the Liberal Democrats seemed well nigh unassailable during the 1960s. Ikeda Hayato led them from 1960 to 1964. When his health failed, he was smoothly replaced by Sato Eisaku – Kishi's brother, adopted into a different branch of the family – who was another ex-bureaucrat with experience at the Ministry of International Trade and Industry. This made him, like Ikeda, a candidate acceptable to business circles, continuing the policies aimed at economic growth. He also won elections: 277 seats in 1967 and 288 in 1969, providing comfortable lower house majorities, which kept him in power for nearly eight years. A by-product of this long tenure was a decision by his party to limit the number of times its president could in future stand for re-election.

It was to be several more years before politicians began to talk of evolving a new pattern of politics to replace that which had been established when the LDP was founded – 'the 1955 system', it came to be called – but there were already some signs in the late 1960s that it was not wholly endorsed by the population at large. Widespread student unrest, for example, expressed dissatisfaction with the nature of Japanese capitalism, as well as grievances about how universities were run. It produced violent demonstrations in the streets, together with strikes and sit-ins thousands-strong at educational establishments – at the peak of the unrest in October 1969 no less than 77 universities were engaged in disputes – which only the newly-formed riot police proved able to subdue. The movement was admittedly short-lived, because doctrinal quarrels destroyed its effectiveness, while the end of the Vietnam war deprived it of the one issue on which factions could readily unite. It left only splinter groups of terrorists as its residue, operating mostly outside Japan. Nevertheless, it had provided unmistakeable evidence that affluence was not everywhere seen as a solution to society's ills. In a different context, so did the protests about industrial pollution, which had reached such a level in 1966 and 1967 that they forced the introduction of anti-pollution laws, notwithstanding objections from businessmen (see chapter 15).

One consequence of the turbulence was a gradual fall in the Liberal Democrats' share of the popular vote. In 1960 they had had over 57 per cent of votes cast. In 1969 the figure was down to 48 per cent, even though the number of their seats was only marginally smaller (Sato won 288, compared with Ikeda's 296 in 1960). Tanaka Kakuei, taking over from Sato, won only 271 seats in December 1972, and even this owed more to management than popularity. One candidate admitted to a newspaper that his election campaign had required 100 million yen – more than twenty times the legal maximum – which he claimed was typical. Some 15 per cent of it had been spent on direct costs, like office expenses, loudspeaker vans and other forms of publicity, but the rest had gone on gifts and entertainment for voters and men of influence in his constituency, plus donations to fellow party members in prefectural and other local assemblies. Such statements, universally believed, were beginning to bring the parliamentary system into disrepute, as it had been earlier in the century. The willingness of the press to give them prominence – the three major dailies, the *Yomiuri*, *Asahi* and *Mainichi*, which were all ostentatiously independent of party, together sold fifteen million copies of their morning editions in 1970 – helped to fuel the public's disenchantment. So did the later career of Tanaka Kakuei (see chapter 16).

FOREIGN RELATIONS

Of the five Prime Ministers who held office between the end of 1954 and the middle of 1972, two, Ishibashi Tanzan and Ikeda Hayato, resigned because of ill health. The other three, Hatoyama Ichiro, Kishi Nobusuke, and Sato Eisaku, fell from power ostensibly, at least, because of controversies over foreign affairs. In one sense this was a tribute to the success of their domestic policies. In another it was an indication of the importance which foreign relations possessed in Japanese politics.

Yoshida Shigeru had planned to restore Japan's fortunes by a concentration on economic development, while engaging in 'low-posture' diplomacy under American protection. His successors followed broadly the same line, seeking respectability through participation in the activities of the United Nations, and reputation through non-political gestures like the Tokyo Olympics of 1964. The geopolitics of Japan's place in the world was left to be determined by the American alliance. The approach was not wholly popular within Japan. There was, for example, some resentment of the terms on which the United States continued to maintain bases in Japan, manifested in October 1956 in large-scale demonstrations against plans to extend an American airfield near the village of Sunakawa at the expense of agricultural land. In 1957 there was another *cause célèbre*, when an American sentry shot a Japanese woman collecting metal for scrap on a firing range. The legal point at issue was whether his trial should be held in a civil – that is, Japanese – court, or an American military one. Since it touched on the constitutions of both countries, as well as carrying emotive overtones of unequal treaties in the nineteenth century, it provoked some acrimony, but in the end, after the Japanese court had been adjudged to have priority, the sentry was released on a suspended sentence.

Disputes about the security treaty itself were of greater substance. Objections to it had existed in Japan from the beginning, coming from both sides of the political divide. Nationalists, especially right-wing conservatives, resented the implications of subservience it contained. Those on the left condemned it as making Japan a partner in what they held to be American imperialism. Kishi Nobusuke, who became Prime Minister in February 1957, therefore decided to renegotiate the agreement in a manner which would provide sops for Japanese pride, together with a clearer statement of the economic advantages to be derived from the relationship. He hoped thereby to damp down opposition, at least on the right.

By January 1960 the terms of a new treaty had been agreed. An exchange of notes, which Kishi signed at that time in Washington, provided for Japan to have a voice – its extent not clearly defined – in the use to which American bases and the forces stationed at them might be put. In the treaty itself, which he also signed, Article II bound both parties to 'seek to eliminate conflict in their international economic policies', while a joint communiqué, issued simultaneously, referred with approval to 'the increasing role the Japanese people are playing in the economic development of free Asia'.[84] Unhappily, this was not enough to overcome public hostility in Japan, due in some measure to the fact that Kishi's own prewar and wartime record, mostly as an economic bureaucrat, made him suspect to the opposition at home in everything he did. By the time the treaty came before the Diet for ratification in April 1960, socialists, communists, trade unions, and the national association of students (Zengakuren) had worked up a tumultuous popular movement against it. There were repeated and violent demonstrations outside the Diet building. Inside, socialist members boycotted the debates and picketed the chamber, until they were forcibly removed by the police. In their absence the government party then voted ratification, thus making the dispute into one of parliamentary rights. Protest mounted to the point of hysteria. There were mass demonstrations throughout Japan on 26 May; student riots in Tokyo causing several hundred casualties, including the death of one girl student; enormous public petitions; and a railway strike at the beginning of June.

It had been arranged that President Eisenhower would pay an official visit to Japan to coincide with the ratification of the treaty, but the disorder, in view of its anti-American tone, made that impossible. On 16 June an emergency cabinet meeting in Tokyo decided to ask the President not to come. Two days later the Diet vote in favour of ratification finally took effect, and on 23 June the United States ratified in its turn. Kishi resigned, to be replaced by Ikeda Hayato.

Surprisingly, these events caused less disturbance than one might have expected in subsequent relations between the two allies, though they made Japanese defence policy of continuing concern to both. Despite a vocal peace movement, dominated by socialists and communists, plus strident minorities which complained about the existence of the treaty and challenged the legality – because of the peace clause in the postwar constitution –of the Self-Defence Force, the majority of Japanese, if one is to judge by their votes and their replies to opinion polls, came within a very few years to accept the necessity of what had been done. True, there was no desire to see Japan become a major military power, if only for financial reasons. There continued to be significant opposition to nuclear weapons and to sending Japanese forces overseas. Within these limits, however, the possession of a modicum of military strength, to be deployed defensively in association with the United States, came by the end of the decade to be generally regarded as legitimate self-interest.

The development of the Self-Defence Force and the plans for its operational use reflected this. From a combatant strength of nearly 165,000 in 1954 it expanded to 235,000 by 1972. Within this total, rather more than 150,000 belonged to a land force, equipped with tanks, aircraft, and surface-to-air missiles. In addition, there was an air arm of 42,000 men, having 900 aircraft, 40 helicopters and 100 Nike missiles, plus a naval one, 37,000 strong, with 200 small combat vessels and a similar number of planes. The annual charge on the national budget that this represented rose from US$509 million in 1961 to three times that much in 1970, then to about $3 billion in 1974. Thereafter costs continued to rise at a regular rate, but this was due to the provision of more sophisticated equipment rather than to any increase in size.

Japanese military forces had originally been brought into being in order to make good the loss of those the United States was in the process of withdrawing (amounting to just over 100,000 men between 1955 and 1960). In July 1961 a more ambitious defence plan was drawn up, under which it was envisaged that Japan should put herself in a position to hold off outside attack, pending American reinforcement or nuclear retaliation. In 1970 a White Paper, produced by Nakasone Yasuhiro as head of the Defence Agency, went a little farther. Japan, it said, was to aim at such a degree of 'military autonomy' as would make it possible to survive if American help were delayed. Though this was seen as a worthwhile gesture of conciliation towards those Americans who had begun to complain that Japan was not assuming her proper share of the military burden, it involved expensive purchases of weapons, to say nothing of arousing fears about a renewal of Japanese militarism among the country's Asian neighbours, and therefore faced hostility in the Diet. Sato Eisaku, the Prime Minister, was wary of it, approaching the whole question much more cautiously than Nakasone. He had already announced in 1967 the 'three non-nuclear principles': that Japan would not manufacture nuclear weapons; nor possess them; nor permit them to be brought into Japan by others. He had also decided to limit defence spending to less than 1 per cent of GNP (a doctrine which did not become official until 1976). All this made him reluctant to approve substantial rearmament, so the proposals had to wait for full endorsement until Nakasone himself became premier in 1982.

Defence was in the end to be a much less serious cause of Japanese–American friction than trade, especially the rise in Japanese exports to the United States, but the issues raised by trade can more appropriately be left for later consideration (see chapter 16). Here we shall consider instead the implications of the American alliance for Japan's relations with other countries in the region. It did, of course, require Japan to stay in line with American policy in Asia, if not to co-operate actively in it. This, too, was often unwelcome to segments of Japanese opinion. The Vietnam war, to take a particularly sensitive case, was often reported in an anti-American manner in Japan, partly because it was seen as a Western intervention in an Asian dispute, partly out of fear that Japan might be unwittingly dragged in. Uneasiness was also expressed about continuing disputes with the Soviet Union. Discussions about the islands to the north remained deadlocked throughout the 1960s and 1970s, despite some improvement in practical matters, such as trade, air routes, and consular representation. To set against this, the alliance made possible a number of specific gains. In April 1968 the Bonin islands were returned to Japan. In the following year Washington promised to return Okinawa in 1972, subject to retaining bases there on the same terms as in the Japanese home islands.

There was also a rapprochement of sorts with America's mainland ally, South Korea. In June 1965 relations with Seoul were 'normalized', a step by which the Liberal Democrats recognized that Korea's strategic importance outweighed the persistent hostile demonstrations in Japan. On the other hand, arguments over Korean fisheries continued; there were constant criticisms from Japanese left-wing groups about Korea's 'reactionary' politics; and when the Korean President made an official visit to Tokyo in 1974, it was thought wise to put 20,000 police on the streets to ensure security. Nevertheless, the President had a meeting with Emperor Hirohito and heard him express regret for Japan's past sins.

For most Japanese the question of what to do about China

policy was an altogether more important matter. American hostility to Peking, coupled with Japanese recognition of Taiwan, made it difficult to promote trade with the mainland, for all that it was left to unofficial business representatives to arrange it. It was December 1962 before the Ikeda cabinet was able to secure an exchange of trade missions, designed to develop an export of industrial plant to the People's Republic; and even that did no more than raise China's share of Japan's foreign trade from 0·1 per cent in 1960 to 2·9 per cent in 1970. This was not enough to persuade the best-known Japanese firms to take part in it. Some companies, which had traditions of dealing with China, or had profited from limited recent contacts, wanted to go ahead and ignore the risks of reprisal from America or Taiwan. Larger ones, whose interests were more diverse and international, hence more at risk in such an eventuality, thought it better to hold aloof. So did their government.

In these circumstances, it took a shift in the international situation generally to bring about a major change in Sino – Japanese relations. This began to take shape in 1970. As China slowly renewed her world contacts after the Cultural Revolution, groups emerged in both the Diet and major business organizations, calling for Japan to emulate Canada in recognizing Peking. China responded by showing a greater willingness to be flexibile about existing Japanese investment in Taiwan. Accordingly, when President Nixon announced in July 1971 that he was to visit Peking for the purpose of restoring the relationship broken off in 1949, there was already a receptive atmosphere in Tokyo. Two Japanese business missions were sent to China in the autumn; China's admission to the United Nations in October then cleared the way for more formal diplomatic action; and only Sato Eisaku's personal sense of commitment to Taiwan seemed to hold it back. His retirement removed that obstacle. Soon after becoming Prime Minister in July 1972, Tanaka Kakuei, strongly supported by senior members of his cabinet, including Nakasone, made plans to visit Peking. Arriving there on 25 September, he had talks with Mao Tse-tung and Chou En-lai before signing a statement which restored relations between the two countries four days later. Japan expressed regret for the sufferings inflicted on China before 1945 and recognized the People's Republic as China's sole legitimate authority. China renounced any claim to a war indemnity, but put once again on record her insistence that Taiwan was part of Chinese territory. At a press conference, Foreign Minister Ohira Masayoshi, who accompanied Tanaka, announced that Japan's treaty with Taiwan was null and void.

15

THE ECONOMIC MIRACLE

Looking back over the past hundred years or so of Japanese history, two things stand out. The first is that the Meiji decision to 'strengthen the army', that is, to acquire such military force as would enable Japan to meet the West on equal terms, was the beginning of disaster. Empire and defeat were a natural, though not inevitable, extension of the drive towards national strength. The second aim of Meiji policy, that of 'enriching the country', was itself not wholly irrelevant to the origins of the Pacific War, but it remains true that economic achievement has proved to be the more successful and durable part of the nineteenth century's legacy. Today, if the Japan of militarism and aggression is not altogether forgotten, it is the Japan of the 'economic miracle' that most holds the attention of the world.

The first task of this chapter is to summarize the nature of Japanese economic growth since the end of the occupation. In addition, one has to recognize that economic prowess has in a number of ways revolutionized the life of the country's inhabitants. Although some of the political and international consequences are considered elsewhere in this book, it seems appropriate to include here an account of the changes that have taken place in conditions of employment and standards of living.

INDUSTRIAL GROWTH, 1955–73

The war left Japan with severe economic problems: some ten million unemployed, if one includes demobilized members of the armed forces; widespread destruction of housing and industrial plant; annual coal production reduced to a million tons; a 1945 rice crop which was only two-thirds of the norm; and rapid inflation. Material losses due to the war have been estimated at a quarter of total national wealth, accounting for all the gains which had been made since 1935. Even so, not all the consequences were bad. Unemployment ensured that there was a pool of labour, much of it skilled, available to be directed towards new tasks. The war had also raised the level of technology and production capacity in heavy industry, notably in iron and steel, machinery, and chemicals, while leaving in place a network of financial controls, devised to give priority to munitions, which were available to governments as instruments of reconstruction.

In making use of these inherited advantages, postwar Japan had the benefit of a great deal of American help. In the early days of the occupation it took the form of emergency shipments of food and raw materials, but after 1948, when the emphasis in United States policy shifted away from 'punishment' towards economic self-reliance for Japan, there were measures to end inflation (the Dodge plan for balanced budgets, 1949), which the Yoshida cabinet might have found it difficult to carry through on its own, plus substantial injections of capital and advanced technology. The outbreak of the Korean war in 1950 led to large-scale American purchases of equipment for the United Nations forces, which gave a major stimulus to Japanese production. Currency earnings on this account were nearly $600 million in 1951, over $800 million in 1952 and again in 1953, making possible important new investment in plant and equipment.

In addition, Washington saw its defence partnership with Japan, following the San Francisco treaty, as requiring efforts on its own part to foster Japanese trade, especially with South East Asia. Under American auspices, reparations treaties were concluded, by which Japan promised to furnish goods and services to countries which she had formerly occupied, rather than sacrificing her own industrial plant for their benefit, as had at first been proposed. $200 million of aid was promised to Burma

(November 1954), $550 million to the Philippines (May 1956), $220 million to Indonesia (January 1958). Coupled with this were Japanese loans to the same three states, totalling $700 million. One result was that by the mid-1960s over 30 per cent of Japan's overseas investment was in the area stretching south and west from Korea to the Indian sub-continent, excluding China.

None of this would have been possible without a regeneration of Japanese industry itself, an aim to which Japanese politicians and officials gave much greater priority than did American ones. Ishibashi Tanzan, prewar economic journalist, whom Yoshida made Finance Minister in 1946, set out to stimulate recovery by creating the Economic Stabilization Board to co-ordinate production, plus the Reconstruction Bank to channel capital into selected industries (food, fertilizer, coal, iron, and steel). He faced objections from SCAP – still in its reforming mood – that the policy favoured the *zaibatsu* and other wartime profiteers, which led to his being purged and removed from office in 1947, but his successors were able in the event to pursue much the same line. In 1948 the Economic Stabilization Board drew up a five-year plan, intended to restore production to approximately the levels of 1934. In the following year the Ministry of International Trade and Industry (MITI) was established, bringing bureaucratic experts on foreign trade into partnership with those who had learnt the techniques of controlling industry in the old Munitions Ministry. Under its aegis, the Reconstruction Bank was replaced by the Development Bank in 1951 as a source of low-interest funds for industrial investment; tax reforms were introduced in the form of investment allowances; a system of foreign exchange allocation was developed, which in practice gave officials the authority to direct raw materials to selected companies; and technical co-operation agreements were made with foreign firms, especially American ones.

MITI used the powers it acquired through these arrangements to improve the competitiveness of Japanese business. It actively sponsored the formation of conglomerates (*keiretsu*) centred on banks, the largest of which were closely related to the prewar *zaibatsu*. Both Mitsubishi and Mitsui, whose trading companies had been dissolved in the first phase of the occupation, were back in large-scale operation by 1955. In addition, producers in several fields (cotton-spinning was the first, soon followed by steel) were encouraged to form cartels, which would allocate production quotas and share out raw materials. Supervision was exercised by means of what was called 'administrative guidance'; and when it was challenged under the anti-monopoly laws in 1952, MITI successfully argued that 'advice' was not legally subject to them. Next year it persuaded the Diet to amend the law so as to authorize government-sponsored cartels in industries that were depressed or undergoing rationalization. From that time on, the department's prestige advanced rapidly. Of the ten Prime Ministers who held office in the thirty years after the resignation of Hatoyama Ichiro (December 1956), no less than seven had at one time been Minister of International Trade and Industry.

By 1955 American assistance and MITI organization had laid the foundations for what was to be an exceptional surge of industrial development. Several factors contributed to it, apart from consistent policies of government support. The world economy as a whole had entered a period of expansion, providing a favourable environment. Japanese industry enjoyed good labour relations, partly a product of postwar hardship, partly a tribute to effective management. This made it easier to move manpower into higher-productivity jobs and industries, which was one key to subsequent growth. Another was technological borrowing, available through Japan's links with America. Social change, such as land reform and the development of trade unions (see chapter 13), helped to spread the gains widely through the community, thus expanding the domestic market, while the Japanese population's high propensity to save ensured that much of the capital required for industrial investment was raised from private domestic sources, channelled through the banks and post office savings. The government's contribution came in the form of central lending to the private banks, plus the provision of infrastructure, such as roads and railways. For example, in 1960 Japan had just under 27,000 km. of paved roads; in 1975 the figure was 340,000km.

Given these stimuli, Japanese industry first recovered, then expanded. In 1948 the industrial production index (1934–6 = 100) had stood at only 55. In 1950 it was 84, by 1955 had risen to 181. Despite a check in 1957 due to balance of payments problems, it jumped to 410 in 1960, a year in which the economy achieved a real growth rate of 13·2 per cent. Something like the same annual rate was then maintained for the following decade.

During the 1960s the Japanese economy was dominated, as it had been in the past, by a relatively small number of large-scale manufacturers. Some of these were within the conglomerates favoured by MITI: Mitsubishi, Mitsui, Sumitomo, and Fuji each had over seventy member firms or affiliates by 1970. They were especially important in basic fields like steel, ship-building, and mining, though they remained strong also in commerce and finance. Outside these groupings were several companies in relatively new types of manufacture, such as electrical goods, electronics, and automobiles. They included some that were to be world-famous names, like Matsushita Electric, Hitachi, Toyota, and Nissan, which were usually part of vertical structures, involving a range of sub-contractors in which the parent concern held stock. All received a measure of protection from foreign competition while they were establishing a market position within Japan, thanks to MITI's control over foreign trade.

A second feature of the economy in this phase was the emphasis given to products that required advanced technology and heavy capital investment: industries like steel and petro-chemicals; the manufacture of consumer goods like cameras, television sets, motorcycles, and eventually automobiles. Metals, chemicals, and engineering already represented about 60 per cent by value of the country's gross factory production in 1960, compared with only 30 per cent in 1930. In the next ten years annual steel output rose from 22 million to 93 million tonnes, crude oil imports increased from 33 million to 205 million kilolitres. Steel ships launched, amounting to 1·76 million grt in 1960, were 12·65 million grt in 1970, helped by expanding world demand, especially for oil tankers after the Suez crisis of 1956. Annual production of television sets rose from 3·6 million to 13·8 million during the same decade, while that of passenger cars, only 165,000 at its beginning, reached over three million at its end. Underlining the character of the change,whereas the index of industrial production as a whole moved from a base of 100 in 1960 to 373 in 1970, that for iron and steel went up to 410, that for chemicals to 424, that for machinery to 579.

By contrast, textiles, which had long held pride of place in both domestic production and foreign trade, were in relative decline by 1960 and made little headway thereafter. Raw silk, facing severe competition from man-made fibres, was produced in much smaller quantities than before the war. Cotton yarn output was also down, while exports of cotton piece-goods proved quite unable to match the prices available from manufacturers in South East Asia. Rayons and other artificial fabrics, relying on the expanding petrochemical industry, to some extent made good the loss, but not entirely so. The textile index rose only from 100 to 226 in the boom years 1960 to 1970.

In 1961 Prime Minister Ikeda Hayato had set out the objective of doubling national income within ten years. Part of the plan was an expansion of exports at approximately 10 per cent a year, concentrating on machinery and on markets in North America and Europe. As a result, Japanese growth in this period was export-oriented in ways that had not been envisaged under the defence agreements with the United States. In particular, export success no longer depended on industries having lower wage rates than their competitors, which would have implied making low-priced goods for underdeveloped areas, but on those whose efficiency was greater, honed by competition in the market at home. Quality and after-sales service became crucial to it. Prices were held down by economies of scale.

When Japan became a party to the General Agreement on Tariffs and Trade (GATT) in June 1955, several countries, including Britain, had refused for some time to accord her its full benefits out of a suspicion that certain commercial practices, like dumping, still lingered in Japan from earlier days. Partly for this reason, partly because of the loss of privileged access to China and other Asian markets since the war, the growth of foreign trade was at first quite slow. After 1960, however, it was rapid. The quantum index of foreign trade (1965 = 100) reveals an increase in imports from 56·6 to 224 between 1960 and 1970, and in exports from 43·9 to 200·8. The composition of the trade reflected the changes taking place in industry. Textile exports less than doubled in value in these years, whereas the index for chemical products rose from 29 to 280, that for machinery from 26 to 263. Japan was becoming one of the world's largest suppliers of ships, cameras, television sets, automobiles, and man-made fibres. The corollary was heavy imports of ore, notably from Australia, and oil, mostly from the Middle East. In 1970 just over 30 per cent of Japanese exports went to the United States, about 15 per cent to Western Europe, and fractionally over 15 per cent to

South East Asia, where the main customers were Hong Kong, the Philippines, Thailand, and Singapore. Imports were drawn more evenly from a wider area, except that the United States provided nearly 30 per cent. For the rest, 13 per cent came from the Middle East, 12 per cent from South East Asia, 10 per cent from Western Europe, and just under 8 per cent from Australia.

TRADE AND INDUSTRY AFTER THE 'OIL SHOCK'

When the Arab oil-producing countries took the decision to quadruple oil prices at the end of 1973, they caused changes in the world economy which brought Japan's phase of exceptionally rapid growth to an end. As a country which depended on oil for two-thirds of its energy supplies and on imports for almost the whole of its oil, Japan inevitably suffered a huge increase in its import bill and a general price rise. The wholesale price index went up by 31 per cent in 1974. Cuts in the use of oil, imposed by the government in order to restrain imports of it, pushed the economy towards recession, with the result that gross national product showed a decline in that year for the first time since the occupation.

In 1975 the position seemed to be improving. Reductions in government spending and a tight money policy, including restrictions on bank lending to industry, began to get inflation under control, while exports expanded, offsetting higher import costs due to the price of oil. Progress was uneven, but by 1977–8 government policy was moving towards greater expenditure again as a means to stimulate the domestic economy. Investment recovered strongly in 1979. At that point came the second 'oil shock', a two-stage increase in oil prices carried out in mid-1979 and early 1980. Japan's import costs rose again, this time by $30 billion, and the wholesale price index went up by 20 per cent. In March 1980 the price of electricity to the consumer was raised by a half. In addition, the cabinet introduced a variety of measures to reduce energy consumption, including a ban on commuting by car for government employees and an end to television broadcasts after midnight. Oil imports for the year fell by 10 per cent in volume. Oil-based production of electric power was reduced, so that by 1982 it accounted for only two-fifths of the total, compared with two-thirds in 1973. Nuclear power stations were built –

despite objections from the peace lobby – and were producing a quarter of the country's electricity by 1985.

As a consequence, Japan threw off the effects of the second oil shock rather more quickly than it had done those of the first. Nevertheless, the two together brought a long-term change in growth rates and in expectations concerning them. Real economic growth, which had averaged at least 10 per cent per annum in the 1960s and was still over 8 per cent in 1972, fell to something like 5 per cent, apart from short periods significantly lower than that in 1974–5 and 1981–3. Unemployment edged slowly higher –from 2 per cent of the workforce in 1980 to nearly 3 per cent in 1987, though it then began to fall back a little – despite the fact that industrial production resumed its upward trend. Japan, it was thought, had now entered a period of 'stable growth', likely to last into the 1990s.

Its characteristics differed in some respects from what had gone before. The rise in the cost of oil had its greatest impact on heavy energy users, such as steel and petrochemicals, while world recession brought a drop in overseas demand for products like ships, machine tools, and ball bearings. Since these changes were also accompanied by the use of more advanced technology by competitors from the newly industrialized countries of Asia, especially South Korea and Taiwan, MITI policy-makers, strongly supported by business, decided to shift the emphasis in manufacturing away from industries which depended heavily on imported raw materials, and towards those which reflected higher values added, mostly through technological innovation. The fact that this included automobiles ensured the continued importance of steel – Japan produced more of both in 1980 than the United States – but there was also a major expansion in the field of information technology, in the form of computers, semiconductors, and related equipment.

As part of this process, some of the giant companies which had previously dominated the export trade began to lose a little of their pride of place, even to the point of shedding some of their labour force. It was this which chiefly explained the growth in unemployment. Firms which were coming to the fore in the 1980s, except automobile manufacturers, tended to be smaller, as well as less committed to the norms of lifetime employment and seniority wages. In addition, attempts to cut labour costs brought about an increase in the proportion of part-time staff, many of whom were women, particularly in the service industries, which were growing faster than the rest. Thus the patterns of industrial organization which the world had taken to be typically Japanese were proving not to be immutable.

As will be evident from much of what is said above, the development of the Japanese economy was still closely related to foreign trade. One feature of it was the much greater pace of growth in exports than imports after 1970. Measured in US dollars (which is customary, but can be misleading for figures after 1980, because of rapid changes in the dollar–yen rate of exchange) Japanese exports totalled $19·3 billion in 1970, $55·7 billion in 1975, $129·8 billion in 1980, $174 billion in 1985, that is, an increase of 800 per cent in fifteen years. Imports stood at $18·9 billion in 1970, $57·9 billion in 1975, $140·5 billion in 1980 (a jump which reflected the short-term effects of the second oil shock), $118 billion in 1985, making a rise of something more than 500 per cent over the same period. There was a decline in the proportion of exports going to the United States, though not in their value, and a substantial increase in both proportion and value of those to the Middle East, as Japan pressed sales to offset the greater cost of oil. Imports from the Middle East, as was to be expected, given the rise in oil prices, came to almost twenty times as much in 1980 as in 1970. Imports from America increased more slowly. South East Asia and Europe (in that order) remained Japan's other main trading partners, the former proving more successful than the latter in keeping its trade approximately in balance. This was not only because it provided raw materials, but also because its emerging industries began to find outlets in Japan for cheap textile and electrical consumer goods.

One significant fact about the composition of foreign trade in these years is that the index of exports of machinery by volume (1965 = 100), which included automobiles, rose from 263 in 1970 to 1070 in 1982. Indeed, Japan exported just under six million motor cars in 1980, when Toyota and Nissan came second and third (after General Motors) in the list of world production by companies. By contrast, the index for textile exports fell from 121 to 52. Among imports, food rather less than doubled (162 to 306); those of machinery increased 2·5 times (269 to 687); while those of fossil fuels were amost unchanged (243 to 285), despite multiplying many times in unit cost. The percentage of manufactured imports continued to rise, if fairly slowly, throughout the period 1982–8. At its end, South Korea had some 3 per cent of the Japanese market for video tape recorders, a little less than that for colour television sets, and about one-sixth of the market for clothing. Taiwan provided about 2 per cent of colour televisions, mainland China much the same proportion of clothing as Korea.

The change in the relationship between imports and exports had brought Japan's trade balance into credit in 1965 for the first time in twenty years. By 1972 the favourable balance was nearly $9 billion. This was cut back sharply by the extra cost of oil in 1973–5, but it recovered in 1976 and grew to over $24 billion in 1978. The second oil shock reduced it to very low levels in 1979 and 1980, but in 1981 the surplus was up to $20 billion again and stayed at about that figure for another two years. Thereafter the rise was resumed, bringing the margin to about $90 billion in both 1986 and 1987. Deficits under the heading of financial services, though sometimes very large, were by no means enough to offset the surplus on trade. Instead, there were substantial outflows of long-term capital, which within a few years made Japan a major international creditor. In its early stages the outflow was mostly used to fund portfolio investment, direct investment being no more than was required to ensure raw material supplies or carry out simple processing (smelting and refining, for instance) in low-cost areas overseas; but from about 1980 Japanese firms began establishing plants or subsidiaries in the more advanced countries of the world, usually for the purpose of securing tax advantages, or avoiding possible restrictions on exports from Japan. By the end of 1987 Japanese direct investment overseas had reached $23 billion. Europe, especially Britain, was becoming a target for it, in anticipation of the creation of a unified European market in 1992, but the United States remained the most important venue. There were over six hundred Japanese-owned factories there, about a hundred of them concerned with electronics, automobiles, or other machinery.

Such success – sometimes called the second economic miracle –was not without its problems. Trade disputes with Europe and the United States became a regular feature of the country's foreign relations. Consequential adjustments to government policies within Japan began to affect the patterns of politics, not only with respect to economic matters. These are topics to which we will turn in the final chapter of this book. One thing did not change, however: the steady rise in the standards of living enjoyed by the Japanese people.

SOCIAL CHANGE AND STANDARDS OF LIVING

Although it was customary in Japan to refer to the Japanese people as 'the hundred million' during the Pacific War, the population of the home islands in fact fell a long way short of that figure. It was still only 83 million in 1950. It continued to grow steadily, however, reaching 100 million towards the end of the 1960s, 120 million in the middle of the 1980s. The birth rate, which had been as high as 33 for every 10,000 people in 1948 (the postwar 'baby boom'), fell to under 14 in 1966, but the fall was balanced by lower death rates, due in large part to better food and health care. For example, national health insurance – funded privately to something like 80 per cent of the total – accounted for an expenditure of 220 billion yen in 1955, almost eight times as much thirty years later, that is, some 5 per cent of GNP. Japanese life expectancy reached over 74 years for men and nearly 80 years for women in the 1980s.

Urbanization increased more rapidly than population. In 1960 towns and cities contained 64 per cent of all Japanese, almost a quarter of the population being located in the 21 cities which had 300,000 inhabitants or more. In 1975 the urban proportion had risen to 76 per cent, with 36 per cent of the whole residing in 49 cities; and visitors to Japan who have travelled by train through the urban sprawl which spreads along the Pacific coast, westward from Tokyo, will have no difficulty in believing these statistics. Much of the increase represented migration from the countryside. In the first phase of postwar industrial development, starting in 1955, a good deal of labour flowed from the villages to the expanding and relatively labour-intensive firms engaged in manufacturing. Later, notably in the 1970s, the influx shifted more to commerce and the service trades. The resulting concentration of people and organizations, most of all in the capital, was by that time causing alarm. One Prime Minister, Tanaka Kakuei, coming to power in 1972, proposed a solution through industrial dispersal, though it was never fully attempted. Another, Takeshita Noboru, formed a committee in February 1988 to consider other possibilities, such as the transfer of the capital or a number of its functions elsewhere.

Population figures also revealed changes in the size and composition of families, partly due to a decline in the ratio of rural to urban households (the former being larger because they provide both labour for the farmer's holding and a measure of welfare for those family members too old to work). Typical of the new Japan was the urban family, which comprised only two generations: a husband, absent at the office or the factory for much of the time; a wife, responsible for running the household and supervising the children's education (she has become increasingly likely to take a part-time job once their schooling is over); and the children themselves, of whom there are not as many as there used to be. Average family size was down to 3·3 in 1980, compared with nearly 5 in 1955.

The predominance of the nuclear family added to the problems which derived from the presence of an increasing proportion of the elderly in the population. Only 5·3 per cent of Japanese people were over 65 years old in 1955. In 1980 the figure was 9 per cent, in 2000 it is expected to be 15 per cent. Given that relatively few of the old will by then belong to the kind of families which offer a welfare substitute for the state, the provision of medical and other care for them, together with the burden which the cost of this will impose on what is assumed from population trends to be a shrinking workforce, is an issue which has come to engage the attention of politicians. Old age pensions, instituted in 1959, were by 1977 paying out 180,000 yen a year to each of 4·6 million Japanese. Both the amount and the numbers are bound to increase.

Since Japan after 1945 had no hereditary ruling class and quite low levels of inherited wealth, a family's position in life came to depend above all on earnings and conditions of employment. There was a total workforce of 47·6 million in 1965. Some 60 per cent were hired employees, the rest divided more or less equally between the self-employed and family workers. By occupation, just under a quarter worked in agriculture, forestry, and fisheries; a little more than 30 per cent in manufacturing and construction; about the same in commerce and the service industries. Ten years later the total had risen to 53·1 million, nearly 70 per cent being hired employees. The largest drop was in the number of family workers, down to 13 per cent, paralleling a decline in the proportion engaged in agriculture, forestry, and fisheries, now only 14 per cent of the whole. The other two occupation categories had increased to almost 34 per cent and 38 per cent of the workforce, respectively.

It is clear from these figures that the farming community no longer played as important a part in the economy as it had done before 1945. Agricultural production had recovered rapidly after the war, as men came back from military service, and supplies of fertilizer were once more made available by industry. It was at prewar levels by 1950, rose by about a third in the next decade, then by a little less than that in the following one. Thereafter it levelled out. Measured by its contribution to gross national product, however, agriculture steadily lost ground: 9 per cent in 1960, 5 per cent in 1970, 2·5 per cent in 1980. Farmers, as we have seen, became a smaller proportion of the working population. They comprised 27 per cent in 1960, only 9 per cent twenty years later.

Rice continued to be the major crop, notwithstanding the fact that Japanese were eating less of it. In 1961, responding to pressure from farming interests, whose disproportionate voting strength gave them a political influence difficult to resist, the Ikeda government passed an agricultural law designed to keep farm earnings tolerably close to those of factory workers. The method chosen was to pay rice producers for their crop at a price calculated in relation to their cost of living, not what it would fetch on the market, the difference being made up by official subsidy. This proved in the long run to have a number of disadvantages. It kept rice prices to Japanese much higher than those ruling in the rest of the world; it enabled inefficient producers to stay in business, so discouraging the consolidation of uneconomically small plots (still averaging no more than a hectare); and persuaded farmers to produce more rice than consumers were willing to buy.

Nor did price support solve all the farmer's problems. It was not only that the high wages paid in the manufacturing and service industries continued to attract labour away from the village. Among the farm households that remained, a substantial proportion of the men took jobs in factories and offices – thanks to an excellent transport system – becoming part-time farmers, who left most of the work of cultivation to their womenfolk, the elderly, and the young. Their place was to some extent taken by machines, mostly small ones, as was appropriate to the size of the average plot. Power cultivators and tractors in use, a mere 38,000 in 1955, numbered half a million in 1960 and seven times as much a decade later. Even so, Japanese agriculture was left with more workers and less machinery than is common in advanced industrial countries.

By the end of the 1960s urban residents in Japan were most likely – and increasingly likely – to work for a company in manufacturing, commerce or the service trades. In the very largest firms, employees fell into three categories. At the top was management, largely recruited from university graduates. A man – there were and are very few women in management posts, though their numbers are slowly increasing – would enter the company with others of his age, expecting to be promoted along with them in accordance with seniority, providing he was suitably conscientious and his health did not break down. The least able would gradually be hived off into less prestigious appointments. The most able could hope eventually to reach the very peak, since family ownership was rare. The price to be paid was hard work, measured by hours spent in the office, and unremitting loyalty, in return for which the 'salaryman' received what was by Western standards a small monthly wage but a fairly generous expense account.

In the next lower category were the company's regular 'permanent' workers, rather less well educated, but not marked off by any obvious status symbols. Pay was good, as was in-job training. There was a high degree of security of employment, made financially possible by a flexible bonus system, plus a willingness on the part of both employer and employee to resort to job changes and re-training, rather than dismissals, when times were hard. Not infrequently there were company housing, company health and pension schemes, and company holidays. Not many of these benefits extended to the lowest cohort, the temporary workers, who were also the people most likely to lose their jobs in a recession.

Medium and smaller companies, which were commonly engaged in sub-contracting for the larger ones, or in the distribution and service industries, had some of the same characteristics, except that they were less elaborately structured and many were family-owned. In the early stages of postwar development they did not pay as well: in 1959 firms with less than 100 employees offered only 60 per cent of the wage rates of those with more than 1,000. They also had fewer welfare facilities. However, as the pool of available labour was slowly whittled away, employers found it better to rely on technological improvement and rationalization, possibly financed by their parent companies or regular suppliers, than to insist on cheaper working practices. Wages in the smaller firms therefore rose. A distinction between the two segments of the dual economy remained, but it was not as great as it had been.

An employee's point of entry into this system, as into the government bureaucracy, was determined by education, which gave the majority of Japanese an interest in ensuring that their children went as far as possible up the educational ladder and attended the best possible schools. This was particularly so, because educational attainment was measured by the reputation of the school or university, rather than by the individual's prowess in it. One consequence was a rapid increase in the number of students who went on from compulsory middle school to voluntary high school: 43 per cent in 1950, 55 per cent in 1960, 82 per cent in 1970, 94 per cent in 1980. Another was a comparable growth in higher education. By 1975 Japan had approximately 400 universities, of which two-fifths had been founded in the previous twenty years, and the total reached almost 500 in the 1980s, some 70 per cent being private foundations. They enrolled two million students, which was a little under 40 per cent of the relevant age group. Not all enjoyed the same esteem, of course. Attendance at the best state universities, headed by Tokyo and Kyoto, or the more famous private ones, like Keio and Waseda, was a guarantee of career opportunities second to none. Graduates from Tokyo University, for example, provided 20 per cent of company executives in 1965 (and twice that proportion of those in the larger firms), as well as 60 per cent of section chiefs in the government ministries concerned with trade and finance. By comparison, many of the newer private establishments of higher education were poorly staffed, thinly provided with books and other facilities, over-provided with students. They were immeasurably inferior as platforms from which to launch a career. It is not surprising, therefore, that there was fierce competition to get into those of the highest reputation; and since this entailed passing entrance examinations, the result was an annual 'examination hell'. What is more, the best schools afforded the best preparation for entry to the best universities, so the struggle extended downwards through the system. A survey published in 1988 showed that of a sample of Tokyo children in their last year of elementary school, three-quarters attended cramming schools (*juku*) during the summer vacation. One in four of these did so every day.

Membership of a trade union, even for employees who had no ambition to be managers, was of a good deal less importance than graduation from high school or university. It did nevertheless have advantages, especially in the larger firms. The growth of trade unions had proceeded quickly after 1945, profiting from American encouragement. Many of the wartime conciliation bodies established in factories had turned themselves into company unions and campaigned vigorously for membership, while nationwide unions were founded for public sector employees, like railway and postal workers, and teachers. There was a setback when a planned general strike was vetoed by SCAP in 1947, again when the purge was extended to communists in industry in 1949, but from 1950 the situation settled down. During the next quarter of a century just over one third of Japanese workers usually belonged to unions, rather more among the permanent workforce in manufacturing, fewer in smaller companies and in the wholesale and retail trades. The largest segment (36 per cent of unionized labour in 1971) was affiliated to Sohyo (General Council of Trade Unions), which supported the Japan Socialist Party. About half as many belonged to Domei (Japan Confederation of Labour), which backed the moderate left-of-centre Democratic Socialists. Most of the rest were in small and unaffiliated enterprise unions – their membership averaged less than 200 in 1971 – whose principal concern was with local wages and conditions of work.

Collectively, the unions, which engaged each year in a 'spring offensive' to settle wages and bonuses, helped the bulk of the Japanese people to a share in the affluence brought by the expansion of national production. Real wages in manufacturing industry were nearly 50 per cent higher in 1960 than they had been in 1934–6 (which is taken to be the prewar norm). In the next ten years they rose by another 80 per cent, while those in commerce grew only a little more slowly. To take a different measure, Japan's per capita income was US$208 in 1955, but five times as much in 1980, even allowing for inflation. In 1987 per capita GNP – though this reflected in part the rapid change in yen–dollar exchange rates – stood at $19,600, exceeding that of the United States.

One benefit conferred by higher incomes was the consumption of a wider range of more expensive foodstuffs, whose greater nutritional value brought significant increases in the height and weight of Japanese youth. To some extent this was made possible by diversification in agriculture. There were increases in the domestic production of milk, pig's meat, and chickens, for example, while fruit and vegetables also became available in greater quantity and variety. Nevertheless, the improvements in diet were purchased at a cost which was not altogether welcome to those who believed – for non-economic reasons – that the country should as far as possible be able to feed itself. Food imports grew rapidly, with the result that by the 1970s Japan was not much more than 70 per cent self-sufficient in farm products as a whole. She produced more rice than she needed, and 90 per cent or more of domestic consumption of eggs, chickens, and vegetables, but had to import at least three-quarters of her requirements of soybeans, wheat, barley, and sugar. The trend accelerated after 1980, as the yen grew stronger in relation to other currencies.

Despite better and more expensive foodstuffs, the amount of the average household budget spent on food fell from 44·5 per cent in 1955 to 27·8 per cent in 1980, bringing it down to approximately American and West European levels. The proportion spent on clothing also dropped, as did that on rent and medical care. This left more for non-essentials, such as extra education, consumer durables, and leisure. By 1965 90 per cent of Japanese households had black-and-white television sets. Ten years later the percentage was the same, but the sets were colour. Moreover, in 1975 80 per cent had telephones, over 90 per cent had refrigerators and washing machines, 40 per cent had private cars. The figure for cars reached 57 per cent in 1980.

In many ways Japanese standards of living were undoubtedly impressive by the 1980s: high real wages, low unemployment rates, excellent health care, above average consumption of goods and services. However, a White Paper issued in 1986 made it clear that in matters touching the quality of life there was still a great deal to be done if Japan were to reach American and European norms. Working hours were very long. Nearly three-quarters of Tokyo's power lines were still above ground; only just over a third of homes were connected to sewers; houses were very small – 'rabbit hutches' they were called in one European report, which provoked hostile reactions in Japan – and so expensive as to cause the introduction of two-generation mortgages. Land prices, which were quite exceptionally high, especially in the cities, were at the heart of the housing problem, serving also as a brake on public works. What is more, they imposed restrictions on the 'leisure boom'. Golf driving ranges and bowling alleys were much more common than activities which required extensive open space.

On the other hand, it sometimes proved possible to overcome difficulties of this kind, where there was the political will. Pollution is a relevant example. Industrial growth in the 1960s, unaccompanied by controls over siting or the disposal of waste, produced not only urban ugliness, but also dangers to health. New diseases were identified, stemming from pollution of the water or the air, which often took their names from the manufacturing centres that gave them birth: Yokkaichi asthma (from petrochemical fumes), and Minamata disease (from mercury poisoning). In cities, smog caused by exhaust emissions became so regular a hazard that Tokyo traffic police were issued with oxygen. The public outcry became vociferous. Eventually it forced action on a government that had hesitated without such prompting to take any step that might imperil economic growth. In 1966 regulations were issued concerning exhaust gases from new cars. In 1967 a Pollution Prevention Law provided a legal framework within which victims could force offending firms to pay compensation. In 1971 the Environment Agency was created to supervise the implementation of the law. Observers of Japanese politics were doubtful whether this would be enough to outweigh the advantages enjoyed by business, not least because enforcement was left to local government; but they proved wrong. Though compensation was never easy to extract, the threat of it proved cogent, with the result that by 1980 only a tiny proportion of water samples failed to conform with the rigid new standards. Tokyo's air at that date contained only a quarter as much sulphur as it had ten years before. Against that, it has to be said that in subsequent years, as oil prices fell and the yen rose in value, oil consumption began to increase again, bringing renewed signs of pollution of the atmosphere.

16

THE END OF THE SHOWA ERA, 1971–1989

The death of Emperor Hirohito in January 1989 was literally the end of an era. The era-name Showa, or Brilliant Harmony, which had identified his reign, passed into history, becoming his posthumous title. Heisei, awkwardly translated as Achieving Peace, was adopted for that of Akihito, his son. The event also had a symbolic significance, appropriate to a ruler whose duties were themselves symbolic. Because Hirohito was the last surviving head of state among the major participants in the Pacific War, his disappearance from the scene, and that of the era with which he was linked, could be said to have closed a chapter which many of the Japanese people had shown a preference to forget. By the same token, however, in some parts of the world it revived bitter memories, manifested in a spate of accusations that Hirohito had himself been a war criminal. Many of those who had fought against Japan voiced complaints about their countries sending senior representatives to the emperor's funeral.

Yet war guilt and the position of the emperor were no longer central to Japan's place in the world in 1989. Much more immediately important were the repercussions of recent economic growth, raising questions about trade and the balance of international payments, which provoked disputes between Japan and other countries. These affected in particular her relations with her ally, the United States. At the same time, they prompted among Japanese an increasing self-confidence, coupled – in apparent contradiction – with a desire to break away from nationalist insularity for the sake of understanding other peoples better. It is not yet clear which of the two impulses will prevail.

TRADE DISPUTES AND ECONOMIC POLICY

Difficulties over the trade imbalance between Japan and the United States had begun some time before the 'oil shock' of 1973. Japanese exports to America had increased from $666 million in 1958 to $9·6 billion fifteen years later, whereas imports from that country had grown over the same period from $980 million to $8·3 billion. In other words, a substantial Japanese import surplus had become an export surplus. The composition of the trade had also changed. By the end of the period Japan's exports were chiefly advanced products of her modern industry, which found ready markets in America, while imports of similar goods had relatively declined, because of the competition they faced from Japanese manufacturers. The advantage enjoyed by the latter was enhanced by the determination of the Ministry of International Trade and Industry to support those Japanese firms which it judged to be crucial to the country's economy.

The complaints made by foreign manufacturers and governments about this situation were focused initially on Japanese exports, whose pricing was determined in many fields, not by the requirements of reasonable profit, but by a desire to expand market share. Japan, in fact, was accused of acting contrary to international rules about 'fair trade'. The earliest specific charges concerned textiles, both natural and synthetic. By 1971, however, Washington was also concerned about the monetary implications of the trade imbalance, which had been exaggerated, it said, by Japan's defence of an unrealistic yen– dollar exchange rate. In the light of this belief, the Nixon administration suddenly took steps in August 1971 to adjust the position, ending the fixed exchange rate between the dollar and other currencies, as well as the dollar's fixed relationship to gold, and imposing a temporary surcharge of 10 per cent on imports. These measures, though of general application, were clearly chosen for their anticipated effect on Japan. And in the short-term they worked. By the end of the year the yen had appreciated 16 per cent against the dollar; the trade gap narrowed; and Japan's balance of payments moved from a surplus of $4·6 billion in 1971 to a deficit of nearly $10 billion in 1973.

This was by no means the end of the story, however. In 1977 there was another long wrangle concerning the price of steel. From about 1980 automobiles became an even more emotive issue – in Europe, as well as America – leading Western producers to demand various forms of restriction on imports from Japan. There was also a dispute with the United States about semi-conductors in 1987, which reached so acrimonious a level that Washington imposed temporary higher tariffs on selected Japanese goods as an act of retaliation.

In a narrow sense, a solution to problems of this kind was usually found through the negotiation of 'voluntary' bilateral agreements, imposing quotas on Japanese shipments of the products concerned. However, this did not suffice to meet another foreign complaint, that Japan protected her own markets against imports from abroad to a degree which prevented foreign firms from redressing the trade imbalance for themselves. Certainly the American and European shares of the goods which Japan imported dropped quite sharply after 1970. In the next ten years, America's share fell from 29 per cent to 17 per cent, Europe's from 8 per cent to under 6 per cent.

Japanese governments therefore thought it desirable to make concessions. In May 1973, in response to Nixon's surcharge on imports almost two years earlier, the Tanaka cabinet announced that it would carry out a 'liberalization' of trade, though in practice it continued to operate non-tariff barriers to protect a number of selected industries. Protests continued, notably from the United States. In 1977–8 there was a series of exchanges over access for American beef and citrus fruits to the Japanese market, temporarily settled by an increase in quotas, but dragging on intermittently until 1988, when agreement was reached to phase out both protection and quotas by 1992. Another long-running disagreement was over the extent to which Japan would permit foreign bidding for contracts and procurement orders, especially in public works and the telecommunications industry. As a result, during the early 1980s attitudes and actions on both sides became settled and predictable: Japanese ministers made announcements about 'market opening' from time to time; foreign firms and governments greeted them sceptically.

Underlying the trade disputes was a very much larger issue, that of the relationship between Japan's balance of payments and world economic growth. During 1977 President Carter enunciated the 'locomotive' thesis, calling for Japan and West Germany to join the United States in stimulating domestic demand within their own countries, in order to aid in the recovery of those economies still suffering from the oil shock. Prime Minister Fukuda Takeo was persuaded to accept a 7 per cent annual growth target for Japan, but failed to achieve it. His successor, Ohira Masayoshi, abandoned the idea as impracticable in the context of the second oil shock of 1979. As a consequence, Japan entered the 1980s under pressure from both America and Europe to adopt a range of economic policies – reducing exports, liberalizing imports, revaluing the yen, and providing improved facilities for foreign banking and finance – not only for the sake of redressing unfavourable balances, but also as a duty owed to the weak by the strong. The cabinets of Suzuki Zenko (1980–2) and Nakasone Yasuhiro (1982–7) denied the charge of selfishness, but decided that it would be politically wise to respond.

One means of doing so was to increase the amounts which Japan allocated for overseas aid, which had been reduced during the difficult years of the 1970s. By 1987 the annual total was up to nearly $7·5 billion, the second highest in the world, and the scope of what was done had been extended to include the relief of Third World debt. Plans were made to increase the amount expended to $50 billion over the next five years. Of more fundamental significance were proposals for structural reform of the Japanese economy. A report submitted in April 1986 by an advisory group, chaired by Maekawa Haruo, former Governor of the Bank of Japan, recommended an increase in domestic demand through greater expenditure on housing and public works, plus tax reforms calculated to raise consumption; a further improvement in market access for foreign goods and investment, effected by reviewing distribution systems and liberalizing trade rules; and a revision of agricultural support, so as to reduce the degree of protectionism it involved. Prime Minister Nakasone publicly welcomed the report. After his term of office had ended (November 1987), another committee, reporting to his successor,

Takeshita Noboru, put the proposals into the form of a five-year plan for 1988–93. It envisaged a real growth rate of 3·75 per cent per annum, based to a greater extent than in the past on domestic demand; a very gradual increase in inflation; an unemployment rate steady at 2·5 per cent; and a higher standard of living for the country's inhabitants, more commensurate with economic performance as a whole. This would entail *inter alia* a reduction in land and commodity prices, plus the institution of a five-day forty-hour week.

There was public support for the last of these proposals, but much of the rest faced strongly-worded opposition from economists and politicians, who were reluctant to abandon the policies of export-dependence which had served so well in the previous thirty years. There were also complaints from vested interests of many kinds. Nevertheless, some headway was made. The national railways were privatized in 1987, as a step towards reducing public subsidies. A small dent was made in the structure of farm price support in the same year (though only after farmers had prevented it in 1986). Nakasone had to abandon his plans for tax reform in 1987 because of Diet opposition, but Takeshita Noboru reintroduced them in a slightly modified form in 1988 and eventually got them through the lower house. As finally agreed, they simplified and lowered the levels of income tax, which was to be levied in five bands, ranging from 10 to 50 per cent; made a small reduction in corporation tax, fully effective in 1990; and brought in two new taxes, a capital gains tax, set at 20 per cent, and a consumption tax, similar to Europe's VAT, at 3 per cent. One object of the reforms was to make tax fairer, especially to employees and middle-income management, by reducing the loopholes available to farmers and the self-employed. Another was to provide a firmer revenue base, in anticipation of the need for higher welfare payments to an ageing population. A third, directly relevant to external problems, was to shift the tax burden in ways which would expand domestic demand.

There was also an important shift of emphasis in the 1980s in the form of stronger economic bonds between Japan and her Asian neighbours. Nakasone's first overseas visit after he became Prime Minister was to South Korea in January 1983, seeking goodwill through the offer of loans and credits to a total of $4 billion. With China there were at first political obstacles to overcome: though formal relations had been resumed in 1972, as we have seen (chapter 14), it was not until 1978 that a peace treaty was concluded, the delay being largely due to the fact that China wanted to include, and Japan to avoid, a clause condemning Russia's world ambitions. However, once this difficulty had been resolved (by a wording which rejected 'hegemony', no matter who pursued it), Sino-Japanese relations, too, came to turn on matters of credit and investment. Most Japanese exports to China – they reached an annual total of $5 billion in 1980 and 1981, nearly twice that much in 1986 – consisted of industrial plant and other high-technology products. They were crucial to China's own industrial development, but she found them difficult to fund, since her return exports to Japan, which included a high proportion of raw materials, never reached the same value. The result was a stop–go policy of Chinese credit controls, making the flow of trade uneven. This was greatly to the inconvenience of Japanese manufacturers. Ohira Masayoshi attempted to solve the problem in 1979 by making available loans to China of $1·5 billion. Nakasone went to Peking in March 1984 to arrange large-scale credits in yen, while Takeshita Noboru, following suit in August 1988, extended the programme of loans until 1995. In return, Japan's business investors were given better access to Chinese raw materials and labour, plus improved facilities for remitting their profits home.

In South East Asia, expanding Japanese trade encountered some hostility after the rapid growth of the 1960s. Most of it reflected fears about potential economic domination by Japan, together with complaints about the failure of Japanese companies to give proper career opportunities to locally-recruited staff, but there were also doubts concerning rearmament, which was held by some to be evidence of renewed Japanese ambitions. Thus when Tanaka Kakuei toured the region early in 1974 he was greeted by anti-Japanese demonstrations in Thailand and Indonesia. The Japanese response was to observe more discretion in business activities and to increase trading credits as a means of winning friends. Tanaka, for example, granted Indonesia a credit of 95 billion yen for the exploitation of natural gas as soon as he returned to Tokyo. Nakasone followed a very similar policy towards the region ten years later. As a result, the newly-industrialized countries of Asia (chiefly South Korea,

Taiwan, Hong Kong, and Singapore) found themselves in a much better position than most to profit from Japanese import liberalization. Often with the help of Japanese capital and technology, they began to sell to Japan items which Japan had been selling to the rest of the world: televisions, tape recorders, and electronic equipment generally.

Looking more widely at Japan's external policies in this period, two points require comment. One was the greater involvement in the Middle East. As an importer of Gulf oil, Japan made moves to placate Arab opinion by adopting an anti-Israeli stance from the end of 1973, sending senior ministers to the area to expound her viewpoint, increasing her diplomatic representation there, giving aid to Palestinian refugees and technical assistance to various Arab countries. The outcome was security of oil supplies, even though in 1979 it also provoked a dispute with the United States, when Japan continued to buy Iranian oil despite the seizure of the American embassy in Tehran.

After 1980 the question of oil gradually became less critical, both because of reductions in Japanese consumption and because of more diverse sources of energy supply. In these years the Japanese government began to develop a different theme around which to co-ordinate its overseas interests. This was first enunciated by Ohira before his unexpected death in 1980, when it was described as a policy for the 'Pacific Rim'. It envisaged using Japanese capital for the purpose of working out economic strategies in the countries forming an arc from Korea south through China and South East Asia into Australasia. The focus was to be on Japan's raw material needs: China's coal; Indonesia's oil; Australia's coal, iron, and bauxite; and supplies of uranium for atomic power. Not surprisingly, the idea prompted hostile comments about the creation of a new Co-prosperity Sphere. After all, the proposals to use Australian iron ore and Japanese technology in China's Baoshan ironworks, or for Japan to finance an improvement in China's transport facilities, in order to get raw materials to the coast, would not have been out of place in 1942. Gradually, however, the concept was expanded to take in Canada and the United States, thereby becoming a plan for what was called the 'Pacific Basin'. In this guise it was less obviously concerned with Japan's particular needs, or a 'vertical' relationship between advanced and less advanced economies. It looked instead to exploit what was thought to be an impending transfer of the world's economic centre of gravity from the 'old' Atlantic to the 'new' Pacific. The future, it was assumed, would depend on a form of Japanese–American co-operation within which the inequalities of the defence agreement and the disputes over trade would both be reconciled. Spreading outward from this would be a much more complex set of relationships between the economies of the region – advanced, newly-industrialized, and underdeveloped – than had ever existed, or even been conceived, for the Co-prosperity Sphere.

CONSERVATISM AND NATIONALISM

Given the wide spread of political attitudes within the Liberal Democrat Party, it is not surprising that the cabinets it produced varied quite substantially in their policies. Indeed, commentators have identified a pattern of alternation during recent years, in which some Prime Ministers, like Ohira Masayoshi (1978–80) and Nakasone Yasuhiro (1982–7), have taken initiatives to break the mould they inherited, while others, like Suzuki Zenko (1980–2) and Takeshita Noboru (1987–9), have devoted their efforts to consolidation. One might nevertheless argue that the result has been a process of change over time, because the consolidators have never entirely put back the clock.

There have been a number of variations in the parliamentary position of the LDP. Against a background of economic misgivings, caused by trade disputes and the oil shock, the party lost for a time its reputation as the architect of affluence in the 1970s. In consequence, its representation declined: 271 seats in the election of 1972, 257 in 1976, 248 in 1979. Since there were just over 500 lower house seats in all at the end of the decade, the 1979 result, even allowing for the recruitment of a few independents after the election, was not enough to provide a working majority. On the other hand, the party seemed in no real danger of losing control. There were conservative splinter groups, with which it could form an alliance, while its opponents remained too diverse to unite against it, despite occasional rumours about a popular front.

It is true that in this situation left-wing members of the Diet, seeing an opportunity to exercise some practical influence for the first time in many years, began to concentrate more on specific measures, less on ideological points. The Communist Party, for example, stopped using the phrase 'dictatorship of the proletariat' or appealing to Marxist–Leninist principles, preferring 'scientific socialism', at least in public. Yet the Socialist Party, which was still the strongest element in opposition, failed to rise to the occasion. As trade union membership grew smaller –the expanding sectors of business were those which were less unionized – the Socialists proved unable to muster any countervailing basis of support. They won only 107 seats in 1979, when another 135 were distributed among Communists, the Komeito, and Democratic Socialists. Thereafter, the speed with which Japan recovered from the second oil shock restored to the Liberal Democrats some measure of their former reputation, leaving the Socialists trailing. The LDP won 284 seats in June 1980, mostly at the expense of Komeito amd the Communists (benefiting, it was said, from a sympathy vote, because its incumbent Prime Minister, Ohira, died during the campaign). It dropped to 250 in 1983, saving its majority by recruiting independents, then swept back under Nakasone with a triumphant 300 seats in July 1986. At this point the Socialists reached their lowest level since 1955, a mere 86 seats. So great was their disarray that the party gambled on electing a woman as leader later in the year: Doi Takako, the first woman to lead a political party in Japan.

Prime Ministers during this period were men of a somewhat different background from those of the 1950s and 1960s. Of the seven who held office between the middle of 1972 and the end of 1988, only Ohira Masayoshi can be described as a former bureaucrat. The rest had been politicians for most of their adult lives. The LDP, in fact, was producing its own successor generation of leaders, able to dominate the civil servants, or at least exploit the disagreements between ministries to get their own way. The party was also evolving a secretariat competent to brief its members on policy issues, plus a forum, the Policy Research Council, in which these could be discussed. The result was a shift in the balance of power at the centre, a little away from the government bureaucracy, a little towards the Diet and the Liberal Democrats.

The role of business was becoming different, too. It still provided the money that the politicians needed: at the time of the

1972 election it was reported that the Liberal Democrats asked Keidanren for 7·5 billion yen, about a third of which was to be distributed as subsidies to individual candidates. On the other hand, for the Liberal Democrats as a party, too great a reliance on business money and 'machine' politics carried the risk of alienating public sympathy. This was evident in the later stages of the career of Tanaka Kakuei. Tanaka had entered politics after 1945, having already put together a private fortune as a building contractor; and in the next twenty years he demonstrated a flair for raising funds and a skill in dispensing them which enabled him to assemble the party's largest faction. After filling a number of appropriate ministerial posts – Finance, as well as International Trade and Industry – he became Prime Minister in July 1972, succeeding Sato. The timing was unfortunate. The principal plank of his policy, a plan to relocate industry more widely through the Japanese archipelago by greater spending on transport and communications, had to be abandoned as too costly in the wake of the oil crisis. The rise in consumer prices, also due to oil, then weakened his popularity with electors. Consequently, when one of the Tokyo journals published material in November 1974, casting doubt on his probity in matters of fund-raising and finance, there were calls for his resignation which he was in no position to resist.

All the same, resignation did not by any means put an end to his power. The membership of his faction rose from 90 in 1974 to 105 in 1982, making him still the acknowledged king-maker among the Liberal Democrats. His immediate successor, Miki Takeo, was a rival, chosen as 'Mr Clean', but two of the next four Prime Ministers were Tanaka protegés. Even after he was arrested in July 1976 on fresh charges of corruption (this time of having accepted huge bribes from Lockheed during his tenure of office, in order to influence the placing of Japanese contracts for aircraft), Tanaka continued to serve in the Diet while on bail. He left the LDP, becoming an independent, but he did not relinquish control of his faction. This anomaly remained at the centre of political debate for several years, during which his friends had to thwart repeated attempts to remove him from the lower house; and though he was tried and convicted on the Lockheed charge in October 1983, subject to appeal, he retained his seat in the election which followed. Many senior members of the LDP must have been profoundly relieved when a cerebral haemorrhage removed him from active politics – and from public view – in February 1985.

Despite this, the issue of fund-raising in politics, especially conservative politics, did not go away. In the closing months of 1988 press and television began to carry reports about the political donations of a property subsidiary, Cosmos, of the Recruit company, in particular the shares which it had distributed to politicians and others at bargain prices, in the expectation that they would be able to make substantial profits after a planned quotation on the stock exchange. Early statements implicated the Finance Minister, Miyazawa Kiichi, and possibly also the former Prime Minister, Nakasone Yasuhiro. Takeshita Noboru, who had succeeded Nakasone, sacrificed Miyazawa in December, then reshuffled his cabinet, supposedly to eliminate those members who had been tainted by the scandal. It transpired, however, that the affair was more far-reaching than he had thought. The new Justice Minister, responsible for pursuing the case against Recruit, and the Chief Cabinet Secretary, were both forced to resign soon after. Several senior bureaucrats were also implicated. A number of arrests were made, including those of some executives in government corporations. At this point Takeshita's own position came under threat, first because of his failure to produce an 'honest' cabinet the second time round, then because it emerged that he had himself received Cosmos money. At the end of April 1989 he announced his intention of resigning, though it was not until 2 June that the Diet elected his Foreign Minister, Uno Sosuke, to succeed him. Uno lasted only two months. Involved in a sex scandal, then held responsible for the party's poor showing in the upper house elections in July, he was replaced by a former Education Minister, Kaifu Toshiki, early in August. It began to look as if the Liberal Democrats would have to change their ways if they were to stay in power. Kaifu appointed a woman as Chief Cabinet Secretary, apparently in a bid to appease women voters, offended by the public revelation of the sexual habits of senior politicians. Nakasone, like Tanaka before him, resigned from the LDP – while retaining control of his faction – amidst indications that some of his more unpopular policies, such as the reduction in farm price support and the introduction of a consumption tax, might be abandoned.

Nakasone had consistently adopted a higher profile in his international dealings than had been customary among Japanese Prime Ministers in the postwar years. In their first meeting early in 1983 he had moved on to 'Ron' and 'Yasu' terms with President Reagan. He also had a forthcoming attitude towards defence, which helped win friends in Washington. Within a week or two of taking office in 1982 he indicated to the Diet that he was not prepared to regard the limitation of defence spending to 1 per cent of GNP as sacrosanct; soon after, he authorized the export of defence technology, a step which America had several times suggested; then a Defence White Paper, approved by the cabinet in August 1983, for the first time envisaged building up Japan's sea and air power to the point at which it would make possible the policing of sea lanes for a thousand miles from the Japanese coast; and the budget for 1986 provided for an increase in missiles and a qualitative upgrading of other weapons. There was even talk of revising the constitution, so as to make the Self Defence Force unmistakably legal, though nothing came of it.

Nakasone's interest in education, motivated in part by his wish to strengthen traditional values, also had an international dimension. In April 1984 he set up a Council of Education to advise the Prime Minister on how to remove those features of the country's education system which seemed outmoded, and how to fit it to be a suitable preparation for the qualities which Japan would need in future in dealing with the outside world. The council produced reports in June 1985 and April 1986, recommending a number of reforms. One was to reduce the rigidities of entrance examinations and teaching methods in schools and universities, in the belief that greater flexibility would make for creativity and independent expression of ideas. Rote learning, in other words, was no longer to be regarded as the norm, partly because it was thought to handicap research. Another proposal was to give Japanese youth a better knowledge of cultures other than their own, including a more practical command of foreign languages.

Because much of this was controversial among Liberal Democrats – they were conservatives, after all – Nakasone tended to look outside the party for some of his support. By making more use of the specialized sections of the Prime Minister's secretariat, plus advisory groups recruited in part from non-government service, he was able at times to bypass the Diet and the regular bureaucratic machinery, and appeal directly to the public. The device was not always successful, to be sure: his proposals for tax reform and education continued to meet with a good deal of expert, as well as political, opposition. All the same, greater openness helped to win votes. The resounding LDP victory in the election of 1986 was so widely attributed to Nakasone's personal qualities that his party voted him another year in office as its president, one more than its constitution technically allowed.

It would be unwise to conclude from this that Japanese politics were becoming presidential in the American sense. Rather, it seems that Nakasone had caught a public mood. It helped that the economy was booming again. It also helped that the workforce was less inclined to vote for the left than it once had been. In the spring wage offensive of 1986 the metal workers (steel, automobiles, electrical appliances, heavy industry generally), who had always been at the heart of union support for the Socialists, won a smaller percentage rise than that of the year before or those of most other workers. November 1987 saw the formation of a federation of private sector unions (Rengo), having well over five million members (which made it larger than Sohyo) and no declared political affiliation. An Equal Employment Act of May 1985 had given a fresh impetus to the employment of women – they amounted to 36 per cent of the workforce in 1986 and 1987 – who were not heavily unionized. There were thus some grounds for accepting Nakasone's claim that he had brought the Liberal Democrats out of the years of uncertainty and back into a strong position once again, even though scandals about the party's finances undermined its position under his immediate successors.

One of the factors that had enabled him to do so was a modest revival of nationalism, or of a sense of Asian identity, in Japan. For a hundred years the conflict between being Asian and being modern – in the Western manner – was a recurrent theme in Japanese life. At first blush, most of what happened after 1945 seemed to strengthen modernity. Parliamentary democracy, bureaucratic government, business structures, trade unions, education in its postwar phase, all had their origins in a culture that is European and American. So do most of the trappings of everyday living: buses and trains, water-taps and refrigerators, the office and the factory, television, the daily newspaper, clothing, even food (except for special occasions). Contemporary Japanese tastes in music are above all for Beethoven, jazz, or one of their Western successors.

The Japanese are no different in this from other non-Western peoples, though they have travelled farther along the road. So one is left with the question, what is there about Japanese society after more than a century of modernization that still justifies the label 'Asian'? It is tempting to give the answer, very little. The intellectuals and the youth of Japan today – indeed, the greater part of the population – have received an education which makes the writing of Goethe or Shakespeare or Tolstoy as familiar to them as that of Murasaki Shikibu or Ihara Saikaku, perhaps more so. If they admit to having a political creed at all it is likely to be a Western-style conservatism, or else Marxism, which remains pervasive, though no longer as universally orthodox as it was for a time just after the surrender. In 1978, when a White Paper reported the results of a poll comparing the attitudes of young people in various parts of the world to work, religion, and service to one's country, the figures for Japan in all three contexts came out very close to those for Britain and West Germany, a long way removed from those for India.

Yet there is more to be said about it than that. To a Japanese, whether young or old, 'ethics' still means in very large part Confucianism. Ever since the end of the occupation in 1952 talk of reforming education has nearly always included some reference to restoring its ethical base, expressed in Confucian terms. Nor can religion be ignored as a link with tradition, even though opinion surveys taken between 1958 and 1983 tended to show that only a quarter or a third of the population admit to having a personal faith. Setting aside festivals, because they are more likely to be attended as a family day out or a community celebration, it remains significant that there has been a considerable array of new religious movements since the war, most of which claim some kind of traditional antecedents. Sokagakkai, the largest and most famous, derives from a Buddhist sect, while others are at least nominally Shinto, or are concerned with semi-religious practices like oracles and fortune-telling, to which one cannot easily attach a doctrinal tag. Aspects of Zen Buddhism are not infrequently to be found in courses on management training. Japanese companies like Mitsubishi and Hitachi have *kami*:

patron deities of business, or deities related in some way to their founder or their place of origin.

However one may explain this, or categorize it, it is not obviously 'modern', except in so far as other modern societies manifest similar phenomena. It is certainly not Western. On the other hand, it may not be sensible to call it 'Asian'. As was said in the first chapter of this book, much of Japanese tradition traced its origins to cultures outside Japan, but elements of these had been so thoroughly assimilated over the centuries as to have become in effect Japanese. And it is in the context of national culture in this sense, rather than Asian identity self-consciously defined, that most recent signs of a turning back to the past can be placed. There have been a variety of symptoms of it in the 1970s and 1980s. The Japan Foundation was established in 1972 to promote the knowledge of Japanese language and culture overseas. Japanese diplomacy has regularly made provision for cultural exchanges, though it has come under attack within Japan for not doing enough. Prime Ministers, starting with Miki Takeo in 1975, have resumed the practice of visiting the Yasukuni Shrine, dedicated to the country's war dead (but have usually claimed that they were doing so 'privately'). Even Ohira Masayoshi, a Christian, thought it proper as Prime Minister to make a New Year visit to the Shinto shrines at Ise. In addition, the Ministry of Education has on several occasions used its authority over the licensing of school textbooks to tone down some of the harsher statements made about Japanese military expansion between 1931 and 1945. In 1982 and 1986 this became a matter of international dispute, calling forth vigorous protests from Peking and Seoul. Japanese scholars also protested, but it is significant that the main thrust of their arguments, unlike those which came from abroad, was against the fact of censorship, rather than the substance of what was changed.

From the Meiji period onwards the focus of Japanese nationalism has been the imperial house, at least until defeat in 1945. By contrast, in the postwar years it became the conventional wisdom that the emperor had a role more concerned with culture than with politics, and that any residual political sentiment attaching to him was to be found chiefly among the old. Then in October 1988 Hirohito fell gravely ill, his death expected hourly. Reactions to this in Japan, as the press and television reported them, showed much more widespread concern than the conventional wisdom would have led one to expect. When he died on 7 January 1989 much the same was true. This may simply have been because he had reigned so long that people throughout the country, unsure of how to behave in unfamiliar circumstance, thought it better to express too much grief than too little; but it could also be that Japanese were suddenly reminded of the imperial institution as something that linked them with their past, a sort of defence against rootlessness. Certainly the emperor's funeral on 24 February was not only a state occasion, bringing together leaders of the world, but also a national one, in which the Japanese people displayed their sense of unity and identity. It is therefore by no means impossible that Akihito's reign will see a more self-confident Japan seeking to build on these foundations, not least with respect to the country's standing overseas.

17

THE POSTWAR PATTERN UNRAVELS, 1989–1999

Japan's politics, foreign relations and economy after the conclusion of the peace treaty in 1951 settled down into a stable pattern, which seemed little affected in its essential character by struggles for power or business cycles, whether in Japan or abroad. Government remained in the hands of the Liberal Democrat Party (LDP), a broadly conservative configuration, which formed close links on the one side with the bureaucracy, its partner in the drafting and implementation of decisions, and on the other with business interests, which provided funding for the political machine. In return, business was guaranteed a framework of tax and legislation that was favourable to its collective needs (a result that was sometimes described, mostly by foreigners, as Japan Inc.). Under this regime the economy was regulated by a mixture of formal rules and bureaucratic 'guidance', originally designed to promote the export of manufactured goods. The production of these was the task of a fairly small number of very large corporations, relying for processed or semi-processed parts on a network of smaller companies, many of which they controlled through contract relationships. They bound their labour force to them through a number of incentives which have come to be recognised as together comprising a distinctively Japanese business system: lifetime employment (though not for all), promotion by seniority, extensive welfare provision for employees, and the active encouragement of loyalty to the concern.

Externally, the corollary was a close bond with the United States. A defence agreement, negotiated at the same time as the peace treaty, gave Japan the protection of a nuclear umbrella in a divided world. In return, she provided air and naval bases which stretched America's strategic reach to China and Asiatic Russia. This partnership also provided Japan in its early years with access to American capital and technology, in its later ones with a rich market for hi-tech consumer goods. Though the relationship was not always smooth, its continuation was for twenty years or more taken for granted by both parties to it.

There were a number of signs that this pattern was under stress by the 1980s (as described in Chapter 16). Events in the first five years of the new emperor's reign were to make the strains increasingly apparent. The collapse of the Soviet Union and the end of the Cold War put in question many of the assumptions on which the American alliance had been founded. Economic frictions therefore tended to loom larger than they had before. At home, the boom years, marked by huge rises in the value of land and stocks, came suddenly to an end, plunging the country into its deepest recession since the immediate aftermath of the war. This undermined many of the economic structures which had developed in the intervening years. It also threatened the political settlement of 1955, under which the dominance of the Liberal Democrats had come to seem assured.

THE DISINTEGRATION OF POLITICS

The death of Emperor Hirohito at the beginning of 1989 prompted speculation in Japan about the future development of the monarchy. The new emperor had been a boy at the time of Japan's surrender in 1945. He had been brought up during the American occupation under the guidance of liberal advisers (including an American Quaker), and had given several indications since then of untraditional behaviour, including marriage to the daughter of a wealthy businessman. It is not surprising, therefore, that some of the more conservative palace officials were thought to fear radical departures from the norm, once he succeeded. In fact very little happened, at least on the surface.

There were a number of small concessions to informality. The new emperor travelled abroad more often than his father had done. He showed himself more frequently to the people. Yet in the last resort he remained a distant figure to the majority of Japanese, shrouded in dignity and surrounded by officialdom. Two events, which seemed to provide opportunities to change this state of affairs, did not do so. These were the accession ceremonies for the emperor himself, starting on 12 November 1990, and the marriage of the Crown Prince on 9 June 1993. Both were treated as occasions for the reaffirmation of tradition, rather than for popular pageantry. The rituals were customary and held within the palace, only the television cameras making them publicly accessible (and then not completely so). Afterwards, again in accordance with tradition, both were reported to the imperial ancestors, including the sun-goddess, Amaterasu. On this evidence, the monarchy seemed to be changing very slowly.

The same could not be said of party politics. In the early years of the reign these centred on two domestic issues. One was that of political funding, linked in the public mind with accusations of corruption. It had already attracted a great deal of attention in the 1980s, when it had been revealed that large secret donations had been made to politicians by companies seeking special advantages. Recruit was the most famous example. After 1990 new disclosures continued to be made, involving major political figures, but discussion of the subject now moved to new ground. It was widely agreed that in most cases the motive for accepting such funds was not personal greed, but the need to finance elections, which were becoming more and more expensive. This was partly because members of the lower house of the Diet were elected from multi-member constituencies. Since the candidates on any given occasion were likely to include more than one from each of the major parties, competing with each other in a contest based more on personality than on principle, gifts and favours played a considerable part in ensuring victory. The overall cost was therefore likely to be huge. Awareness of this brought a call for electoral reform, designed to provide not only restrictions on the contributions that could legally be received – the electoral law already put limits on expenditure, which were universally ignored – but also a revision of the voting system itself. There was a particular call for the introduction of single-member constituencies, but opposition to this came from the smaller parties, who conceived it to be to their disadvantage. In the end, therefore, this proposal was coupled with another, by which elections to a number of the seats would be by a system of proportional representation, to be operated in a nationwide constituency, or several large regional ones. Debate came to focus on the number of seats to be allocated to the different categories.

The second issue was that of taxation. The Finance Minstry had for some years been of the view that the progressive ageing of the Japanese population – persons aged 65 and over comprised 12 per cent of the total in 1990, 13.5 per cent in 1993 – implied the need for a future rise in welfare payments, for which existing revenue would be inadequate. Nakasone had tried without success in 1987 to introduce a consumption tax to increase it. Takeshita, his successor as prime minister, had got the Diet to accept it in 1988, but only at a level of 3 per cent. Government economists believed that this would not suffice for very long. Since continued pressure from the United States to stimulate consumption in Japan as a means of redressing the imbalance in foreign trade translated into plans for a reduction in income tax, while the main opposition party in the Diet, the Socialists, remained unwilling to approve an increase in indirect taxation, the situation contained the seeds of fierce controversy. In the event this opened up divisions within parties, as well as between them, with the result that by the middle of 1993 the distribution of power had been transformed.

Kaifu Toshiki, who became leader of the LDP on 8 August 1989, and was elected more or less automatically to the office of prime minister next day, had not at first been thought likely to last very long, because he commanded no major faction in the party. This expectation proved wrong. His main rivals had been weakened by corruption charges. The public found him personable and thought him honest. In February 1990, therefore, he was able to lead the LDP to victory in a general election, helped by a recurrence of divisions between the socialist left and right. For more than a year thereafter his government remained in power, while the socialists, still in disarray, had resort to various shifts to win support, changing the English-language version of their party name to Social Democrat Party of Japan (SDPJ), and dropping Doi Takako as leader. This did not help them much, to judge by their performance in the local elections of April 1991.

Yet Kaifu's position within the LDP was not very strong. In particular, the reluctance of his colleagues to support electoral reform left him unable to fulfil the promises he had made when coming to office. So in October 1991, when his current term as President of the party came to an end, he decided not to seek re-election. His successor, Miyazawa Kiichi, formed a cabinet which was in several ways more backward-looking. It had no women members, for example, while three of its ministers, in addition to Miyazawa himself, had been implicated in the Recruit corruption scandal. It certainly made little effort to get ahead with political reform. Despite this, Miyazawa's own reputation for economic competence, plus the public's distaste for the methods by which the socialists conducted their opposition to him in the Diet, won him a significant victory in the upper house elections in July 1992. This was enough to keep him in office for another year.

During that year his party began to disintegrate over the issue of electoral reform. Public criticism, already widespread on the subject of political ethics, was made sharper by recession, to the point where a good many of the party's younger members began to complain about the leadership offered by their elders. The Finance Minister, Hata Tsutomu, quit to form a party of his own, the Japan Renewal Party, looking for support to the discontented 'salarymen' of the business world. Over forty others followed him out of the LDP. In June 1993, when Miyazawa faced a no-confidence motion in the Diet, they voted against him. So did the ten members of another splinter group, the New Party Sakigake, together with 106 who belonged to an unofficial 'forum', organised by Kaifu to promote political reform. Miyazawa failed to win the confidence vote; called a general election in July, in which the LDP lost its parliamentary majority; and announced his retirement. Japanese politics was in confusion.

The crisis had been precipitated by Miyazawa's failure to find a viable compromise between the LDP's preference for single-member constituencies, and the demands from smaller parties for a measure of proportional representation. The result this time, however, was more than a change of party leadership. In a contested election to the post of prime minister at the beginning of August, the lower house chose, not the new president of the LDP, Kōno Yōhei, nor the leader of the socialists, but a new man, Hosokawa Morihiro, whose Japan New Party, formed in May

1992, had won a mere 35 seats at the general election. Hosokawa was an electoral reformer, previously a prefectural governor and member of the LDP, as well as a descendant of feudal lords and a grandson of Konoe Fumimaro, who had twice been prime minister before the Pacific War. The socialists decided to give him their support. So did six other small parties, which enabled him to form an eight-party coalition. Hata Tsutomu became his deputy and Foreign Minister.

Hosokawa did not find the implementation of reform a simple task. After weeks of wrangling the lower house accepted his plans (18 November), but it was another two months before the reform committee of the upper house approved them. Then, on 21 January 1994, when they were put formally to the upper house, to everyone's surprise it turned them down, because seventeen members of the SDPJ, ostensibly belonging to Hosokawa's coalition, voted with the LDP against them. This forced the cabinet to compromise with the LDP itself, which settled in the end for 300 single-seat constituencies, plus a further 200 to be filled by proportional representation on a regional basis. The deal was struck just in time to get the bill through before the Diet session ended.

The balance of forces on which this agreement rested was destroyed by disputes over taxation. Early in February Hosokawa announced his intention of replacing the existing 3 per cent consumption tax by a new 'national welfare' tax at a level of 7 per cent, ostensibly to finance greater spending on the aged. Unfortunately he had failed to consult his coalition partners in advance. They promptly required him to withdraw, so raising the prospect of a difficult budget debate in June. Before that could be tested, however, Hosokawa announced his intention to resign (early April), citing as his reason the obstacles to government business in the Diet, which were being caused by rumours about his own fund-raising in the past. Once again the prime minister had taken his political allies by surprise. When the Diet turned to the task of electing a successor (25 April), the vote went this time in favour of Hata Tsutomu, supported by another coalition, engineered on his behalf by Ozawa Ichirō, a former Secretary General of the LDP.

In theory the coalition was to include the socialists. In two important respects, however, the agreement on which it was based ran counter to long-standing socialist beliefs. There was to be a reduction in income tax and a rise in indirect taxation to meet Japan's revenue needs. There was also to be a commitment to a foreign policy which was almost identical to that of the LDP. This was to ride roughshod over cherished leftwing sentiment. For the greater part of their adult lives Japan's socialist politicians had campaigned vigorously, sometimes violently, against certain features of the American alliance, which they held to be contrary to the peace clause of the constitution. In particular, they objected to the presence of nuclear weapons on Japanese soil and the formation of the Self Defence Force (SDF). In 1990 and 1991 they had opposed the plans of an LDP cabinet to send non-military aid to support America and its allies in the Gulf War. In June 1992 they had protested with still greater vehemence, though unsuccessfully, against a proposal to send units of the SDF to cooperate in UN peacekeeping overseas. All this was now to be renounced as the price to be paid for a share of power.

Inevitably, it was more than some of the socialist rank-and-file could stomach, especially those on the left. Their resistance was so strong, in fact, that the party had to withdraw from the Hata cabinet even before it was formed. Hostility was then exacerbated by news that Hata and Ozawa were trying to bring into existence a centre-right grouping which would exclude the SDPJ. In these circumstances it quickly became clear that the socialists would not support budget proposals for an increase in consumption tax, despite the machinations of Ozawa. On 25 June Hata in his turn resigned, having been in office exactly two months.

There followed a remarkable volte-face on the part of the socialists. On 29 June 1994 Murayama Tomiichi, a socialist with a background in local and trade-union politics, who had become leader of the party in September 1993, was elected prime minister with the support of the Liberal Democrats, and formed a cabinet in which the latter held key portfolios. Kaifu Toshiki, who resigned from the LDP when it decided to back Murayama, was the defeated candidate. The terms of this new alliance were in substance the same as those which Ozawa had arranged earlier in the year for Hata (with a different set of participants). Having tested power for the first time since 1948, it seems, the socialists had decided to make some sacrifices to retain it.

Even so, cracks were beginning to show by the end of the year.

Plans were announced for a New Frontier Party, a centre-right organisation, thought capable of challenging the LDP. It was to include all current opposition groups except the communists. Kaifu was elected leader in December, defeating Hata, while Ozawa Ichirō became Secretary General. The move prompted an initiative by Yamahana Sadao, Murayama's predecessor as chairman of the SDPJ, to take rightwing members of the party into a new alliance with other 'liberal' and 'democratic' elements, thereby forming an organisation large enough to profit from the reformed electoral rules. They showed a readiness to abandon the SDPJ as part of this process. Leftwing socialists, meanwhile, continued to be restive about the deal with the LDP. In other words, it began to look as if the fragmentation of Japanese politics had reached a level much like that of forty years before, when socialists were split between separate parties of left and right, while conservatives belonged to either the Liberals or the Democrats.

ECONOMIC RECESSION AND FOREIGN AFFAIRS

In the first half of the 1990s Japan suffered the most severe recession the country had known for forty years. It began when the Finance Ministry, seeking to protect overextended banks from the effects of unwise lending, took steps to start deflating asset prices. The result was a drop in the prices of land and shares, sluggish consumption, falling company profits. The annual rise in GNP for the fiscal year 1992 was the smallest since 1974 (the first 'oil shock' crisis). In the spring of 1992 the Nikkei index of the Tokyo stock exchange went below 20,000 for the first time in five years. In August it was below 15,000, well under half its previous peak. Automobile sales fell in each of the three years 1991, 1992 and 1993. In the last of them the production of four-wheel vehicles fell by 12 per cent, exports by over 18 per cent, while Toyota announced a reduction in profits of nearly 35 per cent in 1992.

One consequence was that consumers turned more and more to lower-cost goods, which were now becoming much more readily available in discount shops. Indeed, Japanese prices as a whole were being driven down by Asian competition. This put the returns from established retail businesses under pressure. It also meant a higher-than-usual degree of unemployment. The official figures for unemployment remained low (of the order of 2.5 per cent), but one needs to add about 4 per cent more to account for 'hidden' unemployment, that is, workers still employed, who were surplus to requirement but enjoyed job security. In 1992 average annual working hours fell to less than 2,000. Although the fall was in line with government policy, which had been seeking to move Japan away from its reputation as a country of workaholics, many observers believed that the change was best explained by recession. A report at the end of 1993 showed no significant reduction in the number of employees who worked over 60 hours a week.

In the ordinary course of events, when Japan suffered a recession the main burden of job losses had fallen on the employees of small and medium companies, or on the so-called 'temporary' staff of larger ones (those not covered by lifetime employment). This time the effect was felt more widely. Companies announcing cuts in the work force, or plans to carry them out, included some of the giants: the electrical concern Hitachi, the computer company Fujitsu, the communications combine NTT. Although efforts were made to ensure that the adjustment was achieved by early retirement and lower levels of recruitment, there was evidence here and there that lifetime employment could no longer be guaranteed. Nor could pensions. As early as 1990 some firms were finding it difficult to keep the retiring age at 65. Increasingly they turned (or reverted) to a compulsory age of 60. Related to these problems was a rise in the number of women workers, who totalled almost 20 million in 1992, or 38.6 per cent of the national work force. Some 30 per cent were part-time. In fact, just over half Japan's households now had two incomes, earned by husband and wife.

The usual response of recent Japanese governments to recession has been a series of economic rescue packages, designed to act as a stimulus to consumer spending. In August 1992 the Miyazawa cabinet announced a spending programme of 10,700 billion yen for public works, loans to small and medium businesses, and help to banks in disposing of real estate which was held as collateral for loans. This was expected to produce a rise of 2.3 per cent in GNP. It was not enough. In April 1993 Miyazawa tried again, this time with 13,200 billion yen, aimed at boosting GNP by 2.8 per cent. It was to include, in addition to help for the domestic economy, measures to increase imports by reviewing regulations and the import licensing system. In February 1994 it was Hosokawa's turn. Having failed to win support for his 'national welfare' tax, he decided to stimulate the economy by spending of 15,300 billion yen, which was to include a one-off income-tax cut of 5,500 billion yen in the coming fiscal year (April to March). The political disputes during the summer held up Diet approval for these proposals, so it was left to the Murayama cabinet to get them through (in modified form) in November: a cut of 5,500 billion yen in income tax in each of the fiscal years 1994 to 1996, reducing to 3,500 billion yen a year thereafter, coupled with an increase in consumption tax from 3 per cent to 5 per cent, starting in April 1997.

Outside government, voices were raised to argue that something more fundamental was needed if the Japanese economy were to cope with the world situation, as it existed after the Cold War. Some were influential ones. In an article published in February 1992 Morita Akio, head of the Sony corporation, who was generally held to be Japan's outstanding postwar entrepreneur, set out his own ideas on what was needed. Japan's success, he stated, had for several decades rested on the manufacture of high-quality goods at low prices through mass production and heavy investment in technology. The achievement had been made possible by long working hours, low dividends, and restrictive arrangements between members of large business combines, a 'company-centred' approach which had had its day. To make Japanese business more acceptable to the outside world, as both foreign critics and Japan's own interests now demanded, there had to be re-thinking.

What Morita appears to have had in mind were measures of 'restructuring and deregulation' that would break down some of the cosy relationship between business and the Liberal Democrats, so as to give less protection to Japanese firms in the domestic market and open it more fully to foreign goods, while bringing about a greater mobility of labour. In one respect this argument was a response to the growing shortage of mostly unskilled labour in Japan, caused by a declining birthrate, plus new attitudes among workers, especially the young, who were no longer wholly satisfied with a company-centred, workaholic way of life. It was also prompted, however, by what others called a submission to foreign demands, such as stemmed from Japan's economic penetration overseas. For this reason, critics included farmers' unions, who feared the effect of market-opening on the price of rice, and bureaucrats, who foresaw a loss of influence from deregulation. Both looked for support to rightwing politicians.

The relationship between recession and foreign affairs was therefore a politically controversial one inside Japan as well as abroad. The direct link between the two was provided by foreign trade and investment, the figures for which remained impressive. Between 1988 and 1990 the country's trade surplus became smaller, as imports, because of the boom, grew faster than exports. Thereafter the onset of recession brought a special effort by manufacturers to increase their sales overseas, raising the current account surplus in the next three fiscal years by 62.7 per cent, 39.4 per cent and 3.3 per cent, respectively. The lowest of these figures, that for 1993, reflected a decline in the second half of the year, which has continued in the incomplete returns for 1994: the surplus for the month of October 1994 was 19.3 per cent down on that for October 1993.

These figures are customarily given in US dollars, which means that they are affected by currency values, as well as by exchange of goods. Throughout the period here under discussion the yen remained stronger than the dollar, partly because of the repatriation of overseas investments, with the result, as Japanese economists have calculated, that about three-quarters of the apparent trade surplus for the years 1991 to 1993 could be attributed to the 'high yen' (*en-daka*). The rise of 3.3 per cent in the last of those years would have been a fall of 10.3 per cent if expressed in yen, not dollars.

The diplomatic impact of the trade balance was chiefly on Japan's relations with the United States. A series of attempts to reduce the bilateral imbalance under Presidents Bush and Clinton ended in failure. Automobiles and auto parts were much the largest item in dispute, accounting for about two-thirds of America's $60 billion annual deficit, but an agreement in principle to increase Japanese purchases in this field, made by Bush in 1992, was not put fully into effect, leaving a threat of trade sanctions still on the table at the end of 1994. Meanwhile, in

February 1994 Hosokawa had taken a stiffer line, rejecting an American demand to set numerical targets for specific aspects of market opening. It would, he claimed, amount to 'managed trade', contrary to Japan's international obligations. Instead, in March he announced an easing of controls with respect to insurance and the purchase overseas of telecommunications and medical equipment.

Another connection between the economy and foreign affairs was the so-called 'hollowing-out' of Japanese industry, that is, the transfer of manufacturing capacity to Japanese-owned factories overseas. Where this took place in the United States and Europe, as it had already done on a considerable scale before 1990, it was largely for the sake of market access: to circumvent the threats of protectionism directed from time to time against Japanese goods. This practice continued in the following years. Supplementing it, however, as the recession forced Japanese business to seek ever greater economies, was the use of overseas subsidiaries to provide for a coming together of Japanese capital and technology with cheap local labour. It was accomplished most successfully in China and the countries of Southeast Asia, which found themselves able as a result, not only to take over certain Japanese export markets, but also to penetrate the Japanese market itself. In the first nine months of 1993, for example, Japan became, albeit by a very narrow margin, a net importer of TV sets, most of them manufactured by Japanese-owned firms in Southeast Asia. Such firms also supplied Japanese manufacturers at home with parts, undermining the profits of small and medium businesses in Japan.

Where America was concerned, economic disputes had begun to undermine political co-operation. In Southeast Asia very nearly the reverse was true, for the nature of Japanese economic activity in the region raised the spectre in Asian eyes of another Greater East Asia Co-prosperity Sphere. These fears were enhanced by occasional incidents in Japan, which implied a reluctance on the part of some Japanese to renounce their wartime past. In January 1990 the mayor of Nagasaki, who had publicly charged Emperor Hirohito with war guilt the year before, was shot and wounded outside his office by a member of a local rightwing group. In August no less than fourteen members of the cabinet attended ceremonials for the war dead at the

Yasukuni Shrine. In May 1994 Nagano Shigeto, Justice Minister in the Hata government, publicly declared that reports of the Rape of Nanking were a fabrication, and denied that the Pacific War was an act of Japanese aggression. Diplomatic protests from Asian countries forced his resignation.

The reactions to such incidents among Japan's Asian neighbours, several of whom were becoming valued economic partners, were a matter of concern in Tokyo. Japan had been the first of the powers to resume making loans to China after the ban on economic aid to that country, imposed as a result of the suppression of the democratic protest movement in Tienanmen Square (June 1989). Kaifu was the first world leader to visit China again (August 1991). South Korea, too, though as much competitor as partner, was given special attention, as were the Philippines, Thailand, Singapore and Malaysia, where Japanese investment, as well as trade, were becoming important. A degree of sensitivity towards them was demonstrated in 1994 by Japan's response to a movement protesting at the Japanese army's wartime recruitment of 'comfort women', in what were then occupied countries, in order to satisfy the sexual needs of Japanese soldiers. The protests had started in Korea in 1992, but they reached their peak in August 1994, when prime minister Murayama, making a goodwill tour of Southeast Asia, was met by demonstrations in Manila and elsewhere. On his return he hurried to announce a compensation package. It was of substantial value, but as it dealt almost entirely with cultural exchanges and historical research it did little to meet the demands of the former comfort women, who wanted cash.

At a more elevated level, Japanese officialdom did what it could to placate opinion in East and Southeast Asia. In May 1990, on the occasion of a state visit to Japan by the South Korean President, Roh Tae Woo, the emperor expressed regret for the sufferings of Koreans under Japanese rule. So did prime minister Kaifu. In November 1993, when visiting Seoul, Hosokawa formally apologised for Japan's colonial rule. A year earlier (October 1992) the emperor and empress had spent six days in China, the first time a reigning emperor of Japan had been there. Akihito expressed regret for the suffering Japan had inflicted on the Chinese people during the war (as Kaifu had already done in August 1991). More comprehensively, Hosokawa, speaking in the Diet in August

1993, apologised to the peoples of the world for Japanese actions during the Pacific War. Murayama expressed his regrets to the countries of Southeast Asia on many occasions during his tour of the region in 1994.

Tokyo was a good deal more inflexible in dealing with other parts of the world. Nearly fifty years after the Japanese surrender there was still no treaty with Russia, largely because both sides remained stubborn about the Kuril islands. No progress was made on the subject when Gorbachev was in Tokyo in April 1991. There was some hope of a deal, involving Japanese aid to Russia in return for an agreement over sovereignty, when Yeltsin planned to go there in September 1991, but this did not materialize. Yeltsin cancelled the visit at very short notice, whereupon Japan refused to make finance available. Another planned meeting was postponed in May 1993, giving rise to speculation that opposition in Russia to any loss of territory was too strong for Yeltsin to ignore. When he did at last arrive in October, the talks were friendly but inconclusive.

Another piece of business which remains unfinished is the normalization of relations with North Korea. A tentative approach to talks was made in January 1991, but a year later stalemate was reached over Korean demands for compensation, arising from Japan's colonial rule (for which Kaifu had apologised in 1990). The matter was then complicated by international disputes over Pyongyang's nuclear capability, dragging on until the death of Kim Il-sung in July 1994, followed by uncertainty in Japan about the ability of Kim Jong-il to establish himself as successor, and even about his health.

Thus at the end of 1994, only a few months before the fiftieth anniversary of Japan's defeat, the Pacific War still exerted an unsettling influence on the country's politics and foreign affairs. Within weeks, however, there was to come a reminder that not all the country's problems were man-made. At dawn on 17 January 1995 the port city of Kobe in central Japan was struck by a severe earthquake, in which 5,000 people were killed and enormous damage was done to property, including roads and railways. To many, this came as a reminder of the uncertainties of human life (not least in Tokyo, where such an event has long been threatened). To others it raised questions about the recovery from recession, since the cost of repairing the region's infrastructure was bound to involve large government borrowing (as it had done in the Kanto earthquake in and after 1923), even though there were likely to be benefits to the construction industry in the longer term.

The Murayama government's position was not strengthened by the widespread public recriminations that followed the earthquake. Complaints about the slow response of central and local services were directed at a leadership already unpopular with its own hard-core followers, because of its surrender of traditional socialist objectives for the sake of a coalition with the Liberal Democrats. They were prolonged by the cabinet's failure to make any substantial headway towards solving the country's financial problems. In January 1996 Murayama resigned.

Because he had not called a general election, the choice of a successor rested on a vote by members of the lower house of the Diet. The largest group of these were the Liberal Democrats, led since September 1995 by the Trade Minister, Hashimoto Ryutaro. On 11 January he was duly elected prime minister, supported in the cabinet by other Liberal Democrats in the departments of foreign affairs, home affairs and defence. The finance ministry (not a popular portfolio in existing circumstances) went to a socialist, to confirm his party's parliamentary support. Since this left Ozawa Ichiro, a former Liberal Democrat, as leader of the strongest opposition party, the conservative right had to all appearances regained its ascendancy.

It did not prove strong enough, however, to carry through in the face of Diet disunity the radical reforms that the Japanese economy needed. Continuing business dissatisfaction, coupled with what was by Japanese standards a high level of unemployment, were to give Hashimoto a rough ride in the early months of 1996. He tried to end it by calling a general election for October. This took place under revised regulations, designed to give the cities larger representation by increasing the number of single-member constituencies; but a low turn-out (under 60 per cent), reflecting popular disillusion with party politicians in general, deprived the LDP of the lower house majority it sought. It was still the largest party (239 seats out of 500), but it had once again to seek partners for a coalition. Despite this, all cabinet posts went to Liberal Democrats when the government was formed on 7 November 1996, though it continued to rely on a promise of support from the socialists on key issues. Policies, it was said, would remain unchanged.

It was not a stable arrangement for a time of unrelenting financial crisis. Nor was Hashimoto's control of his own party strong enough to enable him to survive for very long. Within two years, politics took one more step back towards the post-1955 norm: on 30 July 1998 Hashimoto was replaced as party leader, and hence prime minister, by the leader of the largest LDP faction, Obuchi Keizo. His ally, Miyazawa Kiichi, the leader of the party's second largest faction, became Finance Minister. At first sight this was not a good omen for the economy. Miyazawa, though he had much experience of finance and good business connections, had held the same post in 1990, when the crash occurred. Many blamed him for precipitating it. On the other hand, he now offered promises that markets, both at home and abroad, wanted to hear: tax cuts and less regulation. And as the century drew towards its close there began to be signs of returning optimism and financial stability under the new administration, despite the presence of recurring turmoil, both economic and political, in Southeast Asia, which was an important area of Japanese business interest. Even so, it seemed a long climb yet to the former heights of the 'economic miracle'.

SOME JAPANESE TERMS

BAKUFU: The central administration of Japan under a Shogun (q.v.).

DAIMYO: A feudal lord (vassal-in-chief) of the Tokugawa period whose domain was estimated to yield an annual crop equivalent to 10,000 *koku* of rice or more.

KOKU: Measure of capacity, especially of rice. 1 *koku* = 4·96 bushels.

ROJU: A member of the Shogun's Council of State in the Tokugawa period.

SAMURAI: A member of Japan's feudal ruling class before 1871.

SHOGUN: Theoretically, the emperor's military deputy. In practice, before 1868 the office was that of hereditary military ruler, held by members of the Tokugawa family since 1603.

YEN: Monetary unit of modern Japan, introduced in 1871 at par with the US dollar. By the end of the nineteenth century its value had slipped to approximately half a dollar, remaining at that level until the 1930s, when it declined a little more. For much of the postwar period it was held at 360 to the dollar, but began to strengthen steadily after 1971. At the end of 1988 it exchanged at approximately 130 to the dollar, 225 to the pound sterling.

ZAIBATSU: 'Financial clique'. Term used to describe a handful of large family holding companies in modern Japan, distinguished both by their enormous size and by the wide spread of their business interests.

JAPANESE PRIME MINISTERS, 1885–1999

[The dates given are those of appointment, consecutive terms of office by the same Prime Minister being treated as single units. Alternative versions of the given names of Prime Ministers are given where these are widely used.]

22 Dec. 1885	Itō Hirobumi	8 July 1934	Okada Keisuke
30 Apr. 1888	Kuroda Kiyotaka	9 Mar. 1936	Hirota Kōki
24 Dec. 1889	Yamagata Aritomo	10 Feb. 1937	Hayashi Senjūrō
6 May 1891	Matsukata Masayoshi	4 June 1937	Konoe Fumimaro
8 Aug. 1892	Itō Hirobumi	5 Jan. 1939	Hiranuma Kiichirō
18 Sept. 1896	Matsukata Masayoshi	30 Aug. 1939	Abe Nobuyuki
12 Jan. 1898	Itō Hirobumi	16 Jan. 1940	Yonai Mitsumasa
30 June 1898	Ōkuma Shigenobu	22 July 1940	Konoe Fumimaro
8 Nov. 1898	Yamagata Aritomo	18 Oct. 1941	Tōjō Hideki
19 Oct. 1900	Itō Hirobumi	22 July 1944	Koiso Kuniaki
2 June 1901	Katsura Tarō	7 Apr. 1945	Suzuki Kantarō
7 Jan. 1906	Saionji Kinmochi	17 Aug. 1945	Higashikuni Naruhiko
14 July 1908	Katsura Tarō	9 Oct. 1945	Shidehara Kijūrō
30 Aug. 1911	Saionji Kinmochi	22 May 1946	Yoshida Shigeru
21 Dec. 1912	Katsura Tarō	24 May 1947	Katayama Tetsu
20 Feb. 1913	Yamamoto Gombei	10 Mar. 1948	Ashida Hitoshi
16 Apr. 1914	Ōkuma Shigenobu	15 Oct. 1948	Yoshida Shigeru
9 Oct. 1916	Terauchi Masatake	10 Dec. 1954	Hatoyama Ichirō
29 Sept. 1918	Hara Kei (Takashi)	23 Dec. 1956	Ishibashi Tanzan
13 Nov. 1921	Takahashi Korekiyo	25 Feb. 1957	Kishi Nobusuke
12 June 1922	Katō Tomosaburō	19 July 1960	Ikeda Hayato
2 Sept. 1923	Yamamoto Gombei	9 Nov. 1964	Satō Eisaku
7 Jan. 1924	Kiyoura Keigo	6 July 1972	Tanaka Kakuei
11 June 1924	Katō Kōmei (Takaaki)	9 Dec. 1974	Miki Takeo
30 Jan. 1926	Wakatsuki Reijirō	24 Dec. 1976	Fukuda Takeo
20 Apr. 1927	Tanaka Giichi	7 Dec. 1978	Ōhira Masayoshi
2 July 1929	Hamaguchi Yūkō (Osachi)	17 July 1980	Suzuki Zenko
14 Apr. 1931	Wakatsuki Reijirō	26 Nov. 1982	Nakasone Yasuhiro
13 Dec. 1931	Inukai Ki (Tsuyoshi)	6 Nov. 1987	Takeshita Noboru
26 May 1932	Saitō Makoto	2 June 1989	Uno Sōsuke

9 Aug 1989	Kaifu Toshiki
5 Nov. 1991	Miyazawa Kiichi
6 Aug. 1993	Hosokawa Morihiro
25 Apr. 1994	Hata Tsutomu
29 June 1994	Murayama Tomiichi
11 Jan. 1996	Hashimoto Ryutaro
30 July 1998	Obuchi Keizo

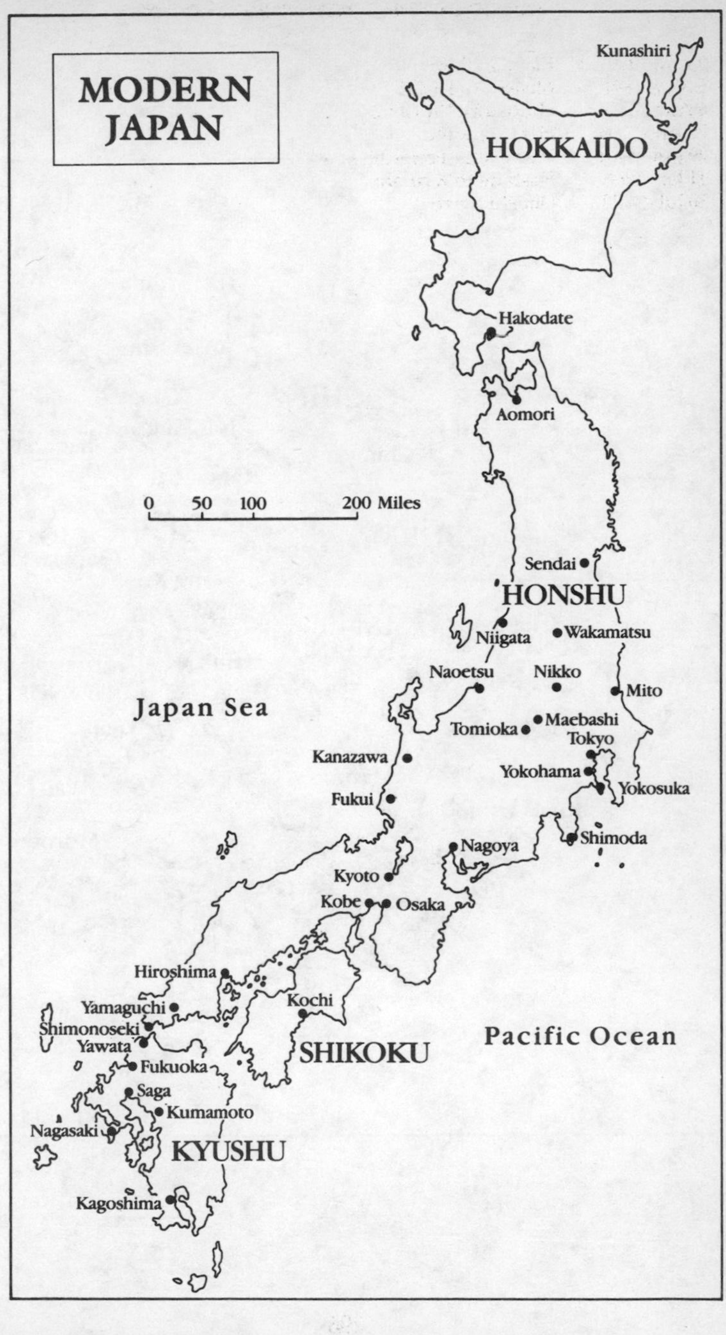
MODERN JAPAN
Kunashiri
HOKKAIDO
Hakodate
Aomori
0 50 100 200 Miles
Sendai
HONSHU
Niigata
Wakamatsu
Naoetsu
Nikko
Mito
Japan Sea
Maebashi
Tomioka
Tokyo
Kanazawa
Yokohama
Yokosuka
Fukui
Shimoda
Nagoya
Kyoto
Kobe
Osaka
Hiroshima
Kochi
Yamaguchi
Shimonoseki
Yawata
Pacific Ocean
SHIKOKU
Fukuoka
Saga
Kumamoto
Nagasaki
KYUSHU
Kagoshima

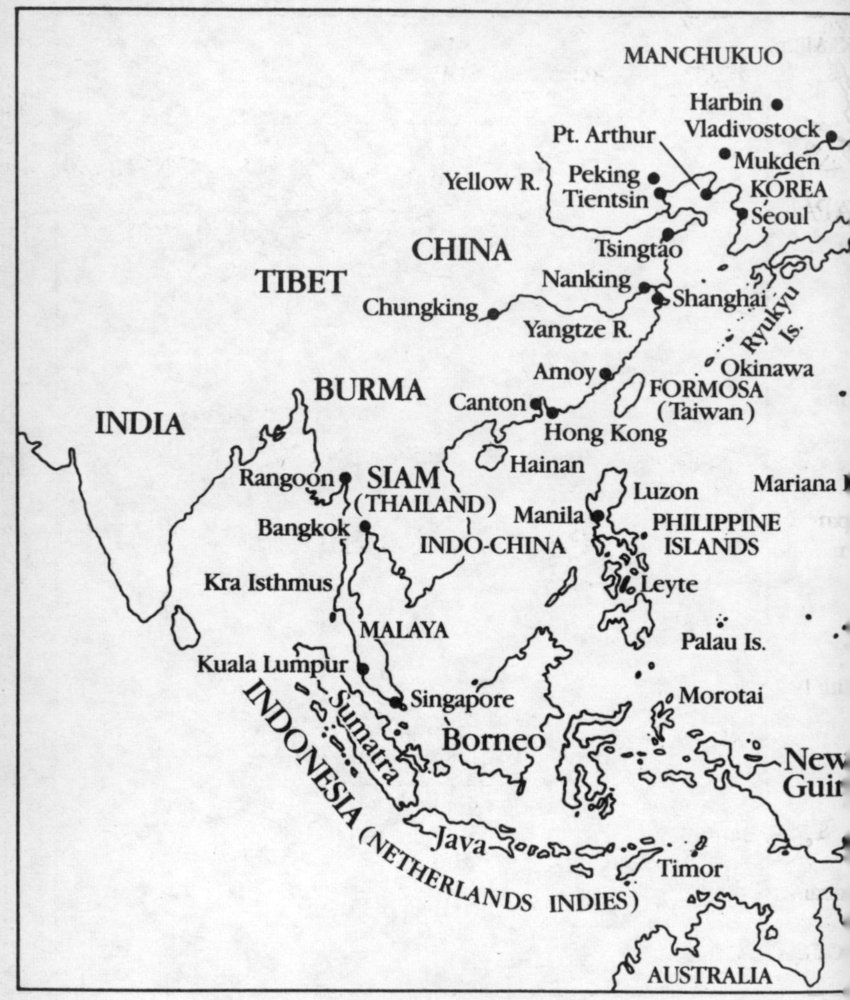
MANCHUKUO
Harbin
Vladivostock
Pt. Arthur
Mukden
Peking
Tientsin
Yellow R.
KOREA
Seoul
CHINA
Tsingtao
TIBET
Nanking
Shanghai
Chungking
Yangtze R.
Ryukyu Is.
Okinawa
Amoy
BURMA
Canton
FORMOSA
(Taiwan)
INDIA
Hong Kong
Hainan
Rangoon
SIAM
(THAILAND)
Luzon
Mariana
Manila
PHILIPPINE
ISLANDS
Bangkok
INDO-CHINA
Kra Isthmus
Leyte
MALAYA
Palau Is.
Kuala Lumpur
Morotai
Singapore
Sumatra
Borneo
INDONESIA (NETHERLANDS INDIES)
Java
Timor
AUSTRALIA

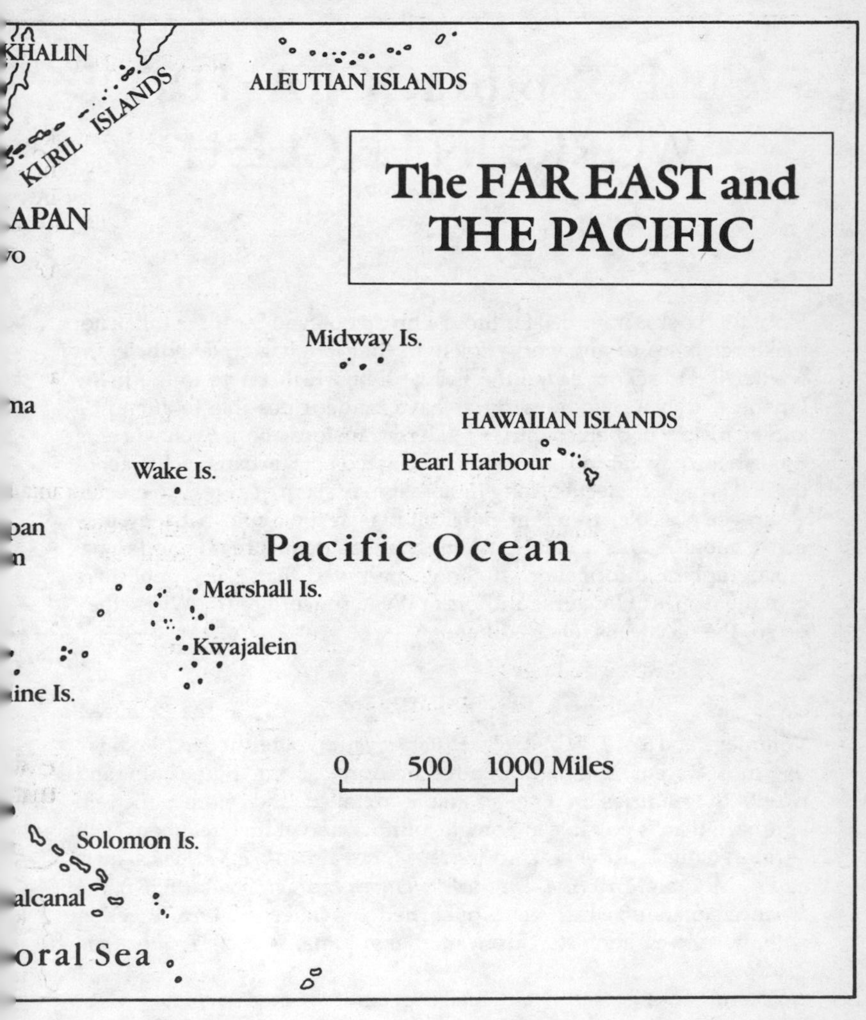

KHALIN
KURIL ISLANDS
ALEUTIAN ISLANDS
The FAR EAST and THE PACIFIC
APAN
na
Midway Is.
HAWAIIAN ISLANDS
Pearl Harbour
Wake Is.
pan
Pacific Ocean
Marshall Is.
Kwajalein
ine Is.
0 500 1000 Miles
Solomon Is.
alcanal
oral Sea

A SELECT BIBLIOGRAPHY OF WORKS IN ENGLISH

Since this book is intended for those who do not read Japanese I shall not make reference to any works solely in that language. Nevertheless, I would like to acknowledge the heavy debt which I owe to the many Japanese scholars whose writings have made it possible to attempt a survey history of their country's modern transformation. Even works in English are now far too numerous to be listed at all exhaustively. Hence this list is highly selective, long though it may seem. It gives preference, wherever possible, to recent publications, in the hope that they may prove more readily available. Almost all of them provide additional bibliographical information. It should be noted that many publishers give the names of Japanese authors in Western word order. Where they do so, the practice is followed here.

GENERAL WORKS

Volumes 5 and 6 of *The Cambridge History of Japan*, published in 1989, give the most recent and authoritative account of the nineteenth and twentieth centuries in English, more detailed and more varied in approach than is possible in a single-author one-volume treatment such as this. For the broader background, see J. K. Fairbank, E. O. Reischauer, and A. M. Craig, *East Asia. The Modern Transformation* (Boston, 1965), the Japan chapters of which were published separately in 1978, together with those on earlier history from another volume, as *Japan. Tradition and Transformation*.

Several books deal with particular aspects of the modern period. G. B. Sansom, *The Western World and Japan* (New York and London, 1950), is an outstanding study of cultural relations with Europe from the sixteenth to the nineteenth centuries. Kurt Steiner, *Local Government in Japan* (Stanford, 1965), is also fundamental, though in a different mould. More controversial is Jon Halliday, *A Political History of Japanese Capitalism*

(New York, 1975), which examines twentieth-century politics from a largely Marxist viewpoint. Masao Maruyama's articles on nationalism and fascism, published in his *Thought and Behaviour in Modern Japanese Politics* (London, 1963), are still of prime importance in the same context.

Among studies of foreign relations, M. B. Jansen's *Japan and China: from War to Peace 1894–1972* (Chicago, 1975), is the best account of one central theme, as Akira Iriye, *Across the Pacific. An Inner History of American–East Asian Relations* (New York, 1967), is of another. Endymion Wilkinson, *Misunderstanding. Europe versus Japan* (Tokyo, 1981; published in England in 1983 under the title *Japan versus Europe*), provides an extended historical introduction to the trade disputes of the later twentieth century.

The development of the Japanese economy is treated reliably and straightforwardly in G. C. Allen, *A Short Economic History of Modern Japan* (3rd. ed., London, 1972). A more recent and analytical study is in two volumes by Takafusa Nakamura: *Economic Growth in Prewar Japan* (New Haven and London, 1983), and *The Postwar Japanese Economy. Its development and structure* (Tokyo, 1981). From a different viewpoint, see Johannes Hirschmeier and Tsunehiko Yui, *The Development of Japanese Business 1600–1973* (London, 1975). Partly economic and partly sociological is Takeo Yazaki, *Social Change and the City in Japan* (Tokyo, 1968). Herbert Passin, *Society and Education in Japan* (New York, 1965), gives an overview of educational history, including some useful documents, and Joseph M. Kitagawa, *Religion in Japanese History* (New York and London, 1966), covers the modern period as well as earlier ones. For the history of ideas more generally, see the later chapters of Ryusaku Tsunoda et al., *Sources of Japanese Tradition* (New York, 1958), which provides translated extracts from Japanese writings, together with introductory comment.

In recent years there have been many compendium volumes on Japan, comprising articles from several contributors, organized round a particular theme. Of these, the most influential have been those arising from a series of conferences on Japanese modernization, published by Princeton U.P.: M. B. Jansen, ed., *Changing Japanese Attitudes Toward Modernization* (1965); W. W. Lockwood, ed., *The State and Economic Enterprise in Modern Japan* (1965); R. P. Dore, ed., *Aspects of Social Change in Modern Japan* (1967); R. E. Ward, ed., *Political Development in Modern Japan* (1968); J. W. Morley, ed., *Dilemmas of Growth in Prewar Japan* (1971); D. H. Shively, ed., *Tradition and Modernization in Japanese Culture* (1971). Their methodological approach has been challenged, not altogether convincingly, in Tetsuo Najita and J. V. Koschmann, eds., *Conflict in Modern Japanese History* (Princeton, 1982).

JAPAN BEFORE 1868

The importance of the Meiji Restoration to an understanding of modern Japan has ensured that there is a voluminous literature concerning it, even in English. My own book, *The Meiji Restoration* (Stanford, 1972), deals with most aspects of it, including immediate post-Restoration policy. Conrad Totman, *The Collapse of the Tokugawa Bakufu 1862–1868* (Honolulu, 1980), concentrates on the factors which explain the Bakufu's weakness. M. B. Jansen, *Sakamoto Ryōma and the Meiji Restoration* (Princeton, 1961), and H. D. Harootunian, *Toward Restoration. The growth of political consciousness in Tokugawa Japan* (Berkeley and London, 1970), adopt different ways of examining the radical samurai movement. On the intellectual background, see Masao Maruyama, *Studies in the Intellectual History of Tokugawa Japan* (Princeton and Tokyo, 1974).

In the field of foreign relations, there are separate accounts of the role of the major powers: P. J. Treat, *The Early Diplomatic Relations between the United States and Japan 1853–1865* (Baltimore, 1917); G. A. Lensen, *The Russian Push Toward Japan. Russo-Japanese relations 1697–1875* (Princeton, 1959); Grace Fox, *Britain and Japan 1858–1883* (Oxford, 1969); Meron Medzini, *French Policy in Japan during the Closing Years of the Tokugawa Regime* (Cambridge, Mass., 1971). I have published a volume, *Select Documents on Japanese Foreign Policy 1853–1868* (London, 1955), treating the formulation of Bakufu policy.

Japanese research on the Tokugawa economy has for some time tended to concentrate on the origins of capitalism, rather than on the Restoration, but not a great deal of it is reflected adequately in English-language works. There are some significant articles by Thomas C. Smith, notably 'Pre-modern economic growth: Japan and the West', *Past and Present*, 60 (1973), 127–60. Also important is Susan B. Hanley and Kozo Yamamura, *Economic and Demographic Change in Preindustrial Japan 1600–1868* (Princeton, 1977). Other aspects of Tokugawa society are well enough covered in the general works, cited above, except, perhaps, for the material in R. P. Dore's *Education in Tokugawa Japan* (London, 1965).

FROM THE RESTORATION TO THE PACIFIC WAR

For the political narrative of this period, R. A. Scalapino, *Democracy and the Party Movement in Prewar Japan* (Berkeley, 1953), has never been entirely superseded, though some of its conclusions have to be modified in the light of later publications, such as Tetsuo Najita, *Hara Kei in the Politics of Compromise 1905–1915* (Cambridge, Mass., 1967); Peter Duus, *Party Rivalry and Political Change in Taishō Japan* (Cambridge, Mass., 1968); and G. M. Berger, *Parties Out of Power in Japan 1931–1941* (Princeton, 1977). Ishii Ryosuke, *Japanese Legislation in the Meiji Era* (Tokyo, 1958), deals with political as well as legal institutions. Also important is David A. Titus, *Palace and Politics in Prewar Japan* (New York and London, 1974). There are a number of useful political biographies, including R. F. Hackett, *Yamagata Aritomo in the Rise of Modern Japan 1838–1922* (Cambridge, Mass., 1971); Haru M. Reischauer, *Samurai and Silk* (Cambridge, Mass., 1986), on Matsukata Masayoshi; Lesley Connors, *The Emperor's Adviser* (London, 1987), on Saionji Kinmochi; Oka Yoshitake, *Konoe Fumimaro* (Tokyo, 1983), and *Five Political Leaders of Modern Japan: Itō Hirobumi, Ōkuma Shigenobu, Hara Takashi, Inukai Tsuyoshi, Saionji Kinmochi* (Tokyo, 1986).

Modern ideology has come in for a great deal of attention because of its links with the origins of the Pacific War: see especially Byron K. Marshall, *Capitalism and Nationalism in Prewar Japan. The ideology of the business élite 1868–1941* (Stanford, 1967); Carol Gluck, *Japan's Modern Myths. Ideology in the late Meiji period* (Princeton, 1985); D. C. Holtom, *Modern Japan and Shinto Nationalism* (Chicago, 1947); Thomas Havens, *Farm and Nation in Modern Japan. Agrarian nationalism 1870–1940* (Princeton, 1974); G. M. Wilson, *Radical Nationalist in Japan: Kita Ikki, 1883–1937* (Cambridge, Mass., 1969). There are, however, other aspects of the subject worth pursuing. See, for example, Joseph Pittau, *Political Thought in Early Meiji Japan 1868–1889* (Cambridge, Mass., 1967), on the Meiji Constitution; Carmen Blacker, *The Japanese Enlightenment. A study of the writings of Fukuzawa Yukichi* (Cambridge, 1964); Earl H. Kinmonth, *The Self-made Man in Meiji Japanese Thought* (Berkeley, 1981); and Sharon H. Nolte, *Liberalism in Modern Japan. Ishibashi Tanzan and his teachers 1905–1960* (Berkeley, 1987).

The best general survey of foreign policy in this period is Ian Nish, *Japanese Foreign Policy 1869–1942* (London, 1977). More detailed bibliographical comment is to be found in J. W. Morley, ed., *Japan's Foreign Policy 1868–1941. A research guide* (New York and London, 1974), which has chapters both on countries and on aspects of the subject. There are two recent studies of Japanese imperialism: Ramon H. Myers and Mark R. Peattie, ed., *The Japanese Colonial Empire 1895–1945* (Princeton, 1984), and W. G. Beasley, *Japanese Imperialism 1894–1945* (Oxford, 1987). Valuable on the 1930s are Mark R. Peattie, *Ishiwara Kanji and Japan's Confrontation with the West* (Princeton, 1975), and Michael Barnhart, *Japan Prepares for Total War. The search for economic security 1919–1941* (Ithaca and London, 1987). James Morley has also edited four volumes, published by Columbia U.P., which derive from the main Japanese study of the origins of the Pacific War: *Deterrent Diplomacy. Japan, Germany, and the USSR 1935–1940* (1976); *The Fateful Choice. Japan's advance into Southeast Asia 1939–1941* (1980); *The China Quagmire. Japan's expansion on the Asian Continent 1933–1941* (1983); and *Japan Erupts. The London Naval Conference and the Manchurian Incident 1928–1932* (1984). There are many accounts of the war itself and its immediate background, some of which are controversial. The following is a representative selection: F. C. Jones, *Japan's New Order in East Asia. Its rise and fall 1937–45* (London, 1954); Robert Butow, *Tojo and the Coming of the War* (Princeton, 1961); Akira Iriye, *Power and Culture. The Japanese–American War 1941–1945* (Cambridge, Mass., 1981); Ronald H. Spector, *Eagle against the Sun* (New York, 1985); and Michael Montgomery, *Imperialist Japan. The Yen to Dominate* (London, 1987). Wartime Japan is described from a Japanese and a non-Japanese viewpoint, respectively, in Saburo Ienaga, *Japan's Last War* (Oxford, 1979), and Ben-Ami Shillony, *Politics and Culture in Wartime Japan* (Oxford, 1981).

It is very difficult to choose books on economic development, since the literature is voluminous and mostly technical. Apart from Allen's book, cited under general works, W. W. Lockwood, *The Economic Development of Japan. Growth and structural change 1868–1938* (rev. ed., Princeton and London, 1968), though in some respects outdated, is probably still the best introduction to the subject. Yujiro Hayami, *A Century of Agricultural Growth in Japan* (Tokyo, 1975), is standard in its field. There are several recent, more specialized volumes which raise important issues: Hugh Patrick, ed., *Japanese Industrialization and its Social Consequences* (Berkeley and London, 1976); Andrew Gordon, *The Evolution of Labor Relations in Japan: heavy industry, 1853–1955* (Cambridge, Mass., 1985); Richard J. Smethurst, *Agricultural Development and Tenancy Disputes in Japan 1870–1940* (Princeton, 1986).

Finally, on the role played by Westerners in Japanese modernization, see especially Ernst Presseisen, *Before Aggression. Europeans prepare the Japanese Army* (Tucson, 1965); Hazel Jones, *Live Machines. Hired Foreigners and Meiji Japan* (Vancouver, 1980); and Ardath W. Burks, ed., *The Modernizers: overseas students, foreign employees, and Meiji Japan* (Boulder, 1985).

JAPAN SINCE 1945

For the postwar period there are relatively few books which cover any substantial part of the subject. Several which are listed in the general section of this bibliography are also useful here, as are one or two of those noted for the years before 1945. For the rest, J. A. A. Stockwin, *Japan: Divided Politics in a Growth Economy* (London, 1975), is a sound introduction to party politics. On the occupation, Kazuo Kawai, *Japan's American Interlude* (Chicago, 1960), is an interesting survey from the Japanese viewpoint, while Robert Ward and Sakamoto Yoshikazu, ed., *Democratizing Japan. The Allied Occupation* (Honolulu, 1987), provides a later perspective from scholars of both sides. There are a number of specialist studies on the politics of this and subsequent decades: J. W.

Dower, *Empire and Aftermath. Yoshida Shigeru and the Japanese experience, 1878–1954* (Cambridge, Mass., 1979); Chitoshi Yanaga, *Big Business in Japanese Politics* (New Haven and London, 1968); and James H. Buck, ed., *The Modern Japanese Military System* (Beverly Hills, 1975). In addition, there are two articles which appeared in the *Journal of Japanese Studies* (Seattle): Fukui Haruhiro, 'The Liberal Democratic Party Revisited' (vol. 10, 1984, pp. 385–435), and Chalmers Johnson, 'Tanaka Kakuei, structural corruption, and the advent of machine politics in Japan' (vol.12, 1986, pp.1–28).

R. A. Scalapino, ed., *The Foreign Policy of Modern Japan* (Berkeley and London, 1977), contains some useful papers, but does not provide a continuous narrative. An excellent monograph is George R. Packard, *Protest in Tokyo. The Security Treaty crisis of 1960* (Princeton, 1966). Leon Hollerman, ed., *Japan and the United States. Economic and Political Adversaries* (Boulder, 1980), examines later Japanese–American conflict.

On the economy, apart from Nakamura's book, listed in the general section, above, Chalmers Johnson, *MITI and the Japanese Miracle. The growth of industrial policy 1925–1975* (Stanford, 1982), is of prime importance. So are two books by Ronald Dore: *Land Reform in Japan* (London, 1959), and *Flexible Rigidities. Industrial policy and structural adjustment in the Japanese economy, 1970–80* (Stanford, 1986). James W. White, *The Sōkagakkai and Mass Society* (Stanford, 1970), has much that is of interest to say about social change, as well as postwar religion, while Tsurumi Shunsuke, *A Cultural History of Postwar Japan 1945–1980* (London, 1987), makes some illuminating comments on popular culture and attitudes.

In conclusion, it should be noted that specific information on both persons and events can often conveniently be found in the *Kodansha Encyclopedia of Japan* (9 vols., Tokyo and New York, 1983).

NOTES

1.

1. Rutherford Alcock, *The Capital of the Tycoon* (2 vols., London, Longman, 1863), I, xix–xx.
2. Thomas C. Smith, *The Agrarian Origins of Modern Japan* (Stanford, Stanford U.P., 1959), 68–9.
3. Translated in R. Tsunoda *et al.*, *Sources of Japanese Tradition* (New York, Columbia U.P., 1958), 357.
4. ibid., 409–10.
5. ibid., 528.
6. G. B. Sansom, *Japan. A short cultural history* (rev. ed., London, Cresset, 1952), 477.

2.

7. Tsunoda, *Sources*, 601.
8. ibid., 543–4.
9. Quoted in G. B. Sansom, *The Western World and Japan* (London, Cresset, 1950), 258.
10. *Edinburgh Review*, XCVI (1852), 383.
11. Perry's letter has been published on a number of occasions; see, for example, F. L. Hawks, *Narrative of the Expedition of an American Squadron to the China Seas and Japan* (3 vols., Washington D.C., 1856), I, 258–9, and W. G. Beasley, ed., *Select Documents on Japanese Foreign Policy 1853–1868* (London, Oxford U.P., 1955), 101–2.
12. M. E. Cosenza, ed., *The Complete Journal of Townsend Harris* (New York, Doubleday, 1930), 357–8.
13. ibid., 507.
14. Translated from a Japanese account of Harris' statement: Beasley, *Select Documents*, 163–4.
15. Beasley, *Select Documents*, 180.
16. ibid., 194.

3.

17. Quoted in Maruyama Masao, *Studies in the Intellectual History of Tokugawa Japan* (Princeton, Princeton U.P., and Tokyo, Tokyo U.P., 1974), 362.
18. Text in Beasley, *Select Documents*, 236–40.
19. ibid., 298.
20. Translation in Marius B. Jansen, *Sakamoto Ryōma and the Meiji Restoration* (Princeton, Princeton U.P., 1961), 299–301.

4.

21. Translation in J. R. Black, *Young Japan* (2 vols., London, Trubner, 1880–1), II, 178–81.
22. The text has been published many times: see for example, Tsunoda, *Sources*, 644, and Ishii Ryosuke, *Japanese Legislation in the Meiji Era* (reprint, Tokyo, Toyo Bunko, 1969), 145.
23. Ito Hirobumi, 'Some reminiscences', in Okuma Shigenobu, ed., *Fifty Years of New Japan* (2 vols., London, Smith, Elder, 1910), I, 122.
24. Quoted in W. G. Beasley, *The Meiji Restoration* (Stanford, Stanford U.P., 1972), 331. There is a slightly different translation in W. W. McLaren, ed., *Japanese Government Documents* (*Trans. Asiatic Soc. Japan*, vol. XLII, Tokyo, 1914), 29–32.

5.

25. The text of the memorial is in McLaren, *Japanese Government Documents*, 440–8.
26. Quoted in G. M. Beckmann, *The Making of the Meiji Constitution* (Lawrence, Kansas U.P., 1957), 149.
27. McLaren, *Japanese Government Documents*, 542.
28. ibid., 503.
29. Ito, 'Some reminiscences', in Okuma, *Fifty Years*, I, 127. The text of the constitution has been published many times in official translation: see, for example, Beckmann, *Making*, 151–6, and Ishii, *Japanese Legislation*, 725–33.
30. Quoted in Johannes Siemes, *Hermann Roesler and the Making of the Meiji State* (Tokyo, Sophia U.P., 1966), 22.
31. Joseph Pittau, *Political Thought in Early Meiji Japan 1868–1889* (Cambridge, Mass., Harvard U.P., 1967), 177–8.
32. Quoted in Richard H. Minear, *Japanese Tradition and Western Law* (Cambridge, Mass., Harvard U.P., 1970), 80.
33. The text is translated in Tsunoda, *Sources*, 705–7.
34. Hibino Yutaka, *Nippon Shindo Ron, or the national ideas of the Japanese people*, trans. A. P. McKenzie (Cambridge, Cambridge U.P., 1928), 94; for other phrases quoted, see ibid., 27, 33, 42, 48.

6.

35. Quoted in Beasley, *Meiji Restoration*, 367–8.
36. H.L. Jones, *Live Machines. Hired Foreigners and Meiji Japan* (Tenterden, Norbury, 1980).
37. *The Autobiography of Fukuzawa Yukichi*, trans. E. Kiyooka (Tokyo, Hokuseido, 1934), 264.
38. Black, *Young Japan*, II, 407.
39. Text of preamble, quoted in Kikuchi Dairoku, *Japanese Education* (London, Murray, 1909), 68–9.
40. The rescript of 1879 is translated in Herbert Passin, *Society and Education in Japan*(New York, Columbia U.P., 1965), 227–8. Translations of the Education Rescript appear in Kikuchi, *Japanese Education*, 2–3, and Tsunoda, *Sources*, 646–7.
41. Fukuzawa Yukichi, *An Outline of a Theory of Civilization*, trans. David A. Dilworth and G. Cameron Hurst (Tokyo, Sophia U.P., 1973), 28, 99.
42. Translated in Kenneth B. Pyle, *The New Generation in Meiji Japan . . . 1885–1895* (Stanford, Stanford U.P., 1969), 94.
43. Quoted in John D. Pierson, *Tokutomi Sohō 1863–1957* (Princeton, Princeton U.P., 1980), 229, 235.
44. Okakura Kakuzō, *The Awakening of Japan* (London, Murray, 1905), 188–9.
45. Nakae Chōmin, *A Discourse by Three Drunkards on Government* (New York and Tokyo, Weatherhill, 1984), 51, 100.

7.

46. Quoted in Masakazu Iwata, *Ōkubo Toshimichi. The Bismarck of Japan* (Berkeley, California U.P., 1964), 236–8.
47. Quoted in Thomas C. Smith, *Political Change and Industrial Development in Japan: Government Enterprise, 1868–1880* (Stanford, Stanford U.P., 1955), 95.

8.

48. J. W. Robertson Scott, *The Foundations of Japan* (London, Murray, 1922), 65.
49. Quoted in Carol Gluck, *Japan's Modern Myths. Ideology in the Late Meiji Period* (Princeton, Princeton U.P., 1985), 188.
50. Quoted in F. G. Notehelfer, *Kōtoku Shūsui* (Cambridge, Cambridge U.P., 1971), 40, 47.
51. Quoted in Delmer M. Brown, *Nationalism in Japan* (Berkeley, California U.P., 1955), 139.

9.

52. The two memoranda are translated in Ian Nish, *Japanese Foreign Policy, 1869–1942* (London, Routledge, 1977), 268–70.
53. Memorandum quoted in W. G. Beasley, *Japanese Imperialism 1894–1945* (Oxford, Clarendon, 1987), 82–3.
54. Minutes of meeting, quoted in Beasley, *Japanese Imperialism*, 96.
55. There is a contemporary English translation of the demands (not quite complete) in Peter Lowe, *Great Britain and Japan 1911–1915* (London, Macmillan, 1969), 258–62.
56. Quoted in Beasley, *Japanese Imperialism*, 120.

10.

57. Quoted in Sharon H. Nolte, *Liberalism in Modern Japan. Ishibashi Tanzan and his teachers, 1905–1960* (Berkeley, California U.P., 1987), 155.
58. Quoted in Brown, *Nationalism*, 139.
59. Quoted in Mark R. Peattie, *Ishiwara Kanji and Japan's Confrontation with the West* (Princeton, Princeton U.P., 1975), 68.
60. Text in Nish, *Japanese Foreign Policy*, 299–300.

11.

61. The argument is set out in Masao Maruyama, *Thought and Behaviour in Modern Japanese Politics* (London, Oxford U.P., 1963), 25–65.
62. Quoted in Lesley Connors, *The Emperor's Adviser. Saionji Kinmochi and pre-war Japanese politics* (London, Croom Helm, 1987), 203.
63. Quoted in Saburo Ienaga, *Japan's Last War* (Oxford, Blackwell, 1979), 98.
64. D. C. Holtom, *Modern Japan and Shinto Nationalism* (Chicago, Chicago U.P.,1947), 166–7.
65. Shunsuke Tsurumi, *An Intellectual History of Wartime Japan, 1931–1945* (London, KPI, 1986), 12.
66. Quoted in an article by G. M. Beckmann in James Morley, ed., *Dilemmas of Growth in Prewar Japan* (Princeton, Princeton U.P., 1971), 169–70.
67. *Kokutai no Hongi. Cardinal Principles of the National Entity of Japan*, trans. J. O. Gauntlett (Cambridge, Mass., Harvard U.P., 1949), 134, 182, 52, 126.
68. John Morris, *Traveller from Tokyo* (London, Cresset, 1943), 121–2.

12.

69. Translation in Nish, *Japanese Foreign Policy*, 301–3.
70. Text in Joyce C. Lebra, ed., *Japan's Greater East Asia Co-Prosperity Sphere in World War II* (Kuala Lumpur, Oxford U.P., 1975), 68–70.
71. Quoted in Beasley, *Japanese Imperialism*, 225.

72. Translation in Lebra, *Japan's Greater East Asia Co-Prosperity Sphere*, 71–2.
73. ibid., 78–81.
74. ibid., 114–16.
75. ibid., 115.

13.

76. There is a full translation of the decree, dated 14 August 1945, in Robert J. C. Butow, *Japan's Decision to Surrender* (Stanford, Stanford U.P., 1954), 248.
77. The full text is given in Edward M. Martin, *The Allied Occupation of Japan* (Stanford, Stanford U.P., 1948), 122–50.
78. Quoted in Robert E. Ward and Sakamoto Yoshikazu, ed., *Democratizing Japan. The Allied Occupation* (Honolulu, Hawaii U.P., 1987), 15–16.
79. Yoshida Shigeru, *The Yoshida Memoirs* (London, Heinemann, 1961), 78.
80. The English text of the 1947 constitution can be found in *Kōdansha Encyclopedia of Japan* (9 vols., Tokyo & New York, Kodansha, 1983), II, 9–12.
81. The translated text is in Passin, *Society and Education*, 301–4.
82. ibid., 278–84.

14.

83. *Yoshida Memoirs*, 288.
84. The texts of the treaty, the notes exchanged, and the communiqué, are given in George M. Packard III, *Protest in Tokyo. The Security Treaty Crisis of 1960* (Princeton, Princeton U.P., 1966), 364–79.

INDEX